The Least
You Should Know
about English

The Least
You Should Know about
English

FORM B
Writing Skills
NINTH EDITION

Paige Wilson
Pasadena City College

Teresa Ferster Glazier
Late, Western Illinois University

THOMSON
WADSWORTH

Australia   Brazil   Canada   Mexico   Singapore   Spain   United Kingdom   United States

The Least You Should Know about English, Form B, Writing Skills, Ninth Edition
Paige Wilson/Teresa Ferster Glazier, Late

Publisher: *Michael Rosenberg*
Development Editor: *Cheryl Forman*
Technology Project Manager: *Joe Gallagher*
Managing Marketing Manager:
   Mandee Eckersley
Senior Marketing Assistant: *Dawn Giovanniello*
Associate Marketing Communications Manager:
   Patrick Rooney

Associate Content Project Manager: *Sarah Sherman*
Senior Art Director: *Bruce Bond*
Print Buyer: *Betsy Donaghey*
Senior Permissions Editor: *Isabel Alves*
Production Service/Compositor: *Interactive
   Composition Corporation*
Text/Cover Printer: *Banta Harrisonburg*
Cover Design: *Gina Petti*

Printed in the United States of America
   2 3 4 5 6 7 09 08 07 06

Library of Congress Control Number: 2006923335

ISBN 1-4130-1701-0

Thomson Higher Education
25 Thomson Place
Boston, MA 02210-1202
USA

For more information about our products, contact us at:
Thomson Learning Academic Resource Center
1-800-423-0563
For permission to use material from this text or product, submit a request online at
http://www.thomsonrights.com
Any additional questions about permissions can be submitted by e-mail to
thomsonrights@thomson.com

CONTENTS

This book is for students who need to review basic English skills and who may profit from a simplified "least you should know" approach. Parts 1 to 3 cover the essentials of word choice and spelling, sentence structure, punctuation and capitalization. Part 4 on writing teaches students the basic structures of the paragraph and the essay, along with the writing skills necessary to produce them.

The "least you should know" approach attempts to avoid the use of linguistic terminology whenever possible. Students work with words they know instead of learning a vocabulary they may never use again.

Abundant exercises include practice writing sentences and proofreading paragraphs. Diligent students learn to use the rules automatically and thus *carry their new skills over into their writing*. Most exercises consist of sets of ten thematically related, informative sentences on both timely and timeless subjects—anything from dogs having plastic surgery and babies learning sign language to the formation of hailstones. Such exercises reinforce the need for coherence and details in student writing. With answers provided at the back of the book, students can correct their own work and progress at their own pace.

The ninth edition includes a new section in Part 1 devoted to Adjectives and Adverbs. In Part 2, the format of exercises to correct Clichés, Awkward Phrasing, and Wordiness has changed from sentences to paragraphs. In addition, comma exercises in Part 3 now allow students to practice using individual comma rules before combining them. Finally, in Part 4, the Writing section, students will find a contemporary poem to read and respond to, along with several other new student and professional sample paragraphs and essays. As always, the Writing section outlines the writing process and stresses the development of the student's written "voice." Writing assignments follow each discussion. Students improve their reading by learning to find main ideas and their writing by learning to write meaningful reactions and concise summaries.

The Least You Should Know about English functions equally well in the classroom and at home as a self-tutoring text. The simple explanations, ample exercises, and answers at the back of the book provide students with everything they need to progress on their own. Students who have previously been overwhelmed by the complexities of English should, through mastering simple rules and through writing and rewriting simple papers, gain enough competence to succeed in further composition courses.

A **Test Booklet** with additional exercises and ready-to-photocopy tests accompanies this text and is available to instructors.

ACKNOWLEDGMENTS

For their thoughtful commentary on the book, we would like to thank the following reviewers:

Brenda J. L. Trottman
Katherine Gibbs School, New York

Michael W. Keathley
Ivy Tech State College

Greta Anderson
Kirkwood Community College

David P. Gonzales
Los Angeles Pierce College

In addition, thanks to our publishing team for their expertise and hard work: Steve Dalphin, Acquisitions Editor; Cheryl Forman, Editorial Assistant; and Sarah Sherman, Associate Content Project Manager.

For their specific contributions to the ninth edition of Form B, we extend our gratitude to the following student writers: Daniel Dominguez, Jessica Ovando, and Herminia Trejo.

As always, we are especially indebted to our family and friends for their support and encouragement.

Paige Wilson
Teresa Ferster Glazier (1907–2004)

This edition is dedicated to the memory of Teresa Ferster Glazier. In creating *The Least You Should Know about English,* she discovered a way to teach grammar and writing that students have actually enjoyed for nearly thirty years. Her explanations and approaches have been constant sources of inspiration for this and the past two coauthored editions, as they will be for all future editions of her text.

What Is the Least You Should Know?

Most English textbooks try to teach you more than you need to know. This book will teach you the least you should know—and still help you learn to write clearly and acceptably. You won't have to deal with grammatical terms like *gerund, modal auxiliary verb,* or *demonstrative pronoun.* You can get along without knowing such technical labels if you learn a few key concepts. You *should* know about the parts of speech and how to use and spell common words; you *should* be able to recognize subjects and verbs; you *should* know the basics of sentence structure and punctuation—but rules, as such, will be kept to a minimum.

The English you'll learn in this book is sometimes called Standard Written English, and it may differ slightly or greatly from the spoken English you use. Standard Written English is the form of writing accepted in business and the professions. So no matter how you speak, you will communicate better in writing when you use Standard Written English. You might *say* something like "That's a whole nother problem," and everyone will understand, but you would probably want to *write,* "That's a completely different problem." Knowing the difference between spoken English and Standard Written English is essential in college, in business, and in life.

Until you learn the least you should know, you'll probably have difficulty communicating in writing. Take this sentence for example:

I hope that the film school will except my application for admission.

We assume that the writer used the *sound,* not the meaning, of the word *except* to choose it and in so doing used the wrong word. If the sentence had read

I hope that the film school will *accept* my application for admission.

then the writer would have communicated clearly. Or take this sentence:

The film school accepted Beth and Hector and I will try again next year.

This sentence includes two statements and therefore needs punctuation, a comma in this case:

> The film school accepted Beth and Hector, and I will try again next year.

But perhaps the writer meant

> The film school accepted Beth, and Hector and I will try again next year.

Punctuation makes all the difference, especially for Hector. With the help of this text, we hope you'll learn to make your writing so clear that no one will misunderstand it.

As you make your way through the book, it's important to remember information after you learn it because many concepts and structures build upon others. For example, once you can identify subjects and verbs, you'll be better able to recognize fragments, understand subject-verb agreement, and use correct punctuation. Explanations and examples are brief and clear, and it shouldn't be difficult to learn from them—*if you want to.* But you have to want to!

HOW TO LEARN THE LEAST YOU SHOULD KNOW

1. Read each explanatory section carefully (aloud, if possible).

2. Do the first exercise. Compare your answers with those at the back of the book. If they don't match, study the explanation again to find out why.

3. Do the second exercise and correct it. If you miss a single answer, go back once more to the explanation. You must have missed something. Be tough on yourself. Don't just think, "Maybe I'll get it right next time." Reread the examples, and *then* try the next exercise. It's important to correct each group of ten sentences before moving on so that you'll discover your mistakes early.

4. You may be tempted to quit after you do one or two exercises perfectly. Instead, make yourself finish another exercise. It's not enough to *understand* a concept or structure. You have to *practice* using it.

5. If you're positive, however, after doing several exercises, that you've learned a concept or structure, take the next exercise as a test. If you miss even one answer, you should do all the rest of the questions. Then move on to the proofreading and sentence composing exercises so that your understanding carries over into your writing.

Learning the basics of word choice and spelling, sentence structure, and punctuation does take time. Generally, college students must study a couple of hours outside of class for each hour in class. You may need to study more. Undoubtedly, the more time you spend, the more your writing will improve.

P A R T 1

Word Choice and Spelling

Anyone can learn to use words more effectively and become a better speller. You can eliminate most of your word choice and spelling errors if you want to. It's just a matter of deciding you're going to do it. If you really intend to improve your word choice and spelling, study each of the following nine sections until you make no mistakes in the exercises.

Your Own List of Misspelled Words

Words Often Confused (Sets 1 and 2)

The Eight Parts of Speech

Adjectives and Adverbs

Contractions

Possessives

Words That Can Be Broken into Parts

Rule for Doubling a Final Letter

Using a Dictionary

Your Own List of Misspelled Words

On the inside cover of your English notebook or in some other obvious place, write correctly all the misspelled words from your previously graded papers. Review the correct spellings until you're sure of them, and edit your papers to find and correct repeated errors.

Words Often Confused (Set 1)

Learning the differences between these often-confused words will help you over-come many of your spelling problems. Study the words carefully, with their examples, before trying the exercises.

a, an

Use *an* before a word that begins with a vowel *sound* (*a, e, i,* and *o,* plus *u* when it sounds like *uh*) or silent *h.* Note that it's not the letter but the *sound* of the letter that matters.

> *an* apple, *an* essay, *an* inch, *an* onion

> *an* umpire, *an* ugly design (The *u*'s sound like *uh*.)

> *an* hour, *an* honest person (The *h*'s are silent.)

Use *a* before a word that begins with a consonant sound (all the sounds except the vowels, plus *u* or *eu* when they sound like *you*).

> *a* chart, *a* pie, *a* history book (The *h* is not silent in *history*.)

> *a* union, *a* uniform, *a* unit (The *u*'s sound like *you*.)

> *a* European vacation, *a* euphemism (*Eu* sounds like *you*.)

accept, except

Accept means "to receive willingly."

> I *accept* your apology.

Except means "excluding" or "but."

> Everyone arrived on time *except* him.

advise, advice

Advise is a verb. (Pronounce the *s* like a *z*.)

> I *advise* you to take your time finding the right job.

Advice is a noun. (It rhymes with *rice*.)

> My counselor gave me good *advice*.

affect, effect

Affect is a verb and means "to alter or influence."

> All quizzes will *affect* the final grade.

> The happy ending *affected* the mood of the audience.

Effect is most commonly used as a noun and means "a result." If *a, an,* or *the* is in front of the word, then you'll know it isn't a verb and will use *effect*.

The strong coffee had a powerful *effect* on me.

We studied the *effects* of sleep deprivation in my psychology class.

all ready, already

If you can leave out the *all* and the sentence still makes sense, then *all ready* is the form to use.

We're *all ready* for our trip. (*We're ready for our trip* makes sense.)

The banquet is *all ready*. (*The banquet is ready* makes sense.)

But if you can't leave out the *all* and still have a sentence that makes sense, then use *already* (the form in which the *al* has to stay in the word).

They've *already* eaten. (*They've ready eaten* doesn't make sense.)

We have seen that movie *already*.

are, our

Are is a verb.

We *are* going to Colorado Springs.

Our shows we possess something.

We painted *our* fence to match the house.

brake, break

Brake used as a verb means "to slow or stop motion." It's also the name of the device that slows or stops motion.

I had to *brake* quickly to avoid an accident.

Luckily I just had my *brakes* fixed.

Break used as a verb means "to shatter" or "to split." It's also the name of an interruption, as in "a coffee break."

She never thought she would *break* a world record.

Enjoy your spring *break*.

choose, chose

The difference here is one of time. Use *choose* for present and future; use *chose* for past.

I will *choose* a new major this semester.

We *chose* the wrong time of year to get married.

clothes, cloths

Clothes are something you wear; *cloths* are pieces of material you might clean or polish something with.

I love the *clothes* that characters wear in movies.

The car wash workers use special *cloths* to dry the cars.

coarse, course   *Coarse* describes a rough texture.

I used *coarse* sandpaper to smooth the surface of the board.

Course is used for all other meanings.

Of *course* we saw the golf *course* when we went to Pebble Beach.

complement, compliment   The one spelled with an *e* means to complete something or bring it to perfection.

Use a color wheel to find a *complement* for purple.

Juliet's personality *complements* Romeo's: she is practical, and he is a dreamer.

The one spelled with an *i* has to do with praise. Remember "*I* like compliments," and you'll remember to use the *i* spelling when you mean praise.

My evaluation included a really nice *compliment* from my coworkers.

We *complimented* them on their new home.

conscious, conscience   *Conscious* means "aware."

They weren't *conscious* of any problems before the accident.

Conscience means that inner voice of right and wrong. The extra *n* in *conscience* should remind you of *No,* which is what your conscience often says to you.

My *conscience* told me to turn in the expensive watch I found.

dessert, desert   *Dessert* is the sweet one, the one people like two helpings of. So give it two helpings of *s.*

We had a whole chocolate cheesecake for *dessert.*

The other one, *desert,* is used for all other meanings and has two pronunciations.

I promise that I won't *desert* you at the party.

The snake slithered slowly across the *desert.*

do, due   *Do* is a verb, an action. You *do* something.

I always *do* my best work at night.

But a payment or an assignment is *due;* it is scheduled for a certain time.

Our first essay is *due* tomorrow.

Due can also be used before *to* in a phrase that means *because of.*

The outdoor concert was canceled *due to* rain.

feel, fill   *Feel* describes *feel*ings.

Whenever I stay up late, I *feel* sleepy in class.

Fill is the action of pouring into or packing a container fully.

Why did he *fill* the pitcher to the top?

fourth, forth   The word *fourth* has *four* in it. (But note that *forty* does not. Remember the word *forty-fourth.*)

This is our *fourth* quiz in two weeks.

My grandparents celebrated their *forty-fourth* anniversary.

If you don't mean a number, use *forth*.

We wrote back and *forth* many times during my trip.

✱ **have, of**   *Have* is a verb. Sometimes, in a contraction, it sounds like *of.* When you say *could've,* the *have* may sound like *of,* but it is not written that way. Always write *could have, would have, should have, might have.*

We should *have* planned our vacation sooner.

Then we could *have* used our coupon for a free one-way ticket.

Use *of* only in a prepositional phrase. (See p. 68.)

She sent me a box *of* chocolates for my birthday.

hear, here   The last three letters of *hear* spell "ear." You *hear* with your ear.

When I listen to a seashell, I *hear* ocean sounds.

The other spelling *here* tells "where." Note that the three words indicating a place or pointing out something all have *here* in them: *here, there, where.*

I'll be *here* for three more weeks.

✷ **it's, its**	*It's* is a contraction and means "it is" or "it has."
	It's hot. (*It is* hot.)
	It's been hot all week. (*It has* been hot all week.)
	Its is a possessive. (Words such as *its, yours, hers, ours, theirs,* and *whose* are already possessive forms and never need an apostrophe. See p. 44.)
	The jury had made *its* decision.
	The dog pulled at *its* leash.
knew, new	*Knew* has to do with knowledge. Both start with *k.*
	New means "not old."
	Her friends *knew* that she wanted a *new* bike.
know, no	*Know* has to do with knowledge. Both start with *k.*
	By Friday, I must *know* all the state capitals.
	No means "not any" or the opposite of "yes."
	My boss has *no* patience. *No,* I am not exaggerating.

E X E R C I S E S

Circle the correct words in parentheses. Don't guess! If you aren't sure, turn back to the explanatory pages. When you've finished ten sentences, compare your answers with those at the back of the book. Correct each set of ten sentences before continuing so you'll catch your mistakes early.

Exercise 1

1. I just finished reading (a, an) article that offers some interesting (advise, advice).

2. If (a, an) male athlete wants to win, he should (choose, chose) red as the color of his uniform.

3. Scientists recently studied the (affect, effect) of wearing red on the results of competition at the 2004 Olympics in Athens, Greece.

4. Experts had (all ready, already) looked into the ways red may (affect, effect) animal behavior.

5. They (knew, new) it increased the status and success of certain animals who "wore" it.

6. Red seems unique in (it's, its) ability to help male athletes win in competition.

7. The results of the study in Athens showed that wearing red (clothes, cloths) during competition did have a positive impact.

8. The winning (affect, effect) was the same for both individuals and teams.

9. These results may be hard for some people to (accept, except).

10. (Know, No) such studies have included female athletes yet.

Source: Discover, August 2005

Exercise 2

1. Frozen dinners (are, our) part of most of (are, our) lives.

2. They come in trays with separate sections for each (coarse, course).

3. They usually include (a, an) entree, some vegetables, and (a, an) baked (dessert, desert).

4. Swanson started selling (it's, its) first frozen dinners in 1953.

5. That year, the company had ended up with too many turkeys after Thanksgiving (due, do) to (a, an) ordering mistake.

6. A Swanson salesperson, Gerry Thomas, (knew, new) that he could find a way to sell the turkeys somehow.

7. Thomas used airline meals as a model and invented a (knew, new) kind of convenience for the American family, the frozen "TV Dinner."

8. He had the idea to (feel, fill) sleek metal trays with simple, satisfying meals.

9. These quick meals were the perfect (complement, compliment) to a night in front of the television.

10. No one could (have, of) predicted how successful the TV dinner would become.

Source: Smithsonian, December 2004

Exercise 3

1. You probably (know, no) something about Stonehenge, but did you ever (hear, here) of Seahenge?

2. (It's, Its) like Stonehenge, (accept, except) (it's, its) made of wood, and it was discovered in 1998 at the edge of the sea on the coast of England.

3. (It's, Its) shape is similar to Stonehenge's in that they (are, our) both circular.

4. Stonehenge is (a, an) ancient stone circle—one of many nearly 4000-year-old stone structures found throughout Great Britain that still baffle scientists.

5. Seahenge is (a, an) timber circle from even earlier in the Bronze Age, but (it's, its) the very first wooden circle to be found intact.

6. Previous to (it's, its) discovery, scientists (knew, new) about timber circles only from the indentations the wooden posts had left in the earth.

7. Seahenge became visible after (a, an) especially severe storm removed the peat it had been buried under for thousands of years.

8. At the center of Seahenge's circle of wooden posts was (a, an) huge upside-down tree trunk that many (feel, fill) must (have, of) been used as (a, an) altar of some kind.

9. Almost against their (conscious, conscience), British experts decided to dig up Seahenge (do, due) to the vulnerable nature of (it's, its) newly exposed wood.

10. This (brake, break) with the traditional preservation instinct angered many but has (all ready, already) led to several scientific discoveries about the people and tools that created one of the world's newest mysteries—Seahenge.

Source: Smithsonian, July 2002

Exercise 4

1. I've lived on my own for two years, and I'm (all ready, already) tired of trying to decide what to (do, due) for dinner every night.

2. When I lived at home, I used to come home from school, change my (clothes, cloths), and (choose, chose) from all of the things my mom, dad, or siblings were eating for dinner.

3. I could (have, of) taken a plate of Dad's famous macaroni and cheese back to my room and then gone downstairs later for a slice of Mom's lemon pie with (it's, its) fluffy meringue on top.

4. Now I have to come up with a main (coarse, course) and a (dessert, desert) all by myself.

5. (Do, Due) to my lack of cooking experience, dinners of my own are either burned or bought.

6. I'm beginning to (feel, fill) a little self-(conscience, conscious) about my limitations in the kitchen.

7. I could call my parents for (advise, advice), but I don't want them to worry about me.

8. Without a doubt, I should (have, of) paid more attention when both my parents were cooking, not just have (complemented, complimented) them on the results.

9. I guess I could take a cooking (coarse, course) or get a roommate to (do, due) the cooking for reduced rent.

10. I like everything about living away from home (accept, except) making my own dinner.

Exercise 5

1. There is (a, an) old, commonly held belief that if you (choose, chose) to wash your car today, it will rain tomorrow.

2. Of (coarse, course), that's just a saying; (it's, its) not true.

3. However, if you take my (advise, advice) and wash your car at home, you will at least save the cost of (a, an) expensive car wash should this happen to you.

4. To avoid the undesirable (affect, effect) of clouding or streaking of the finish, never wash your car in direct sunlight.

5. But don't park your car under a tree to take advantage of (it's, its) shade, or you may be sorry later (do, due) to the possibility of sap falling from the tree.

6. Also, be sure that the (clothes, cloths) you use to wipe the surface are clean and have (know, no) (coarse, course) stitching or texture that might scratch the finish.

7. You don't want to (brake, break) your antenna, so it should be removed if possible.

8. Once your car is (all ready, already) to be washed, use circular motions and (feel, fill) the surface with your hand every now and then to be sure (it's, its) been thoroughly cleaned.

9. Take the time to dry the whole surface of the car with a chamois if you want to get a lot of (complements, compliments) from your friends.

10. If you've done a good job, the (clothes, cloths) you're wearing will be wet, but your car will be dry and as shiny as it was the day you bought it.

PROOFREADING EXERCISE

Find and correct the ten errors contained in the following student paragraph. All of the errors involve Words Often Confused (Set 1).

Its hard to except criticism from friends. The other day, my friend Jane told me that my voice is always too loud when I talk on the phone. She said that the way I talk hurts her ears and makes her hold the phone away from her head. I no that she didn't mean to hurt my feelings, but that was the affect of what she said. I should of told her that she snores whenever we go camping in the dessert. Next time, I will record her snoring so that she can here herself. I don't really want Jane's criticism to brake up are friendship, so I'll probably just talk to her and tell her how I fill.

SENTENCE WRITING

The surest way to learn these Words Often Confused is to use them immediately in your own writing. Choose the five pairs or groups of words that you most often confuse from Set 1. Then use each of them correctly in a new sentence. No answers are provided at the back of the book, but you can see if you are using the words correctly by comparing your sentences to the examples in the explanations. Use your own paper, and keep all of your sentence writing results in a folder.

Words Often Confused (Set 2)

Study this second set of words carefully, with their examples, before attempting the exercises. Knowing all of the word groups in these two sets will take care of many of your spelling problems.

lead, led	*Lead* is the metal that rhymes with *head.*
	Old paint is dangerous because it often contains *lead.*
	The past form of the verb "to lead" is *led.*
	What factors *led* to your decision?
	I *led* our school's debating team to victory last year.
	If you don't mean past time, use *lead,* which rhymes with *bead.*
	I will *lead* the debating team again this year.
loose, lose	*Loose* means "not tight." Note how *l o o s e* that word is. It has plenty of room for two *o*'s.
	My dog has a *loose* tooth.
	Lose is the opposite of win.
	If we *lose* this game, we will be out for the season.
✶**passed, past**	The past form of the verb "to pass" is *passed.*
	She easily *passed* her math class.
	The runner *passed* the baton to her teammate.
	I *passed* your house on my way to the store.
	Use *past* when it's not a verb.
	I drove *past* your house. (Meaning "I drove *by* your house.")
	I try to learn from *past* experiences.
	In the *past,* he worked for a small company.
personal, personnel	Pronounce these two correctly, and you won't confuse them—*pérsonal, personnél.*
	She shared her *personal* views as a parent.
	Personnel means "a group of employees."
	I had an appointment in the *personnel* office.

piece, peace   Remember "piece of pie." The one meaning "a *piece* of something" always begins with *pie*.

Some children asked for an extra *piece* of candy.

The other one, *peace,* is the opposite of war.

The two sides finally signed a *peace* treaty.

principal, principle   *Principal* means "main." Both words have *a* in them: princip*a*l, m*a*in.

The *principal* concern is safety. (main concern)

We paid both *principal* and interest. (main amount of money)

Also, think of a school's "princi*pal*" as your "*pal*."

An elementary school *principal* must be kind. (main administrator)

A *principle* is a "rule." Both words end in *le*: princip*le*, ru*le*.

I am proud of my *principles*. (rules of conduct)

We value the *principle* of truth in advertising. (rule)

⭐ **quiet, quite**   Pronounce these two correctly, and you won't confuse them. *Quiet* means "free from noise" and rhymes with *diet*.

Tennis players need *quiet* in order to concentrate.

Quite means "very" and rhymes with *bite*.

It was *quite* hot in the auditorium.

right, write   *Right* means "correct" or "proper."

You will find your keys if you look in the *right* place.

It also means in the exact location, position, or moment.

Your keys are *right* where you left them.

Let's go *right* now.

Write means to compose sentences, poems, essays, and so forth.

I asked my teacher to *write* a letter of recommendation for me.

⭐ **than, then**   *Than* compares two things.

I am taller *than* my sister.

Then tells when. (*Then* and *when* rhyme, and both have *e* in them.)

> I always write a rough draft of a paper first; *then* I revise it.

their, there, they're

Their is a possessive, meaning belonging to them.

> *Their* cars have always been red.

There points out something. (Remember that the three words indicating a place or pointing out something all have *here* in them: *here, there, where.*)

> I know that I haven't been *there* before.

> *There* was a rainbow in the sky.

They're is a contraction and means "they are."

> *They're* living in Canada now. (*They are* living in Canada now.)

threw, through

Threw is the past form of "to throw."

> We *threw* snowballs at each other.

> I *threw* away my application for a scholarship.

If you don't mean "to throw something," use *through*.

> We could see our beautiful view *through* the new curtains.

> They worked *through* their differences.

two, too, to

Two is a number.

> We have written *two* papers so far in my English class.

Too means "extra" or "also," and so it has an extra *o*.

> The movie was *too* long and *too* violent. (extra)

> They are enrolled in that biology class *too*. (also)

Use *to* for all other meanings.

> They like *to* ski. They're going *to* the mountains.

weather, whether

Weather refers to conditions of the atmosphere.

> Snowy *weather* is too cold for me.

Whether means "if."

I don't know *whether* it is snowing there or not.

Whether I travel with you or not depends on the weather.

were, wear, where   These words are pronounced differently but are often confused in writing.

Were is the past form of the verb "to be."

We *were* interns at the time.

Wear means to have on, as in wearing clothes.

I always *wear* a scarf in winter.

Where refers to a place. (Remember that the three words indicating a place or pointing out something all have *here* in them: *here, there, where.*)

Where is the mailbox? There it is.

Where are the closing papers? Here they are.

who's, whose   *Who's* is a contraction and means "who is" or "who has."

Who's responsible for signing the checks? (*Who is* responsible?)

Who's been reading my journal? (*Who has* been reading my journal?)

Whose is a possessive. (Words such as *whose, its, yours, hers, ours,* and *theirs* are already possessive forms and never need an apostrophe. See p. 44.)

Whose keys are these?

woman, women   The difference here is one of number: wo*man* refers to one adult female; wo*men* refers to two or more adult females.

I know a *woman* who has bowled a perfect game.

I bowl with a group of *women* from my work.

you're, your   *You're* is a contraction and means "you are."

You're as smart as I am. (*You are* as smart as I am.)

Your is a possessive meaning belonging to you.

I borrowed *your* lab book.

E X E R C I S E S

Circle the correct words in parentheses. When you've finished ten sentences, compare your answers with those at the back of the book. Do only ten sentences at a time so that you will catch your mistakes early.

Exercise 1

1. James Dean was a famous actor in the (passed, past).

2. Even though he had a (principal, principle) role in only three films of the 1950s, James Dean's work still inspires audiences.

3. Dean's acting style was (quiet, quite) and intense.

4. His most famous (piece, peace) was the movie *Rebel Without a Cause*.

5. At the time, his performances (lead, led) him (right, write) into the spotlight and made him an instant star.

6. Unfortunately, audiences would (loose, lose) (their, there, they're) opportunity to know him better.

7. At the age of 24, Dean (passed, past) away in a legendary car crash.

8. Dean and his mechanic (wear, were, where) speeding along in his silver convertible near Bakersfield, California, when another driver wandered over the center line at a fork in the road and hit them.

9. James Dean died, but his mechanic survived, and the other driver did, (two, too, to).

10. Although 50 years have (passed, past), devoted fans still visit that bit of highway every year on September 30, the anniversary of James Dean's death.

Source: Westways, September/October 2005

Exercise 2

1. You've probably been (threw, through) this experience.

2. (You're, Your) in a theater, auditorium, or intimate restaurant, and someone's cell phone rings.

3. The person (who's, whose) phone it is becomes (two, to, too) embarrassed (two, to, too) answer it.

4. In the (passed, past), (their, there, they're) was no way to keep this unfortunate event from happening.

5. Now scientists have invented a type of magnetic wood paneling that will maintain the (piece, peace) and (quiet, quite) of public places even if people still refuse to turn off (their, there, they're) cell phones.

6. This new wood will block radio signals and therefore keep such calls from going (threw, through) the walls of a theater, auditorium, restaurant, or anywhere else (their, there, they're) not wanted.

7. Of course, (their, there, they're) are people who do not want to (loose, lose) (their, there, they're) (right, write) to make (personal, personnel) calls wherever they want.

8. One of the best uses of magnetic wood will be to protect areas (were, wear, where) signals interfere with each other.

9. (Than, Then) wooden panels will be used (two, too, to) divide wireless signals rather (than, then) block calls altogether.

10. (Weather, Whether) (you're, your) for it or against it, magnetic wood will probably be used worldwide (quiet, quite) soon.

Source: New Scientist, June 27, 2002

Exercise 3

1. The three days following September 11, 2001, (were, wear, where) unique.

2. They offered an unprecedented opportunity to study an aspect of the (whether, weather) that could not be studied under normal conditions.

3. The situation that (lead, led) to the study was the temporary ban on nearly all airline flights over America.

4. In the (passed, past), scientists had wondered (whether, weather) the clouds produced by airplane engines affected temperatures on land.

5. These man-made clouds, called contrails, are the streaks left behind after an airplane has (passed, past) across the sky.

6. Never in the recent (passed, past) had (their, there, they're) been days when the skies were clear of contrails.

7. The absence of air traffic also produced an eerie kind of (quiet, quite).

8. Not wanting to (loose, lose) the chance to discover the effects of contrails, (two, too, to) scientists went (right, write) to work.

9. David Travis and Andrew Carleton discovered, (threw, through) comparisons of temperatures from the three days without air traffic and the same days for the (passed, past) thirty years, that the contrails do cause temperatures to cool slightly.

10. This (piece, peace) of scientific data may lead to a greater understanding of our impact on the planet's (whether, weather) overall.

Source: Discover, August 2002

Exercise 4

1. I don't know (weather, whether) I should (right, write) my own resume or pay a service to do it for me.

2. I have a friend (who's, whose) just been hired by a law firm; he told me, "(You're, Your) crazy if you don't let an expert put together (you're, your) resume."

3. Maybe he's (right, write); he's been (threw, through) the process already and was (quiet, quite) satisfied with the result.

4. He has never (lead, led) me astray before, and I'm not (two, too, to) sure I know how to (right, write) all of my (personal, personnel) information in a clear format.

5. For instance, I can't decide how much of my (passed, past) experience I should include.

6. (Personal, Personnel) offices do have strict requirements about the length and styles of documents.

7. (Their, There, They're) often harder to get (passed, past) (than, then) the people on the hiring committees.

8. In fact, the one (woman, women) who helped me the last time I tried to get a job told me that the (principal, principle) problem with my file was the poor quality of my resume.

9. I think I'll ask my friend (were, wear, where) he got his resume done and how much it cost.

10. I would rather (loose, lose) a little money (than, then) (loose, lose) another job opportunity.

Exercise 5

1. Lately, it seems people have forgotten the (principal, principle) "Mind (you're, your) own business, and let other people mind theirs."

2. Private moments are becoming more public (than, then) ever, especially when it comes (two, too, to) marriage proposals.

3. In the (passed, past), people asked each other the big question in the secure setting of a home or perhaps in a (quiet, quite) corner of a restaurant.

4. Now a stadium full of baseball fans, the entire readership of a newspaper, or a whole TV audience must be (their, there, they're) to witness the event.

5. One man decided to (right, write) a crossword puzzle that would spell out the question "Will you marry me?" for his beloved to discover.

6. The (woman, women) he wanted to marry did the puzzle in the newspaper every morning.

7. On the morning of the proposal, she went (threw, through) the clues, answered all of them correctly, and when she saw the proposal and her name spelled out in the puzzle, she looked up at her boyfriend and said, "Yes!"

8. Some men and (woman, women) don't think it's (right, write) to be put on the spot in public, however.

9. In one instance, the intended (threw, through) the ring overboard after being asked in front of the entire population of a cruise ship.

10. (Weather, Whether) it's other people's cell phone calls or marriage proposals, we (loose, lose)—or maybe we give away—a little more privacy every day.

PROOFREADING EXERCISE

See if you can correct the ten errors in this student paragraph. All errors involve Words Often Confused (Set 2).

In the passed, if you wanted to here a peace of music, you turned on you're stereo. Later, you could even listen too tunes on your computer. Now, with the write equipment, you can play music threw a vase of flowers. The sound doesn't come from the vase, but from the flowers themselves. Let's Corp., a company in Japan, has created a gadget called Ka-on, which means "flower sound" in Japanese. With the Ka-on device, sound is past up the stems of the flowers, into the delicate blossoms, and out into the room. If you touch the petals, you can feel there vibrations. The Ka-on sound is supposed to be softer then music played through ordinary speakers.

Source: Current Science, May 6, 2005

SENTENCE WRITING

Write several sentences using any words you missed in the exercises for Words Often Confused (Set 2). Use your own paper, and keep all of your sentence writing results in a folder.

The Eight Parts of Speech

Choosing the right word is an important aspect of writing. Some words sound alike but are spelled differently and have different meanings (*past* and *passed,* for instance), and some words are spelled the same but sound different and mean different things (*lead,* for the action of "leading," and *lead,* for the stuff inside pencils).

One way to choose words more carefully is to understand the roles that words play in sentences. Just as one actor can play many different parts in movies (a hero, a villain, a humorous sidekick), single words can play different parts in sentences (a noun, a verb, an adjective). These are called the *eight parts of speech,* and they are briefly defined with examples below.

1. **Nouns** name some*one, thing, place,* or *idea* and are used as subjects and objects in sentences. (See pp. 62, 68, and 140 for more about nouns as subjects and objects.)

    The **technician** installed the **computers** in the **lab.**

2. **Pronouns** are special words—such as *I, she, him, it, they,* and *us*—that replace nouns to avoid repeating them. (See p. 158 for more about pronouns.)

    She (the technician) installed **them** (the computers) in **it** (the lab).

3. **Adjectives** add description to nouns and pronouns—telling *which one, how many, what kind, color,* or *shape* they are. (See p. 29 for more about adjectives.)

    The **best** technician installed **thirty new** computers in the **writing** lab.

    The words *a, an,* and *the* are special forms of adjectives called **articles.** They always point to a noun or a pronoun. They are used so often that there is no need to label them.

4. **Verbs** show action or state of being. (See p. 62 for more about verbs.)

    The technician **installed** the new computers in the writing lab; Terri **is** the technician's name.

5. **Adverbs** add information—such as *when, where, why,* or *how*—to verbs, adjectives, and other adverbs. (See p. 30 for more about adverbs.)

    Yesterday Terri **quickly** installed the **brand** new computers in the writing lab.

6. **Prepositions** show position in *space* and *time* and are followed by noun objects to form prepositional phrases. (See p. 68 for more about prepositions.)

    The computers arrived **in** the writing lab **at** noon.

7. **Conjunctions** are connecting words—such as *and, but,* and *or*—and words that begin dependent clauses—such as *because, since, when, while,* and *although.* (See p. 74 and p. 90 for more about conjunctions.)

    Students still visited the lab **and** the media center **while** Terri installed the computers.

8. **Interjections** interrupt a sentence to show surprise or other emotions and are rarely used in Standard Written English.

>   **Wow**, Terri is a valuable employee.

To find out what parts of speech an individual word can play, look it up in a good dictionary. (See p. 55.) A list of definitions beginning with an abbreviated part of speech (*n, adj, prep,* and so on) will catalog its uses. However, seeing how a word is used in a particular sentence is the best way to identify its part of speech. Look at these examples:

>   Our **train** arrived at exactly three o'clock.
>
>   (*Train* is a noun in this sentence, naming the vehicle we call a "train.")
>
>   Sammy and Helen **train** dolphins at Sea World.
>
>   (*Train* is a verb in this example, expressing the action of teaching skills we call "training.")
>
>   Doug's parents drove him to the **train** station.
>
>   (*Train* is acting as an adjective here, adding description to the noun "station," telling what *kind* of station it is.)

All of the words in a sentence work together to create meaning, but each one serves its own purpose by playing a part of speech. Think about how each of the words in the following sentence plays the particular part of speech labeled:

>   n   prep   adj   n   adv   v   adj   n   prep   n conj v
>   Students at community colleges often attend several classes in a day and are
>
>   adv adj conj pro adv   v   adv
>   very tired when they finally go home.

Below, you'll find an explanation for each label:

>   Students   n (*names the people* who are the subject of the sentence)
>
>   at   prep (*begins a prepositional phrase* showing position in space)
>
>   community   adj (*adds description* to the noun *colleges,* telling what
>   kind)
>
>   colleges   n (*names the place* that is the object of the preposition *at*)
>
>   often   adv (*adds to the verb,* telling when students attend classes)
>
>   attend   v (*shows an action,* telling what the students do)

several	adj (*adds description* to the noun *classes,* telling how many)
classes	n (*names the things* that the students *attend*)
in	prep (*begins a prepositional phrase* showing position in time)
a	no label (an article that *points to the noun day*)
day	n (*names the thing* that is the object of the preposition *in*)
and	conj (*joins* the two verbs *attend* and *are*)
are	v (*shows a state of being,* linking the subject *students* with the descriptive word *tired*)
very	adv (*adds to the adjective tired,* telling how tired the students are)
tired	adj (*describes the noun* subject *students*)
when	conj (*begins a dependent clause*)
they	pro (*replaces* the word *students* as a new subject to avoid repetition)
finally	adv (*adds to the verb,* telling when they *go* home)
go	v (*shows an action,* telling what they do)
home.	adv (*adds to the verb,* telling where they *go*)

Familiarizing yourself with the parts of speech will help you spell better now and understand phrases and clauses better later. Each of the eight parts of speech has characteristics that distinguish it from the other seven, but it takes practice to learn them.

E X E R C I S E S

Label the parts of speech above all of the words in the following sentences using the abbreviations **n, pro, adj, v, adv, prep, conj,** and **interj.** For clarity's sake, the sentences here are very brief, and you may ignore the words *a, an,* and *the.*

Refer back to the definitions and examples of the parts of speech whenever necessary. When in doubt, leave a word unmarked until you check the answers at the back of the book after each set of ten sentences.

Exercise 1

1. I really love cookies.

2. They are my favorite snack.

3. I prefer the ones with chocolate chips or nuts.

start 4. Cookies taste best when they are fresh.

5. Sometimes, I have cookies and milk for breakfast.

6. Now some fast-food restaurants offer fresh-baked cookies.

7. Oatmeal cookies are delicious when they are still warm.

8. Companies release new versions of traditional cookies.

9. One variety of Oreos now has chocolate centers.

10. Wow, are they yummy!

Exercise 2

1. When babies want something, they often cry.

2. Now some parents teach sign language to their babies.

3. One professor of psychology tried sign language with her baby in the 1980s.

4. Then she repeated the experiment with other children.

5. The results showed that at twelve months of age, most babies are ready.

6. They can control their hands fairly well.

7. If a parent repeats signs for a few months, a child can learn them.

8. Studies report benefits for babies who learn sign language.

9. Later, their verbal test scores are high.

10. Also, they score very well on IQ tests.

Source: Psychology Today, November/December 2004

Exercise 3

1. In the summer of 2005, London Zoo opened a temporary exhibit.

2. The title of the exhibit was "The Human Zoo."

3. Zoo officials selected eight human volunteers.

4. Then they put the humans on display for several days.

5. Dozens of people had applied online for the project.

6. The exhibit showcased three males and five females.

7. They dressed in fake fig leaves that covered their shorts and bikini tops.

8. With its rocky ledges and cave-like structures, the enclosure had previously housed bears.

9. The eight humans talked, played games, and received a lot of attention.

10. Outside the exhibit, the zoo posted signs about human diet, habitat, and behavior.

Source: BBC News, August 25, 2005

Exercise 4

1. Plants need water and sunlight.
   - N · v · n · conj · n
2. Sometimes houseplants wither unexpectedly.
   - adv · n · v · adv

3. People often give them too much water or not enough water.

4. I saw an experiment on a television show once.

5. It involved two plants.

6. The same woman raised both plants with water and sunlight.

7. The plants grew in two different rooms.

8. She yelled at one plant but said sweet things to the other.

9. The verbally praised plant grew beautifully, but the other one died.

10. Plants have feelings, too.

Exercise 5

1. Rabies is a disease that is usually fatal.

2. Only five people with rabies symptoms have ever survived.

3. Most people who are bitten get rabies shots before any symptoms begin.

4. These patients can avoid the deadly results of the disease.

5. Jeanna Giese from Wisconsin is unique.

6. She recently survived rabies after a bat bit her at her church.

7. She already showed symptoms of rabies when she went to the hospital.

8. Doctors did not give Giese the rabies vaccine.

9. They put the teenager into a coma instead.

10. Their treatment worked, and it promised hope for rabies patients in the future.

Source: Los Angeles Times, June 16, 2005

PARAGRAPH EXERCISE

Here is a brief excerpt from a book called *The Question and Answer Book of Everyday Science,* by Ruth A. Sonneborn. This excerpt answers the question "Why do our eyes blink?" We have modified some of the phrasing in the excerpt for this exercise. Label the parts of speech above as many of the words as you can before checking your answers at the back of the book.

Your eyelids blink regularly all day long. They stop only when you sleep. Blinking protects your delicate eyes from injury. When something flies toward you, usually your lids shut quickly and protect your eyes.

Blinking also does a kind of washing job. It keeps your eyelids moist. If a speck of dirt gets past your lids, your moist eyeball traps it. Then your eyes fill with water, your lids blink, and the speck washes out of your eye.

SENTENCE WRITING

Write ten sentences imitating those in Exercises 1–5. Keep your sentences short (under 10 words each), and avoid using to _____ forms of verbs. Label the parts of speech above the words in your imitation sentences. Use your own paper, and keep all of your sentence writing results in a folder.

Adjectives and Adverbs

Two of the eight parts of speech, adjectives and adverbs, are used to *add* information to other words. "To modify" means to change or improve something, usually by adding to it. English has only two kinds of modifiers: adjectives and adverbs. Try to remember that both *ad*jectives and *ad*verbs *add* information.

ADJECTIVES

- Adjectives *add to nouns and pronouns* by answering these questions: *Which one? What kind? How much or how many? What size, what color, or what shape?*

       adj   n   adj   n   adj adj adj
   She bought a *new* backpack with *multicolored* pockets. It has *one large blue*

     n   adj   adj   adj   n   adj   adj   adj pro
   pocket, *two medium yellow* pockets, and *three small red* ones.

- Adjectives usually come *before the nouns they modify.*

       adj n   adj   n   adj adj adj   n
   An *oak* tree stands in the *front* yard of *that big green* house.

- However, adjectives can also come *after the nouns they modify.*

           n   adj   adj
   The cake, *plain* and *undecorated,* sat in the middle of the table.

- Adjectives may also come *after linking verbs* (is, am, are, was, were, feel, seem, appear, taste . . .) to add description to the subject. For further discussion of these special verbs, see page 140.

           n   lv   adj   adj
   The branches are *sturdy* and *plentiful.*

          n   lv   adj   adj   n   lv   adj   adj
   The cake tasted *sweet* and *delicious.*   (or)   The cake was *sweet* and *delicious.*

- Adjectives can be *forms of nouns and pronouns* that are used to add information to other nouns.

       adj   n   adj   n   adj   adj   n
   The *tree's* owner always trims *its* branches during *his summer* vacation.

       adj   n   adj   n
   I love *chocolate* cake for *my* birthday.

ADVERBS

- Adverbs *add to verbs, adjectives, and other adverbs* by answering these questions: *How? In what way? When? Where? Why?*

<blockquote>

     adv   v   adv   v

I *quickly* called my sister, who *sleepily* answered her cell phone.

        v adv   v

She did *not* recognize my voice at first.

        adv adj   n

He wore his *light* blue shirt to the party.

        adv   adj n

It was an *extremely* tall tree.

          adv   adj   adv   adj

Its branches were *very* sturdy and *quite* plentiful.

        adv   adv adv

People *often* drive *really fast* in the rain.

</blockquote>

- Unlike adjectives, some adverbs can move around in sentences without changing the meaning.

<blockquote>

 adv

Now I have enough money for a vacation.

   adv

I *now* have enough money for a vacation.

              adv

I have enough money *now* for a vacation.

                    adv

I have enough money for a vacation *now*.

</blockquote>

Notice that many—but not all—adverbs end in *ly*. Be aware, however, that adjectives can also end in *ly*. Remember that a word's part of speech is determined by how the word is used in a particular sentence. For instance, in the old saying "The early bird catches the worm," *early* adds to the noun, telling which bird. *Early* is acting as an adjective. However, in the sentence "The teacher arrived early," *early* adds to the verb, telling when the teacher arrived. *Early* is an adverb.

    Now that you've read about adjectives and adverbs, try to identify the question that each modifier (adj or adv) answers in the example below. Refer back to the questions listed under Adjectives and Adverbs.

<blockquote>

   adj   n   adj   n   adv   adv   v

My family and I went to the farmer's market yesterday. We excitedly watched the

             adj   adj   n   adv   v   adv   adj

decoration of a huge wedding cake. The baker skillfully squeezed out colorful

</blockquote>

n   adj   n   adv adj   adj   n   adj   adj
flowers, leaf patterns, and pale pink curving letters made of smooth, creamy

n
frosting.

NOTE—Although we discuss only single-word adjectives and adverbs here, phrases and clauses can also function as adjectives and adverbs following the same patterns.

CHOOSING BETWEEN ADJECTIVES AND ADVERBS

Knowing how to choose between adjectives and adverbs is important, especially in certain kinds of sentences. See if you can make the correct choices in these three sentences:

We did (good, well) on that test.

I feel (bad, badly) about quitting my job.

She speaks (really clear/really clearly).

Did you choose *well, bad,* and *really clearly?* If you missed *bad,* you're not alone. You might have reasoned that *badly* adds to the verb *feel,* but *feel* is acting in a

v
special way here—not naming the action of feeling with your fingertips (as in "I *feel*

adv   n
the fabric *carefully*"), but describing the feeling of it (as in "The *fabric* feels

adj
smooth"). To test your understanding of this concept, try substituting "I feel (happy, happily)" instead of "I feel (bad, badly)" and note how easy it is to choose.

Another way that adjectives and adverbs work is to compare two or more things by describing them in relation to one another. The *er* ending is added to both adjectives and adverbs when comparing two items, and the *est* ending is added when comparing three or more items.

adj   n   adj   adj   n   adj   adj   n
The red pockets are *big*. The yellow pockets are *bigger.* The blue pocket is

adj   pro
the *biggest* one of all.

v   adv   v   adv   v   adv
She works *hard*. He works *harder.* I work *hardest.*

In some cases, such comparisons require the addition of a word (*more* or *most, less* or *least*) instead of a change in the ending from *er* to *est.* Longer adjectives and adverbs usually require these extra adverbs to help with comparisons.

adj   adv   adj   adv   adj
Food is *expensive*. Gas is *more expensive*. Rent is *most expensive*.

adv   adv   adv   adv   adv
You danced *gracefully*. They danced *less gracefully*. We danced *least gracefully*.

E X E R C I S E S

Remember that adjectives add to nouns and pronouns, while adverbs add to verbs, adjectives, and other adverbs. Check your answers frequently.

Exercise 1

Identify whether each *italicized* word is used as an adjective or an adverb in the sentence.

1. We have *many* beautiful trees on our campus. (adjective, adverb)

2. The *two* magnolias by the auditorium are especially pretty. (adjective, adverb)

3. Huge *white* flowers cover them when they're in bloom. (adjective, adverb)

4. The magnolia blossoms have such *thick* petals. (adjective, adverb)

5. *Eventually*, their heavy petals fall to the ground. (adjective, adverb)

6. The gardeners *usually* sweep the petals up in the morning. (adjective, adverb)

7. I like to walk by the auditorium in the *late* afternoon. (adjective, adverb)

8. *Then* the fallen petals look like tiny boats all over the sidewalk and grass. (adjective, adverb)

9. By the next morning, the ground is *clean* again. (adjective, adverb)

10. Those gardeners work *very* hard. (adjective, adverb)

Exercise 2

Identify whether the word *only* is used as an adjective or an adverb in the following sentences. In each sentence, try to link the word *only* with another word to figure out if *only* is an adjective (adding to a noun or pronoun) or an adverb (adding to a verb, adjective, or other adverb). Have fun with this exercise!

1. I reached into my wallet and pulled out my *only* coupon.

2. I had *only* one coupon.

3. *Only* I had a coupon.

4. That company *only* sells the software; it doesn't create the software.

5. That company sells *only* software, not hardware.

6. Other companies deal in hardware *only*.

7. In my Spanish class, the teacher speaks in Spanish *only*.

8. *Only* the students use English to ask questions or to clarify something.

9. My best friend is an *only* child, and so am I.

10. *Only* she understands how I feel.

Exercise 3

Choose the correct adjective or adverb form required to complete each sentence.

1. We have many (close, closely) relatives who live in the area.

2. We are (close, closely) related to many of the people in this area.

3. During the holidays, we feel (close, closely) to everyone in town.

4. My sister suffered (bad, badly) after she fell and broke her leg.

5. She felt (bad, badly) about tripping on a silly little rug.

6. Her leg itched really (bad, badly) under her cast.

7. The classroom hamster runs (very happy, very happily) on his exercise wheel.

8. The children are always (very happy, very happily) when he exercises.

9. My group received a (good, well) grade on our project.

10. The four of us worked (good, well) together.

Exercise 4

Choose the correct adjective or adverb form required to complete each sentence.

1. Of all my friends' cars, Jake's is (small, smaller, the smallest).

2. Janna has (a small, a smaller, the smallest) car, too.

3. Her car is (small, smaller, smallest) than mine.

4. Ken bought his car last week, so it's (a new, a newer, the newest) one.

5. Mine has (new, newer, newest) tires than Ken's since my tires were put on yesterday.

6. Jake's car is (new, newer, newest) than Janna's.

7. Ken looked for a car with (good, better, best) gas mileage than his old one.

8. Of course, Jake's tiny car gets (good, better, the best) gas mileage of all.

9. I do get (good, better, best) gas mileage now that I have new tires.

10. These days, gas mileage is (important, more important, most important) than it used to be.

Exercise 5

Label all of the adjectives (adj) and adverbs (adv) in the following sentences. Mark the ones you are sure of; then check your answers at the back of the book and find the ones you missed.

1. I took a very unusual art class over the summer.

2. The intriguing title of the class was "Frame-Loom Tapestry."

3. We created small colorful tapestries on a wooden frame.

4. We started with four wooden stretcher bars, two long ones and two short ones.

5. Then we carefully joined them at the corners to make a rectangular frame.

6. Next, we wound white cotton string around the frame lengthwise.

7. We finally had the basis for our tapestries.

8. We took brightly colored yarns and fabric strips and wove them between the strings.

9. I was very happy with the results.

10. My first tapestry looked like a beautiful sunset.

PROOFREADING EXERCISE

Correct the five errors in the use of adjectives and adverbs in the following student paragraph. Then try to label all of the adjectives (adj) and adverbs (adv) in the paragraph for practice.

I didn't do very good in my last year of high school. I feel badly whenever I think of it. I skipped my classes and turned in messy work. My teachers warned me about my negative attitude, but I was real stubborn. Now that I am a college student, I am even stubborner. I go to every class and do my best. Now, success is only my goal.

SENTENCE WRITING

Write a short paragraph (five to seven sentences) describing your favorite class in grade school or high school. Then go back through the paragraph and label your single-word adjectives and adverbs. Use your own paper, and keep all of your sentence writing results in a folder.

Contractions

When two words are shortened into one, the result is called a *contraction:*

is not ········▶ isn't   you have ········▶ you've

The letter or letters that are left out are replaced with an apostrophe. For example, if the two words *do not* are shortened into one, an apostrophe is put where the second *o* is left out.

do not   don't

Note how the apostrophe goes in the exact place where the letter or letters are left out in these contractions:

I am	I'm
I have	I've
I shall, I will	I'll
I would	I'd
you are	you're
you have	you've
you will	you'll
she is, she has	she's
he is, he has	he's
it is, it has	it's
we are	we're
we have	we've
we will, we shall	we'll
they are	they're
they have	they've
are not	aren't
cannot	can't
do not	don't
does not	doesn't
have not	haven't

let us	let's
who is, who has	who's
where is	where's
were not	weren't
would not	wouldn't
could not	couldn't
should not	shouldn't
would have	would've
could have	could've
should have	should've
that is	that's
there is	there's
what is	what's

One contraction does not follow this rule: *will not* becomes *won't.*

In all other contractions that you're likely to use, the apostrophe goes exactly where the letter or letters are left out. Note especially that *it's, they're, who's,* and *you're* are contractions. Use them when you mean *two* words. (See p. 44 for more about the possessive forms—*its, their, whose,* and *your*—which *don't* need apostrophes.)

E X E R C I S E S

Add the missing apostrophes to any contractions in the following sentences. Then compare your answers with those at the back of the book. Be sure to correct each exercise before going on to the next so you'll catch your mistakes early.

Exercise 1

1. Theres a new house in China thats famous in the world of architecture for what it doesnt have.

2. Its called "The Suitcase House" because it doesnt seem to have any rooms.

3. At least the rooms arent there above the floor.

4. If you were standing inside the house, youd see just an empty rectangular space with a shiny wooden floor.

5. The rooms are all there, but theyre hidden beneath the floor.

6. The Suitcase House's floor is unique; its actually a patchwork of lifting panels.

7. Underneath each panel is a room that you cant get to unless you lift up the panel in the floor.

8. When you want to cook your dinner, you lift up the panel for the kitchen.

9. When you dont need the kitchen any more, you close the panel, and its gone.

10. If youre interested, you can rent the Suitcase House and see it for yourself.

Source: Residential Architect Magazine, September 1, 2004

Exercise 2

1. Theres a new kind of addiction to be worried about.

2. Experts call it "infomania," and its having an impact on people's lives.

3. If someones addicted to e-mail, cell phone calls, and text messages, that person suffers from infomania.

4. That persons not alone.

5. A recent study shows that around sixty percent of us have at least a mild case of infomania.

6. If theres a computer around, well check our e-mail, even if were in the middle of a meeting or some other important activity.

7. Well check our messages when we should be resting at home or on vacation.

8. The results of the study showed that theres a price to be paid.

9. People lose approximately 10 points of their IQ scores if theyre distracted by e-mails and phone calls.

10. Thats double the amount of a decline in intelligence than if they were smoking marijuana.

Source: BBC News, April 22, 2005

Exercise 3

1. My friends and I needed some extra money for a trip wed planned, so we decided to have a group yard sale.

2. I didnt think that Id find very many items to sell in my own house.

3. But I couldnt believe how much stuff I discovered that I hadnt ever used.

4. There wasnt any reason to hang onto an old exercise bicycle, for instance.

5. And I knew I didnt want to keep the cat-shaped clock that hung in my room when I was a kid.

6. My parents werent willing to part with the clock, though; I guess theyre more sentimental than I am right now.

7. It isnt easy to get rid of some things, and my friends didnt have any better luck with their parents than Id had.

8. Still, since there were so many of us, we ended up with a yard full of merchandise.

9. We spent the weekend selling a cup here and a bike there until wed made over three hundred dollars.

10. Now were convinced that without our yard-sale profits, we couldnt have had such a fun-filled trip.

Exercise 4

1. Charles F. Brannock is someone whos not as well-known as the machine he invented.

2. Im sure you remember having your foot measured at some point in your life.

3. Youre in a shoe store, and the salesperson wants to sell you a shoe that fits perfectly.

4. So the clerk grabs a metal device thats behind the counter and plops it on the floor.

5. Its a silver and black metal tray, ruler, and vise all in one.

6. My parents wouldnt let anyone sell us a pair of shoes when I was young unless wed been measured using one of these contraptions.

7. Theyre called Brannock Devices, named for Charles F. Brannock, the man who invented them.

8. He got the idea while he was still in college and working in his father's shoe store, where he noticed that the wooden stick they used to measure customers' feet wasnt practical.

9. Brannock spent countless hours in his dorm room designing a metal device thats able to measure three parts of a person's foot at once.

10. The Brannock Device is still used and manufactured today, and its design hasnt been greatly altered since its original patent in 1928.

Source: Invention & Technology, Summer 2000

Exercise 5

1. Every semester, theres a blood drive at my school, and usually I tell myself Im too busy to participate.

2. But this time, Ive decided to give blood with a couple of my friends.

3. Weve all wanted to donate before, but individually we havent had the nerve.

4. Well visit the "bloodmobile" together and support each other if any of us cant do it.

5. My friend Carla has donated before, so shes the one weve asked about how it feels.

6. She described the whole process and assured us that its easy and painless.

7. First, a volunteer asks us some questions and takes a small blood sample from one of our earlobes to see if we are or arent able to give blood.

8. Once were cleared to donate, well be asked to lie down and have one of our arms prepared for the actual donation.

9. Thats the part Ill be dreading, but Carla says its just the first stick that stings a little.

10. After that, she says that theres no sensation at all except the satisfaction of helping with such a worthy cause.

PROOFREADING EXERCISE

Can you correct the ten errors in this student paragraph? They could be from any of the areas we have studied so far.

Ive just learned about Web site created to allow people to share there books with complete strangers. Its called BookCrossing.com, and when your finished reading a book, it can be past on to a knew reader just by leaving it on a park bench, at a cafe, or wherever you like. Before you pass it on, you just register the book on the web site, get its ID number, and tell wear you're going to leave it. Then you place a note or a sticker in the book with a identification number and the web address telling the person whose going to find it what to do next. This way, people can keep track of the books they decide to "release into the wild," which is how the Web site phrases it. The best part about "bookcrossing" is it's anonymous, and its free!

Source: Book, March/April 2002

SENTENCE WRITING

Doing exercises will help you learn a rule, but even more helpful is using the rule in writing. Write ten sentences using contractions. You might write about your own ability (or inability) to tell jokes and make people laugh, or you can choose your own subject. Use your own paper, and keep your sentence writing results in a folder.

Possessives

Words that clarify ownership are called *possessives*. The trick in writing possessives is to ask the question "Who (or what) does the item belong to?" Modern usage has made *who* acceptable when it begins a question. More correctly, of course, the phrasing should be *"Whom* does the item belong to?" or even *"To whom* does the item belong?"

In any case, if the answer to this question does not end in *s* (e.g., *player, person, people, children, month*), simply add an apostrophe and *s* to show the possessive. Look at the first five examples in the following chart.

However, if the answer to the question already ends in *s* (e.g., *players, Brahms*), add only an apostrophe after the *s* to show the possessive. See the next two examples in the chart and say them aloud to hear that their sound does not change.

Finally, some *s*-ending words need another sound to make the possessive clear. If you need another *s* sound when you *say* the possessive (e.g., *boss* made possessive is *boss's*), add the apostrophe and another *s* to show the added sound.

a player (uniform)	Whom does the uniform belong to?	a player	Add *'s*	a player's uniform
a person (clothes)	Whom do the clothes belong to?	a person	Add *'s*	a person's clothes
people (clothes)	Whom do the clothes belong to?	people	Add *'s*	people's clothes
children (games)	Whom do the games belong to?	children	Add *'s*	children's games
a month (pay)	What does the pay belong to?	a month	Add *'s*	a month's pay
players (uniforms)	Whom do the uniforms belong to?	players	Add *'*	players' uniforms
Brahms (Lullaby)	Whom does the Lullaby belong to?	Brahms	Add *'*	Brahms' Lullaby
my boss (office)	Whom does the office belong to?	my boss	Add *'s*	my boss's office

The trick of asking "Whom does the item belong to?" will always work, but you must ask the question every time. Remember that the key word is *belong*. If you ask the question another way, you may get an answer that won't help you. Also, notice that the trick does not depend on whether the answer is *singular* or *plural*, but on whether it ends in *s* or not.

> **TO MAKE A POSSESSIVE**
>
> **1.** Ask "Whom (or what) does the item belong to?"
> **2.** If the answer doesn't end in *s*, add an apostrophe and *s*.
> **3.** If the answer already ends in *s*, add just an apostrophe *or* an apostrophe and *s* if you need an extra sound to show the possessive (as in *boss's office*).

EXERCISES

Follow the directions carefully for each of the following exercises. Because possessives can be tricky, we include explanations in some exercises to help you understand them better.

Exercise 1

Cover the right column and see if you can write the following possessives correctly. Ask the question "Whom (or what) does the item belong to?" each time. Don't look at the answer before you try!

1. the men (reaction)   _____ the men's reaction

2. an umpire (decision)   _____ an umpire's decision

3. Jess (remarks)   _____ Jess's or Jess' remarks

4. Alice (company)   _____ Alice's company

5. the Porters (cat)   _____ the Porters' cat

6. Mr. Deeds (ears)   _____ Mr. Deeds' ears

7. parents (values)   _____ parents' values

8. a butterfly (wings)   _____ a butterfly's wings

9. two butterflies (wings)   _____ two butterflies' wings

10. a novel (success)   _____ a novel's success

(Sometimes you may have a choice when the word ends in *s*. *Jess's remarks* may be written *Jess' remarks*. Whether you want your reader to say it with or without an extra *s* sound, be consistent when given such choices.)

> **CAUTION**—Don't assume that every word that ends in *s* is a possessive. The *s* may indicate more than one of something, a plural noun. Make sure the word actually possesses something before you add an apostrophe.

A few commonly used words have their own possessive forms and don't need apostrophes added to them. Memorize this list:

our, ours	its
your, yours	their, theirs
his, her, hers	whose

Note particularly *its, their, whose,* and *your.* They are already possessive and don't take an apostrophe. (These words sound just like *it's, they're, who's,* and *you're,* which are *contractions* that use an apostrophe in place of their missing letters.)

Exercise 2

Cover the right column and see if you can write the required form. The answer might be a *contraction* or a *possessive.* If you miss any, go back and review the explanations.

1. (She) the best friend I have.	She's
2. (They) remodeling next door.	They're
3. Does (you) computer work?	your
4. (Who) traveling with us?	Who's
5. My parrot enjoys (it) freedom.	its
6. (They) car needs new tires.	Their
7. (Who) shoes are those?	Whose
8. My apartment is noisy; (it) by the airport.	it's
9. (He) going to give his speech today.	He's
10. (There) someone at the gate.	There's

Exercise 3

Here's another chance to check your progress with possessives. Cover the right column again as you did in Exercises 1 and 2, and add apostrophes correctly to any possessives. Each answer is followed by an explanation.

1. My cousins spent the weekend at my parents mountain cabin.

parents' (You didn't add an apostrophe to *cousins,* did you? The cousins don't possess anything.)

2. The border guard collected all of the tourists passports.

tourists' (Whom did the passports belong to?)

3. I attended my sisters graduation.

sister's (if it is one sister) sisters' (two or more sisters)

4. Two of my friends borrowed the camp directors boat.

director's (The friends don't possess anything.)

5. Patricks salad tasted better than hers.

Patrick's (*Hers* is already possessive and doesn't take an apostrophe.)

6. After a moments rest, the dog wagged its tail again.

moment's (*Its* is already possessive and doesn't take an apostrophe.)

7. Overnight, someone covered the Smiths house with tissue.

Smiths' (The house belongs to the Smiths.)

8. Childrens shoe sizes differ from adults sizes.

children's, adults' (Did you use the "Whom do they belong to" test?)

9. The sign read, "Buses only."

No apostrophe, no possessive.

10. A toothpastes flavor affects its sales.

toothpaste's (*Its* is already possessive and doesn't take an apostrophe.)

Exercises 4 and 5

Now you're ready to add apostrophes to the possessives that follow. But be careful. *First,* make sure the word really possesses something; not every word ending in *s* is a possessive. *Second,* remember that certain words already have possessive forms and don't use apostrophes. *Third,* even though a word ends in *s,* you can't tell where the apostrophe goes until you ask the question, "Whom (or what) does the item belong to?" The apostrophe or apostrophe and *s* should follow the answer to that question. Check your answers at the back of the book after the first set.

Exercise 4

1. In July of 2005, a baby stroller saved a childs life.

2. A 7-month-old babys nanny was pushing her stroller down a street in Manhattan.

3. Suddenly, an empty buildings roof caved in, and its outer wall collapsed on top of them.

4. The nannys arm and leg were broken by falling debris.

5. Amazingly, none of the babys bones were broken.

6. The strollers frame had protected her from the debris and saved her life.

7. Due to many bystanders quick efforts, both the nanny and the baby were rescued.

8. In response to the incident, officials were flooded with parents requests for the name of that stroller.

9. Its official name is the Mountain Buggy Urban Double Stroller.

10. Understandably, that particular models sales increased as a result.

Source: New York Daily News, July 15, 2005

Exercise 5

1. Claude Monets paintings of water lilies are world famous.

2. Monet also created a series of paintings that captured the beauty of Londons bridges at the turn of the twentieth century.

3. Monet was inspired by the fogs influence on light, color, and texture.

4. He wrote about the foggy weathers positive effect on his mood and creativity.

5. Now historians and scientists know more about the unusually thick fog that hung over London at that time.

6. It was really smog—fog mixed with soot, smoke, and other pollutants.

7. Peoples health suffered so much that hundreds died each week at its worst.

8. Monet himself had lung disease.

9. The artists views of London in the fog went on tour as an exhibition in 2005.

10. The exhibit was called "Monets London."

Source: Discover, September 2005

PROOFREADING EXERCISE

Find the six errors in this student paragraph. All of the errors involve possessives.

My houses' windows are old and out of style. They have single panes of glass, so they don't provide any insulation from heat or cold. Last months heating bills were the highest I've ever had. My next-door neighbors name is Don. Dons' house has new windows. At his carpenters suggestion, Don put in double-paned windows, and it really makes a difference in his energy bills. The new windows design includes another fancy feature. They have shades installed between the two panes of glass. Since they're protected by glass, the shades don't get dirty. I plan to replace my old windows with new ones like Don's as soon as I can.

SENTENCE WRITING

Write ten sentences using the possessive forms of the names of your family members or the names of your friends. You could write about a recent event that brought your friends and family together. Just tell the story of what happened that day. Use your own paper, and keep all of your sentence writing results in a folder.

REVIEW OF CONTRACTIONS AND POSSESSIVES

Here are two review exercises. First, add the necessary apostrophes to the following sentences. Try to get all the correct answers. Don't excuse an error by saying, "Oh, that was just a careless mistake." A mistake is a mistake. Be tough on yourself.

1. Theres a popular tradition most of us celebrate on Valentines Day.

2. We give each other little candy hearts with sayings on them, such as "Im Yours," "Youre Cute," and "Be Mine."

3. Americas largest maker of these candies is Necco; thats short for New England Confectionery Company.

4. Necco calls its version of the candies "Sweethearts Brand Conversation Hearts," and Neccos sayings have only two basic requirements: theyve got to be short and "sweet."

5. The candy hearts recipe is very sweet indeed—its ninety percent sugar.

6. The companys history goes back to the mid-1800s, and at first the sayings were printed on paper and placed inside a shell-shaped candy, more like a fortune cookies design than the tiny printed hearts we buy now.

7. In 1902, the candys shape was changed to a heart, and the sayings were printed directly on the candy.

8. Necco now makes eight billion of its candy hearts each year to satisfy the countrys desire to continue the hundred-year-old tradition.

9. Stores may begin stocking boxes of conversation hearts as early as New Years Day, but statistics show that over seventy-five percent of each years boxes are purchased in the three days before Valentines Day.

10. And if a couple of boxes are left over after February 14th, theyll stay fresh for up to five years.

Source: The Washington Post, February 11, 1998

Second, add the necessary apostrophes to the following short student essay.

BOWLING FOR VALUES

Growing up as a child, I didnt have a set of values to live by. Neither my mother nor my father gave me any specific rules, guidelines, or beliefs to lead me through the complicated journey of childhood. My parents approach was to set me free, to allow me to experience lifes difficulties and develop my own set of values.

They were like parents taking their young child bowling for the first time. They hung their values on the pins at the end of the lane. Then they put up the gutter guards and hoped that Id hit at least a few of the values theyd lived by themselves.

If I had a son today, Id be more involved in developing a set of standards for him to follow. Id adopt my mom and dads philosophy of letting him discover on his own what hes interested in and how he feels about life. But Id let him bowl in other lanes or even in other bowling alleys. And, from the start, hed know my thoughts on religion, politics, drugs, sex, and all the ethical questions that go along with such subjects.

Now that Im older, I wish my parents wouldve shared their values with me. Being free wasnt as comfortable as it mightve been if Id had some basic values to use as a foundation when I had tough choices to make. My childrens lives will be better, I hope. At least theyll have a base to build on or to remodel—whichever they choose.

Words That Can Be Broken into Parts

Breaking words into their parts will often help you spell them correctly. Each of the following words is made up of two shorter words. Note that the word then contains all the letters of the two shorter words.

chalk board	. . .	chalkboard	room mate	. . .	roommate
over due	. . .	overdue	home work	. . .	homework
super market	. . .	supermarket	under line	. . .	underline

Becoming aware of prefixes such as *dis, inter, mis,* and *un* is also helpful. When you add a prefix to a word, note that no letters are dropped, either from the prefix or from the word.

dis appear	disappear	mis represent	misrepresent
dis appoint	disappoint	mis spell	misspell
dis approve	disapprove	mis understood	misunderstood
dis satisfy	dissatisfy	un aware	unaware
inter act	interact	un involved	uninvolved
inter active	interactive	un necessary	unnecessary
inter related	interrelated	un sure	unsure

Have someone dictate the preceding list for you to write and then mark any words you miss. Memorize the correct spellings by noting how each word is made up of a prefix and a word.

Rule for Doubling a Final Letter

Most spelling rules have so many exceptions that they aren't much help. But here's one worth learning because it has very few exceptions.

Double a final letter (consonants only) when adding an ending that begins with a vowel (such as *ing, ed, er*) if all three of the following are true:

1. The word ends in a single consonant,

2. which is preceded by a single vowel (the vowels are *a, e, i, o, u*),

3. and the accent is on the last syllable (or the word only has one syllable).

We'll try the rule on a few words to which we'll add *ing, ed,* or *er.*

begin   **1.** It ends in a single consonant—*n,*
       2. preceded by a single vowel—*i,*
       3. and the accent is on the last syllable—be gín.
          Therefore, we double the final consonant and write *beginning,
          beginner.*

stop   **1.** It ends in a single consonant—*p,*
       2. preceded by a single vowel—*o,*
       3. and the accent is on the last syllable (only one).
          Therefore, we double the final consonant and write *stopping,
          stopped, stopper.*

filter   **1.** It ends in a single consonant—*r,*
       2. preceded by a single vowel—*e,*
       3. But the accent isn't on the last syllable. It's on the first—*filter.*
          Therefore, we don't double the final consonant. We write *filtering,
          filtered.*

keep   **1.** It ends in a single consonant—*p,*
       2. but it isn't preceded by a single vowel. There are two *e*'s.
          Therefore, we don't double the final consonant. We write *keeping,
          keeper.*

NOTE 1—Be aware that *qu* is treated as a consonant because *q* is almost never written without *u.* Think of it as *kw.* In words like *equip* and *quit,* the *qu* acts as a consonant. Therefore, *equip* and *quit* both end in a single consonant preceded by a single vowel, and the final consonant is doubled in *equipped* and *quitting.*

NOTE 2—The final consonants *w, x,* and *y* do not follow this rule and are not doubled when adding *ing, ed,* or *er* to a word (as in *bowing, fixing,* and *enjoying*).

EXERCISES

Add *ing* to these words. Correct each group of ten before continuing so you'll catch any errors early.

Exercise 1

1. toss
2. clip
3. intend
4. meet
5. pick

6. buy
7. ask
8. call
9. map
10. target

Exercise 2

1. sew
2. review
3. deal
4. clog
5. click

6. unhook
7. quiz
8. push
9. aim
10. deliver

Exercise 3

1. snip
2. buzz
3. mix
4. row
5. tamper

6. perform
7. confer
8. gleam
9. clip
10. permit

Exercise 4

1. pat
2. saw
3. feed
4. play
5. occur

6. brush
7. gather
8. knot
9. offer
10. hog

Exercise 5

1. help
2. flex
3. assist
4. need
5. select

6. wish
7. cook
8. construct
9. polish
10. lead

PROGRESS TEST

This test covers everything you've studied so far. One sentence in each pair is correct. The other is incorrect. Read both sentences carefully before you decide. Then write the letter of the incorrect sentence in the blank. Try to isolate and correct the error if you can.

1. _____ **A.** Kyle and Tracy missed the bus to the airport and arrived there late.

    B. They enjoyed the rest of there vacation.

2. _____ **A.** That new hairstylist gave the twins bad haircuts.

    B. Their parents felt badly about taking them to him.

3. _____ **A.** My teacher complimented me on my clear writing style.

    B. He said that my details perfectly complimented my ideas.

4. _____ **A.** I've heard that your looking for a new car.

    B. A hybrid would suit your lifestyle, don't you think?

5. _____ **A.** That movie was just two hours and forty minutes of special effects.

    B. The final battle scene could of been much shorter.

6. _____ **A.** Driving a car was easier then I thought it would be.

    B. I learned the basics from my brother; then I took driving lessons.

7. _____ **A.** My computer has a problem with it's CD drawer.

    B. It's not opening when I eject the CD.

8. _____ **A.** I am more mature than I was in high school.

    B. I also feel more closer to my family now.

9. _____ **A.** Yesterday, our band teacher was absent, so a student lead the rehearsal.

    B. My feet felt as heavy as lead after marching for so long.

10. _____ **A.** College counselors give good advise.

    B. They advise most students to take general education classes first.

Using a Dictionary

Some dictionaries are more helpful than others. A tiny pocket-sized dictionary or one that fits on a single sheet in your notebook might help you find the spelling of very common words, but for all other uses, you will need a complete, recently published dictionary. Spend some time at a bookstore looking through the dictionaries to find one that you feel comfortable reading. Look up a word that you have had trouble with in the past, and see if you understand the definition. Try looking the same word up in another dictionary and compare. If all else fails, stick with the big names and you probably can't go wrong.

Complete the following exercises using a good dictionary. Then you will understand what a valuable resource it is.

1. Pronunciation

Look up the word *jeopardize* and copy the pronunciation here.

_____

_____

For help with pronunciation of the syllables, you'll probably find key words at the bottom of one of the two dictionary pages open before you. Note especially that the upside-down *e* (ə) always has the sound of *uh* like the *a* in *ago* or *about.* Remember that sound because it's found in many words.

Slowly pronounce *jeopardize,* giving each syllable the same sound as its key word.

Note which syllable has the heavy accent mark. (In most dictionaries the accent mark points to the stressed syllable, but in others it is in front of the stressed syllable.) The stressed syllable in *jeopardize* is *je.* Now say the word, letting the full force of your voice fall on that syllable.

When more than one pronunciation is given, the first is preferred. If the complete pronunciation of a word isn't given, look at the word above it to find the pronunciation.

Find the pronunciation of these words, using the key words at the bottom of the dictionary page to help you pronounce each syllable. Then note which syllable has the heavy accent mark, and say the word aloud.

depot   graphically   ambivalence   temperate

2. Definitions

The dictionary may give more than one meaning for a word. Read all the meanings for each italicized word and then write a definition appropriate to the sentence.

1. People used to drink *phosphates* for fun. _____

_____

2. The archer hit the *wand* every time. _____

_____

3. The audience listened to the lovely *bagatelle.* _____

_____

4. We didn't mean to *gloss* over his accomplishment. _____

_____

3. Spelling

By making yourself look up each word you aren't sure how to spell, you'll soon become a better speller. When two spellings are given in the dictionary, the first one (or the one with the definition) is preferred.

Use a dictionary to find the preferred spelling for each of these words.

catalog, catalogue   _____   canceled, cancelled   _____

millennium, millenium _____   judgement, judgment   _____

4. Parts of Speech

English has eight parts of speech: noun, pronoun, verb, adjective, adverb, preposition, conjunction, and interjection. At the beginning of each definition for a word, you'll find an abbreviation for the part of speech that the word is performing when so defined (n, pron, v, adj, adv, prep, conj, interj). For more discussion of parts of speech, see page 23.

Identify the parts of speech listed in all the definitions for each of the following words.

hit   _____   mean   _____

each   _____   calico _____

5. Compound Words

If you want to find out whether two words are written separately, written with a hyphen between them, or written as one word, consult your dictionary. Look at these examples:

half sister	two words
father-in-law	a hyphenated word
stepson	one word

Write each of the following as listed in the dictionary (as two words, as a hyphenated word, or as one word):

full time _____   card board _____

hand made _____   good will _____

6. Capitalization

If a word is capitalized in the dictionary, that means it should always be capitalized. If it is not capitalized in the dictionary, then it may or may not be capitalized, depending on how it is used (see p. 198). For example, *American* is always capitalized, but *college* is capitalized or not, according to how it is used.

Last year, she graduated from college.
Last year, she graduated from Monterey Peninsula College.

Write the following words as they're given in the dictionary (with or without a capital) to show whether they must always be capitalized or not. Take a guess before looking them up.

calculus _____   jazz   _____

muzac   _____   scotch _____

7. Usage

Just because a word is in the dictionary doesn't mean that it's in standard use. The following labels indicate whether a word is used today and, if so, where and by whom.

obsolete	no longer used
archaic	not currently used in ordinary language but still found in some biblical, literary, and legal expressions
colloquial, informal	used in informal conversation but not in formal writing
dialectal, regional	used in some localities but not everywhere
slang	popular but nonstandard expression
nonstandard, substandard	not used in Standard Written English

Look up each italicized word and write the label indicating its usage. Dictionaries differ. One may list a word as slang whereas another will call it colloquial. Still another may give no designation, thus indicating that that particular dictionary considers the word in standard use.

1. My sister said it was *OK* to borrow her car. _____

2. That last pitch was a *duster,* wasn't it? _____

3. Her new job comes with plenty of *perks.* _____

4. I'm just going to *scoot* down to the store for a minute. _____

5. The substitute teacher was a real *softie.* _____

8. Derivations

The derivations or stories behind words will often help you remember the current meanings. For example, if you read that someone is *narcissistic* and you consult your dictionary, you'll find that *narcissism* is a condition named after Narcissus, who was a handsome young man in Greek mythology. One day Narcissus fell in love with his own reflection in a pool, but when he tried to get closer to it, he fell in the water and drowned. A flower that grew nearby is now named for Narcissus. And *narcissistic* has come to mean "in love with oneself."

Look up the derivation of each of these words. You'll find it in square brackets either just before or just after the definition.

boycott _____

Luddite _____

jovial _____

Florida _____

9. Synonyms

At the end of a definition, a group of synonyms is sometimes given. For example, at the end of the definition of *injure,* you'll find several synonyms, such as *damage* or *harm.* And if you look up *damage* or *harm,* you'll be referred to the same synonyms listed under *injure.*

List the synonyms given for the following words.

dodge _____

knock _____

argue _____

10. Abbreviations

Find the meaning of the following abbreviations.

FYI _____   MPG _____

ID   _____   UN   _____

11. Names of People

The names of famous people will be found either in the main part of your dictionary or in a separate biographical names section at the back.

Identify the following famous people.

Albert Einstein _____

Beryl Markham _____

Margaret Mead _____

Harriet Tubman _____

12. Names of Places

The names of places will be found either in the main part of your dictionary or in a separate geographical names section at the back.

Identify the following places.

Rostock _____

Flushing _____

Tabasco _____

Reindeer Lake _____

13. Foreign Words and Phrases

Find the language and the meaning of the italicized expressions.

1. We walked around the *piazza* before we decided to have lunch. _____

_____

2. For an example of *deus ex machina,* just watch the end of that new movie.

_____

3. We used *tromp l'œil* to paint a doorway on the garden wall. _____

_____

4. Let's go back to the *hacienda.* _____

_____

14. Miscellaneous Information

Find these miscellaneous bits of information in a good dictionary. Don't just guess; look them up.

1. What is the purpose of a *divining rod?* _____

_____

2. What kind of animal is a *koala?* _____

_____

3. A *gable* is what kind of decoration? _____

_____

4. How long is a *fortnight?* _____

_____

5. How often does *bimonthly* mean? _____

_____

PART 2

Sentence Structure

Sentence structure refers to the way sentences are built using words, phrases, and clauses. Words are single units, and words link up in sentences to form clauses and phrases. Clauses are word groups *with* subjects and verbs, and phrases are word groups *without* subjects and verbs. Clauses are the most important because they make statements—they tell who did what (or what something is) in a sentence. Look at the following sentence for example:

We bought oranges at the farmer's market on Main Street.

It contains ten words, each playing its own part in the meaning of the sentence. But which of the words together tell who did what? *We bought oranges* is correct. That word group is a clause. Notice that *at the farmer's market* and *on Main Street* also link up as word groups but don't have somebody (subject) doing something (verb). Instead, they are phrases to clarify *where* we bought the oranges.

Importantly, you could leave out one or both of the phrases and still have a sentence—*We bought oranges*. However, you cannot leave the clause out. Then you would just have *At the farmer's market on Main Street*. Remember, every sentence needs at least one clause that can stand by itself.

Learning about the structure of sentences helps you control your own. Once you know more about sentence structure, then you can understand writing errors and learn how to correct them.

Among the most common errors in writing are fragments, run-ons, and awkward phrasing.

Here are some fragments:

Wandering around the mall all afternoon.

Because I tried to do too many things at once.

By interviewing the applicants in groups.

They don't make complete statements—not one has a clause that can stand by itself. Who was *wandering*? What happened *because you tried to do too many things at once*? What was the result of *interviewing the applicants in groups*? These incomplete sentence structures fail to communicate a complete thought.

In contrast, here are some run-ons:

Computer prices are dropping they're still beyond my budget.

The forecast calls for rain I'll wait to wash my car.

A truck parked in front of my driveway I couldn't get to school.

Unlike fragments, run-ons make complete statements, but the trouble is they make *two* complete statements; the first *runs on* to the second without correct punctuation. The reader has to go back to see where there should have been a break.

So fragments don't include enough information, and run-ons include too much. Another problem occurs when the information in a sentence just doesn't make sense.

Here are a few sentences with awkward phrasing:

The problem from my grades started to end.

It was a time at the picnic.

She won me at chess.

Try to find the word groups that show who did what, that is, the clauses. Once you find them, then try to put the clauses and phrases together to form a precise meaning. It's difficult, isn't it? You'll see that many of the words themselves are misused or unclear, such as *from, it,* and *won*. These sentences don't communicate clearly because the clauses, phrases, and even words don't work together. They suffer from awkward phrasing.

Fragments, run-ons, awkward phrasing, and other sentence structure errors confuse the reader. Not until you get rid of them will your writing be clearer and easier to read. Unfortunately, there is no quick, effortless way to learn to avoid errors in sentence structure. First, you need to understand how clear sentences are built. Then you will be able to avoid common errors in your own writing.

This section will describe areas of sentence structure one at a time and then explain how to correct errors associated with the different areas. For instance, we start by helping you find subjects and verbs and by helping you understand dependent clauses; then we show you how to avoid fragments. You can go through the whole section yourself to learn all of the concepts and structures. Or your teacher may assign only parts based on errors that students in the class are making.

Finding Subjects and Verbs

The most important words in sentences are those that make up its independent clause—the subject and the verb. When you write a sentence, you write about a noun or pronoun (a person, place, thing, or idea). That's the *subject*. Then you write what the subject *does* or *is*. That's the *verb*.

Lightning strikes.

The word *Lightning* is the thing you are writing about. It's the subject, and we'll underline all subjects once. *Strikes* tells what the subject does. It shows the action in the sentence. It's the verb, and we'll underline all of them twice. Most sentences do not include only two words (the subject and the verb). However, these two words still make up the core of the sentence even if other words and phrases are included with them.

Lightning strikes back and forth from the clouds to the ground very quickly.

It often strikes people on golf courses or in boats.

When many words appear in sentences, the subject and verb can be harder to find. Because the verb often shows action, it's easier to spot than the subject. Therefore, always look for it first. For example, take this sentence:

The neighborhood cat folded its paws under its chest.

Which word shows the action? The action word is folded. It's the verb, so we'll underline it twice. Now ask yourself who or what folded? The answer is cat. That's the subject, so we'll underline it once.

Study the following sentences until you understand how to pick out subjects and verbs.

Tomorrow our school celebrates its fiftieth anniversary. (Which word shows the action? The action word is celebrates. It's the verb, so we'll underline it twice. Who or what celebrates? The school does. It's the subject. We'll underline it once.)

The team members ate several boxes of chocolates. (Which word shows the action? Ate shows the action. Who or what ate? Members ate.)

Internet users crowd the popular services. (Which word shows the action? The verb is crowd. Who or what crowd? Users crowd.)

Often the verb doesn't show action but merely tells what the subject *is* or *was*. Learn to spot such verbs—*is, am, are, was, were, seems, feels, appears, becomes, looks*.... (For more information on these special verbs, see the discussion of sentence patterns on p. 140).

Marshall is a neon artist. (First spot the verb is. Then ask who or what is? Marshall is.)

The bread appears moldy. (First spot the verb appears. Then ask who or what appears? Bread appears.)

Sometimes the subject comes after the verb, especially when a word like *there* or *here* begins the sentence without being a real subject. It's best not to start sentences with "There is . . . " or "There are . . . " for this reason.

In the audience were two reviewers from the *Times*. (Who or what were in the audience? Two reviewers from the *Times* were in the audience.)

There was a fortune-teller at the carnival. (Who or what was there? A fortune-teller was there at the carnival.)

There were name tags for all the participants. (Who or what were there? Name tags were there for all the participants.)

Here are the contracts. (Who or what are here? The contracts are here.)

NOTE—Remember that *there* and *here* (as used in the last three sentences) are not subjects. They simply point to something.

In commands, often the subject is not expressed. An unwritten *you* is understood by the reader.

Sit down. (You sit down.)

Place flap A into slot B. (You place flap A into slot B.)

Meet me at 7:00. (You meet me at 7:00.)

Commonly, a sentence may have more than one subject.

Toys and memorabilia from the 1950s are high-priced collectibles.

Celebrity dolls, board games, and even cereal boxes from that decade line the shelves of antique stores.

A sentence may also have more than one verb.

Water boils at a consistent temperature and freezes at another.

The ice tray fell out of my hand, skidded across the floor, and landed under the table.

E X E R C I S E S

Underline the subjects once and the verbs twice in the following sentences. When you've finished the first set, compare your answers carefully with those at the back of the book.

Exercise 1

1. Many people saw the movie *March of the Penguins.*

2. It was one of the most popular films of 2005.

3. The movie followed the lives of a group of emperor penguins.

4. The filmmakers lived in the penguins' world for over a year.

5. Luc Jacquet directed the documentary.

6. Jacquet and his crew recorded the birds' incredible journey to their breeding grounds.

7. The penguins and humans endured extreme storms and hungry predators.

8. There were moments of joy and sadness in the film.

9. In one of the saddest parts, an egg slid away from its parents and froze on the ice.

10. Audiences loved the relationships between the penguin parents and their chicks.

Exercise 2

1. Travelers often carry food and other products from one country to another.

2. They ride trains or take planes to their new destinations.

3. Customs officials check passengers for illegal foods or other contraband.

4. Sometimes, customs officers catch smugglers of very unusual items.

5. One woman from Australia made the news recently.

6. There were two odd things about her skirt.

7. It looked very puffy and made a sloshing noise.

8. Customs officers found fifty-one live tropical fish in an apron under her skirt.

9. The apron had special pockets and held fifteen plastic bags.

10. Officials arrested the woman and confiscated her cargo.

Source: UnderwaterTimes.com, June 6, 2005

Exercise 3

1. Chris Lindland had a simple idea.

2. He used an ordinary fabric in an extraordinary way.

3. Lindland invented "Cordarounds."

4. Cordarounds are corduroy pants with a twist.

5. The corduroy ridges go across instead of down the pant legs.

6. These new pants have their own Web site.

7. The Web site is, predictably, cordarounds.com.

8. There are different colors and styles of Cordarounds.

9. They cost a little more than regular corduroy pants.

10. Lindland sees other new styles of clothes in his future.

Exercise 4

1. Cats are extremely loyal and determined pets.

2. They form strong attachments to their families.

3. One cat recently showed her love for the Sampson family very clearly.

4. The Sampsons made a temporary move and took Skittles, the cat, with them.

5. The Sampsons and Skittles spent several months 350 miles away from home.

6. Before the end of their stay, Skittles disappeared.

7. The family returned home without their beloved cat and considered her lost.

8. Seven months later, there was a surprise on their doorstep.

9. Skittles somehow navigated her way home but barely survived the 350-mile trip.

10. This incredible story proves the loyalty and determination of cats.

Source: Current Science, May 3, 2002

Exercise 5

1. There are a number of world-famous trees in California.

2. One of them is the oldest tree on the planet.

3. This tree lives somewhere in Inyo National Forest.

4. The type of tree is a bristlecone pine.

5. Scientists call it the Methuselah Tree.

6. They place its age at five thousand years.

7. The soil and temperatures around it seem too poor for a tree's health.

8. But the Methuselah Tree and its neighbors obviously thrive in such conditions.

9. Due to its importance, the Methuselah Tree's exact location is a secret.

10. Such important natural specimens need protection.

Source: Current Science, May 3, 2002

PARAGRAPH EXERCISE

Underline the subjects once and the verbs twice in the following student paragraph.

My most valuable possession at the moment is a pair of chopsticks. These chopsticks are not worth a lot of money. In fact, they are the disposable kind and still have the white paper wrapper on them. Their value lies in my memories of an evening with someone very special. It happened almost a year ago. As a favor to my friend Tressa, I agreed to a blind date with her cousin Marcus. Marcus and I met at a restaurant, ate sushi, and talked for hours. That night was the start of a wonderful relationship. On my way out of the restaurant that evening, I looked for a souvenir. There was a tall glass of take-out chopsticks by the door. I grabbed a pair and treasure it to this day.

SENTENCE WRITING

Write ten sentences about any subject—your favorite dessert, for instance. Keeping your subject matter simple in these sentence writing exercises will make it easier to find your sentence structures later. After you have written your sentences, go back and underline your subjects once and your verbs twice. Use your own paper, and keep all of your sentence writing results in a folder.

Locating Prepositional Phrases

Prepositional phrases are among the easiest structures in English to learn. Remember that a phrase is just a group of related words (at least two) without a subject and a verb. And don't let a term like *prepositional* scare you. If you look in the middle of that long word, you'll find a familiar one—*position*. In English, we tell the *positions* of people and things in sentences using prepositional phrases.

Look at the following sentence with its prepositional phrases in parentheses:

Our field trip (to the desert) begins (at 6:00) (in the morning) (on Friday).

One phrase tells where the field trip is going (*to the desert*), and three phrases tell when the trip begins (*at 6:00, in the morning,* and *on Friday*). As you can see, prepositional phrases show the position of someone or something in space or in time.

Here is a list of some prepositions that can show positions in space:

under	across	next to	against
around	by	inside	at
through	beyond	over	beneath
above	among	on	in
below	near	behind	past
between	without	from	to

Here are some prepositions that can show positions in time:

before	throughout	past	within
after	by	until	in
since	at	during	for

These lists include only individual words, *not phrases.* Remember, a preposition must be followed by a noun or pronoun object—a person, place, thing, or idea—to create a prepositional phrase. Notice that in the added prepositional phrases that follow, the position of the balloon in relation to the object, *the clouds,* changes completely:

The hot-air balloon floated *above the clouds.*
below the clouds.
within the clouds.
between the clouds.
past the clouds.
around the clouds.

Now notice the different positions in time:

The balloon landed *at 3:30.*
                    by 3:30.
                    past 3:30.
                    before the thunderstorm.
                    during the thunderstorm.
                    after the thunderstorm.

NOTE—A few words—*of, as,* and *like*—are prepositions that do not fit neatly into either the space or time category, yet they are very common prepositions (box *of candy,* note *of apology,* type *of bicycle;* act *as a substitute,* use *as an example,* testified *as an expert;* thinks *like a computer,* acts *like a child,* moves *like a snake*).

By locating prepositional phrases, you will be able to find subjects and verbs more easily. For example, you might have difficulty finding the subject and verb in a long sentence like this:

> During the rainy season, one of the windows in the attic leaked at the corners of its molding.

But if you put parentheses around all the prepositional phrases like this

> (During the rainy season), one (of the windows) (in the attic) leaked (at the corners) (of its molding).

then you have only two words left—the subject and the verb. Even in short sentences like the following, you might pick the wrong word as the subject if you don't put parentheses around the prepositional phrases first.

> Two (of the characters) lied (to each other) (throughout the play).

> The waves (around the ship) looked real.

NOTE—Don't mistake *to* plus a verb for a prepositional phrase. Special forms of verbals always start with *to,* but they are not prepositional phrases (see p. 130). For example, in the sentence "I like to run to the beach," *to run* is a verbal, not a prepositional phrase. However, *to the beach* is a prepositional phrase because it begins with a preposition (to), ends with a noun (beach), and shows position in space.

E X E R C I S E S

Put parentheses around the prepositional phrases in the following sentences. Be sure to start with the preposition itself (*in, on, to, at, of* . . .) and include the word or words that go with it (*in the morning, on our sidewalk, to Hawaii* . . .). Then underline the sentences' subjects once and verbs twice. Remember that subjects and verbs are not found inside prepositional phrases, so if you locate the prepositional phrases *first,* the subjects and verbs will be much easier to find. Review the answers given at the back for each set of ten sentences before continuing.

Exercise 1

1. Roald Dahl is the author of *Charlie and the Chocolate Factory.*

2. In his youth, Dahl had two memorable experiences with sweets.

3. One of them involved the owner of a candy store.

4. Dahl and his young friends had a bad relationship with this particular woman.

5. On one visit to her store, Dahl put a dead mouse into one of the candy jars behind her back.

6. The woman later went to his school and demanded his punishment.

7. He and his friends received several lashes from a cane in her presence.

8. During his later childhood years, Dahl became a taste-tester for the Cadbury chocolate company.

9. Cadbury sent him and other schoolchildren boxes of sweets to evaluate.

10. Dahl tried each candy and made a list of his reactions and recommendations.

Source: Sweets: A History of Candy (Bloomsbury, 2002)

Exercise 2

1. A killer whale at MarineLand in Canada recently invented his own stunt.

2. After the whale's feeding time, gulls often ate the leftover fish on the surface of the water.

3. This orca found a way to benefit from the gulls' habit.

4. He filled his mouth with fish chunks and squirted them on top of the water.

5. Then he sank beneath the surface and waited for a gull.

6. The whale caught the gull and had it for dessert.

7. This whale then taught his new trick to some of the other whales.

8. One main aspect of the whales' behavior fascinates scientists.

9. These whales taught the trick to themselves and to each other without human guidance.

10. Luckily, cameras captured all of the learning on film for study in the future.

Source: Science News, August 20, 2005

Exercise 3

1. My family and I live in a house at the top of a hilly neighborhood in Los Angeles.

2. On weekday mornings, nearly everyone drives down the steep winding roads to their jobs or to school.

3. In the evenings, they all come back up the hill to be with their families.

4. For the rest of the day, we see only an occasional delivery van or compact school bus.

5. But on Saturdays and Sundays, there is a different set of drivers on our roads.

6. On those two days, tourists in minivans and prospective home buyers in convertibles cram our narrow streets.

7. For this reason, most of the neighborhood residents stay at home on weekends.

8. Frequently, drivers unfamiliar with the twists and turns of the roads in this area cause accidents.

9. The expression "Sunday driver" really means something to those of us on the hill.

10. In fact, even "Saturday drivers" are a nuisance for us.

Exercise 4

1. Most of us remember playing with Frisbees in our front yards in the early evenings and at parks or beaches on weekend afternoons.
2. Fred Morrison invented the original flat Frisbee for the Wham-O toy company in the 1950s.
3. Ed Headrick, designer of the professional Frisbee, passed away at his home in California in August of 2002.
4. Working at Wham-O in the 1960s, Headrick improved the performance of the existing Frisbee with the addition of ridges in the surface of the disc.
5. Headrick's improvements led to increased sales of his "professional model" Frisbee and to the popularity of Frisbee tournaments.
6. After Headrick's redesign, Wham-O sold 100 million of the flying discs.
7. Headrick also invented the game of disc golf.
8. Like regular golf but with discs, the game is played on special disc golf courses like the first one at Oak Grove Park in California.
9. Before his death, Headrick asked for his ashes to be formed into memorial flying discs for select family and friends.
10. Donations from sales of the remaining memorial discs went toward the establishment of a museum on the history of the Frisbee and disc golf.

Source: Los Angeles Times, August 14, 2002

Exercise 5

1. An engraved likeness of Pocahontas, the famous Powhatan Indian princess, is the oldest portrait on display at the National Portrait Gallery.
2. In 1607, Pocahontas—still in her early teens—single-handedly helped the British colonists in Virginia to survive.
3. Later, in 1616, Pocahontas traveled to England after her marriage to John Rolfe and after the birth of their son.
4. She visited the court of King James I and impressed the British with her knowledge of English and with her conversion to Christianity.
5. For her new first name, Pocahontas chose Rebecca.

6. During her seven-month stay in England, she became extremely ill.

7. At some point before or during her illness, Simon Van de Passe engraved her portrait on copper.

8. The portrait shows Pocahontas in a ruffled collar and fancy English clothes but with very strong Indian features.

9. Successful sales of prints from the portrait illustrate her fame abroad.

10. Pocahontas died on that trip to England at the age of twenty-two.

PARAGRAPH EXERCISE

Put parentheses around the prepositional phrases in the following excerpt from *Meet Me in St. Louis*, a book about the 1904 World's Fair by Robert Jackson:

Even the Liberty Bell came to the fair during that summer—after seventy-five thousand St. Louis school children had signed a petition requesting its visit. On June 8, the cracked bell arrived on a flat wagon pulled by a team of horses and surrounded by policemen from Philadelphia. Crowds lined the edges of the Plaza of St. Louis, hoping to get a glimpse of this famous artifact. Mayor Rolla Wells pronounced the occasion Liberty Bell Day and called off school in the city so that children could come to the fair.

SENTENCE WRITING

Write ten simple sentences on the topic of your favorite place to relax—or choose any topic you like. When you go back over your sentences, put parentheses around your prepositional phrases and underline your subjects once and your verbs twice. Use your own paper, and keep all of your sentence writing results in a folder.

Understanding Dependent Clauses

All clauses contain a subject and a verb, yet there are two kinds of clauses: *independent* and *dependent*. Independent clauses have a subject and a verb and make complete statements by themselves. Dependent clauses have a subject and a verb but don't make complete statements because of the words they begin with. Here are some of the words (conjunctions) that begin dependent clauses:

after	since	where
although	so that	whereas
as	than	wherever
as if	that	whether
because	though	which
before	unless	whichever
even if	until	while
even though	what	who
ever since	whatever	whom
how	when	whose
if	whenever	why

When a clause starts with one of these dependent words, it is usually a dependent clause. To see the difference between an independent and a dependent clause, look at this example of an independent clause:

We ate dinner together.

It has a subject (We) and a verb (ate), and it makes a complete statement. But as soon as we put one of the dependent words in front of it, the clause becomes *dependent* because it no longer makes a complete statement:

After we ate dinner together . . .

Although we ate dinner together . . .

As we ate dinner together . . .

Before we ate dinner together . . .

Since we ate dinner together . . .

That we ate dinner together . . .

When we ate dinner together . . .

While we ate dinner together . . .

Each of these dependent clauses leaves the reader expecting something more. Each would depend on another clause—an independent clause—to make a sentence. For the rest of this discussion, we'll place a broken line beneath dependent clauses.

After we ate dinner together, we went to the evening seminar.

We went to the evening seminar *after* we ate dinner together.

The speaker didn't know *that* we ate dinner together.

While we ate dinner together, the restaurant became crowded.

As you can see in these examples, *when a dependent clause comes before an independent clause, it is followed by a comma.* Often the comma prevents misreading, as in the following sentence:

When he returned, the DVD was on the floor.

Without a comma after *returned,* the reader would read *When he returned the DVD* before realizing that this was not what the author meant. The comma prevents misreading. Sometimes if the dependent clause is short and there is no danger of misreading, the comma can be left off, but it's safer simply to follow the rule that a dependent clause coming before an independent clause is followed by a comma. You'll learn more about the punctuation of dependent clauses on pages 95 and 178, but right now just remember the previous rule.

Note that a few of the dependent words (*that, who, which, what*) can do "double duty" as both the dependent word and the subject of the dependent clause:

Thelma wrote a poetry book *that* sold a thousand copies.

The manager saw *what* happened.

Sometimes the dependent clause is in the middle of the independent clause:

The book *that* sold a thousand copies was Thelma's.

The events *that* followed the parade delighted everyone.

The dependent clause can even be the subject of the entire sentence:

What you do also affects me.

How your project looks counts for ten percent of the grade.

Also note that sometimes the *that* of a dependent clause is omitted:

I know *that* you feel strongly about this issue.

I know you feel strongly about this issue.

Everyone received the classes *that* they wanted.

Everyone received the classes they wanted.

Of course, the word *that* doesn't always introduce a dependent clause. It may be a pronoun and serve as the subject or object of the sentence:

That was a long movie.

We knew *that* already.

That can also be an adjective, a descriptive word telling *which one:*

That movie always makes me laugh.

We took them to *that* park last week.

E X E R C I S E S

Exercise 1

Each of the following sentences contains *one* independent and *one* dependent clause. Draw a broken line beneath the dependent clause in each sentence. Start at the dependent word and include all the words that go with it. Remember that dependent clauses can be in the beginning, middle, or end of a sentence.

Example: I jump whenever I hear a loud noise.

1. Two men created a Web site that offers an unusual service.

2. After one of their friends died, they discovered the need for a place online to store a person's important information.

3. Because most people keep this information a secret, family and friends lack necessary details after their deaths.

4. People who subscribe to this service control the release of their private information.

5. The site stores the members' information until they pass away.

6. Members pay about a hundred dollars for the service, which lasts a lifetime.

7. Once people become members, they enter their bank accounts, passwords, life insurance policies, and specifics of their wills.

8. Since current technology is so advanced, pre-written e-mails and pre-recorded video messages are very popular additions to members' last wishes.

9. Members can communicate exactly what they want to say to their loved ones in these final messages.

10. Anyone can visit the site, which is called LastWishes.com.

Source: Newsweek, September 6, 2004

Exercises 2–5

Identify the dependent clauses as before. Then go back to both the independent and dependent clauses and mark their subjects and verbs. Draw a single underline beneath subjects and a double underline beneath verbs. There may be more than one dependent clause.

Example: I jump whenever I hear a loud noise.

Exercise 2

1. The world is a miserable place when you have an upset stomach.

2. Whether you get carsick, airsick, or seasick, you probably welcome any advice.

3. Motion sickness is most common when people are between the ages of seven and twelve.

4. Motion sickness happens to some people whenever the brain receives mixed messages.

5. If the inner ear feels movement but the eyes report no movement, the brain gets confused.

6. This confusion results in dizziness and the feeling that all is not well.

7. Experts suggest that you sleep well and eat lightly to avoid motion sickness.

8. When you travel by car, you should sit in the middle of the back seat and look straight out the windshield.

9. On an airplane or a boat, the best seat is one that allows a view of the clouds or horizon.

10. Whenever the queasy feeling comes, you should sip small amounts of water.

Exercise 3

1. The Breathalyzer is a machine that measures a person's blood alcohol level.

2. Police officers use the device when they suspect a drunk driver.

3. Robert F. Borkenstein was the man who invented the Breathalyzer.

4. Before Borkenstein created the portable measuring device, officers took suspects' breath samples in balloons back to a laboratory for a series of tests.

5. Borkenstein's Breathalyzer was an improvement because all testing occurred at the scene.

6. The Breathalyzer was so reliable and became so feared that one man went to extremes to avoid its results.

7. While this man waited in the back of the police car, he removed his cotton underwear and ate them.

8. He hoped that the cotton cloth would soak up all the alcohol in his system.

9. When the desperate man's case went to court, the judge acquitted him.

10. The judge's decision came after spectators in the court laughed so hard that they could not stop.

Source: Los Angeles Times, August 18, 2002

Exercise 4

1. On June 8, 1924, George Mallory and Andrew Irvine disappeared as they climbed to the top of Mount Everest.

2. Earlier, when a reporter asked Mallory why he climbed Everest, his response became legendary.

3. "Because it is there," Mallory replied.

4. No living person knows whether the two British men reached the summit of Everest before they died.

5. Nine years after Mallory and Irvine disappeared, English climbers found Irvine's ice ax.

6. In 1975, a Chinese climber spotted a body that was frozen in deep snow on the side of the mountain.

7. He kept the news secret for several years but finally told a fellow climber on the day before he died himself in an avalanche on Everest.

8. In May 1999, a team of mountaineers searched the area that the Chinese man described and found George Mallory's frozen body, still intact after seventy-five years.

9. After they took DNA samples for identification, the mountaineers buried the famous climber on the mountainside where he fell.

10. The question remains whether Mallory was on his way up or down when he met his fate.

Exercise 5

1. I read an article that described the history of all the presidents' dogs.

2. George Washington cared so much about dogs that he interrupted a battle to return a dog that belonged to a British general.

3. Abraham Lincoln, whose dog's name was actually Fido, left his loyal pet in Illinois after the Lincolns moved to the White House.

4. Teddy Roosevelt met and adopted Skip, the dog that he loved best, after the little terrier held a bear at bay in the Grand Canyon.

5. Franklin Delano Roosevelt made a U.S. Navy ship return to the Aleutians to pick up his dog Fala up after the diplomatic party accidentally left the dog behind.

6. Warren G. Harding's Laddie Boy was the most pampered of the presidential dogs since the Hardings gave him birthday parties and ordered a special chair for Laddie Boy to sit in during presidential meetings.

7. Nikita Khrushchev traveled from Russia with Pushinka, a dog that he gave to John F. Kennedy's daughter Caroline.

8. At a gas station in Texas, Lyndon Johnson's daughter Luci found a little white dog, Yuki, whom President Johnson loved to have howling contests with in the Oval Office.

9. Of course, Nixon had his famous Checkers, and George Bush Sr. had a spaniel named Millie, who wrote her own best-selling book with the help of Barbara Bush.

10. And just when it seemed that all presidents prefer dogs, Bill Clinton arrived with Socks, a distinctively marked black-and-white cat.

PARAGRAPH EXERCISE

Draw a broken line beneath the dependent clauses in this modified excerpt from *The Question and Answer Book of Everyday Science*. These paragraphs describe the cycle of dew forming on grass overnight. When looking for dependent clauses, remember to find the dependent words (*when, since, that, because, after . . .*) and be sure they are followed by subjects and verbs. Underline the subjects once and the verbs twice in both the independent and dependent clauses.

Why Is the Grass Wet in the Morning?

All day long, the grass is warm and dry. The sun has made it so. Then the sun goes down. And when the sun goes down, the warmth goes away, and the grass grows colder. The air that touches the cold grass leaves little beads of water on it.

All air has water vapor in it. Warm air holds more of this water vapor than cold air does. So when the night air turns colder, it releases its water vapor. The water clings to the blades of grass and forms dew. The dew remains until the sun rises again the next day. Then, as the heat of the sun transforms the beads of water into vapor again, the grass grows warm and dry.

SENTENCE WRITING

Write ten sentences about your morning routine (getting ready for school, eating breakfast, driving or riding to school, etc.). Try to write sentences that contain both independent and dependent clauses. Then draw a broken line beneath your dependent clauses, underline your subjects, and double underline your verbs. Use your own paper, and keep all of your sentence writing results in a folder.

Correcting Fragments

Sometimes a group of words looks like a sentence—with a capital letter at the beginning and a period at the end—but it may be missing a subject or a verb or both. Such incomplete sentence structures are called *fragments*. Here are a few examples:

Just ran around with his arms in the air. (*Who* did? There is no subject.)

Paul and his sister with the twins. (*Did* what? There is no verb.)

Nothing to do at night. (This fragment is missing a subject and a real verb. *To do* is a verbal, see p. 130.)

To change these fragments into sentences, we must make sure each has a subject and a real verb:

The lottery winner just ran around with his arms in the air. (We added a subject.)

Paul and his sister with the twins reconciled. (We added a verb.)

The jurors had nothing to do at night. (We added a subject and a real verb.)

Sometimes we can simply attach such a fragment to the previous sentence.

I want a fulfilling job. A teaching career, for example. (fragment)

I want a fulfilling job—a teaching career, for example. (correction)

Or we can add a subject or a verb to the fragment and make it a complete sentence.

I want a fulfilling job. A teaching career is one example.

PHRASE FRAGMENTS

By definition, phrases are word groups without subjects and verbs, so whenever a phrase is punctuated as a sentence, it is a fragment. Look at this example of a sentence followed by a phrase fragment beginning with *hoping* (see p. 130 for more about verbal phrases):

Actors waited outside the director's office. Hoping for a chance at an audition.

We can correct this fragment by attaching it to the previous sentence.

Actors waited outside the director's office, hoping for a chance at an audition.

Or we can change it to include a subject and a real verb.

> Actors waited outside the director's office. They hoped for a chance at an audition.

Here's another example of a sentence followed by a phrase fragment:

> Philosophy classes are challenging. When taken in summer school.

Here the two have been combined into one complete sentence:

> Philosophy classes taken in summer school are challenging.

Or a better revision might be

> Philosophy classes are challenging when taken in summer school.

Sometimes, prepositional phrases are also incorrectly punctuated as sentences. Here a prepositional phrase follows a sentence, but the word group is a fragment—it has no subject and verb of its own. Therefore, it needs to be corrected.

> I live a simple life. With my family on our farm in central California.

Here is one possible correction:

> I live a simple life with my family on our farm in central California.

Or it could be corrected this way:

> My family and I live a simple life on our farm in central California.

DEPENDENT CLAUSE FRAGMENTS

A dependent clause punctuated as a sentence is another kind of fragment. A sentence needs a subject, a verb, *and* a complete thought. As discussed in the previous section, a dependent clause has a subject and a verb, but it begins with a word that makes its meaning incomplete, such as *after, while, because, since, although, when, if, where, who, which,* and *that.* (See p. 74 for a longer list of these words.) To correct such fragments, we need to eliminate the word that makes the clause dependent *or* add an independent clause.

FRAGMENT

While some of us wrote in our journals.

CORRECTED

Some of us wrote in our journals.

or

While some of us wrote in our journals, the fire alarm rang.

FRAGMENT

Which kept me from finishing my journal entry.

CORRECTED

The fire alarm kept me from finishing my journal entry.

or

We responded to the fire alarm, *which* kept me from finishing my journal entry.

Are fragments ever permissible? Professional writers sometimes use fragments in advertising and other kinds of writing. But professional writers use these fragments intentionally, not in error. Until you're an experienced writer, it's best to write in complete sentences. Especially in college writing, you should avoid using fragments.

E X E R C I S E S

Some of the following word groups are sentences, and some are fragments. The sentences include subjects and verbs and make complete statements. Write the word "correct" next to each of the sentences. Then change the fragments into sentences by making sure that each has a subject, a real verb, and a complete thought.

Exercise 1

1. Some people get tattoos on a whim.

2. Not thinking about the consequences.

3. Studies of people with tattoos reveal interesting facts.

4. Many people change their minds after being tattooed.

5. About half of the people, to be exact.

6. Removing a tattoo is not easy.

7. Involving lasers to remove the pigment in the skin.

8. Alexandrite, YAG, and ruby are the three types of lasers.

9. Used on different colors and in different combinations.

10. A good dermatologist can remove most of a tattoo with lasers.

Source: Scientific American, July 2005

Exercise 2

1. One of Jerry Seinfeld's props was recently inducted into the Smithsonian Institution.

2. It's the white pirate shirt from the famous "Puffy Shirt" episode of *Seinfeld.*

3. The shirt that Jerry had to wear on TV.

4. To help Kramer's friend, a fashion designer.

5. The shirt is now on display at the National Museum of American History.

6. Along with Dorothy's ruby slippers from *The Wizard of Oz.*

7. And other famous objects, like the original Kermit the Frog from *Sesame Street.*

8. Jerry Seinfeld spoke at the ceremony to commemorate the shirt.

9. He explained why he thought the "Puffy Shirt" episode was so funny.

10. Because the shirt had the combination of a funny design and a funny name.

Source: Smithsonian, March 2005

Exercise 3

Each pair contains one sentence and one phrase fragment. Correct each phrase fragment by attaching the phrase to the complete sentence before or after it. Or rewrite the fragment to make it a complete sentence.

1. Finding a parking space on the first day of classes seems impossible. Driving endlessly around campus and looking for an empty spot.

2. With the hope that the situation will improve. I always spend forty dollars for a parking permit.

3. My old car's engine doesn't like the long periods of idling. Stalling a lot and not starting up again easily.

4. In order to get a space close to my first class. I always follow anyone walking through the parking lot closest to the science building.

5. I am usually disappointed by this method, however. Most people just walking through the parking lot to get to farther lots or to the bus stop.

6. I was really lucky on the first day of classes two semesters ago. Driving right into a spot vacated by a student from an earlier class.

7. Maybe I should get up before dawn myself. A foolproof way to secure a perfect parking place.

8. Every morning, I see these early birds in their cars with their seats back. Sleeping there for hours before class but in a great spot.

9. I don't think I can solve the problem this way. Finding it hard to get out of bed in the dark.

10. Due to the rise in college populations. Campus parking problems will most likely only get worse.

Exercise 4

Each pair contains one sentence and one dependent clause fragment. Correct each dependent clause fragment by eliminating its dependent word or by attaching the dependent clause to the independent clause before or after it.

1. We were writing our in-class essays. When suddenly the emergency bell rang.

2. Everyone in the class looked at each other first and then at the teacher. Who told us to gather up our things and follow him outside.

3. The series of short rings continued. As we left the room and noisily walked out into the parking lot beside the main building.

4. The sunlight was very warm and bright compared to the classroom's fluorescent lights. Which always make everything look more clinical than natural.

5. As we stood in a large group with students and teachers from other classes. We wondered about the reason for the alarm.

6. I have never heard an emergency alarm. That was anything but a planned drill.

7. Without the danger of injury, a party atmosphere quickly developed. Since we all got a break from our responsibilities.

8. I've noticed that the teachers seem the most at ease during these situations. Because they don't have to be in control.

9. After we students and the teachers chatted for ten minutes or so. The final bell rang to signal the end of the drill.

10. When we sat down at our desks again. The teacher asked us to continue writing our essays until the end of the hour.

Exercise 5

All of the following word groups are individual fragments punctuated as sentences. Make the necessary changes to turn each fragment into a sentence that makes sense to you. Your corrections will most likely differ from the sample answers at the back of the book. But by comparing your answers to ours, you'll see that there are many ways to correct a fragment.

1. Whenever I see a seagull up close.

2. After lunch on Tuesdays, our club meeting in the gym.

3. After we turned in our research assignments.

4. Traveling overseas without a lot of planning.

5. The pizza arriving within thirty minutes of our call.

6. It being the hardest question on the test.

7. That people often stretch the truth.

8. Discussing the topic with the person next to you.

9. Even though "wet paint" signs were still on the walls.

10. How a series of paragraphs becomes an essay.

PROOFREADING EXERCISE

Find and correct the five fragments in the following paragraph.

Fred Astaire was one of the most popular dancers of all time. Dancing in over forty movies in his fifty-year career. Born in Omaha, Nebraska, with the real name of Frederick Austerlitz. Fred Astaire and his sister were stage stars when they were still children. Appearing as a miniature married couple dancing on top of a huge wedding cake and as a lobster and a glass of champagne. Astaire was eventually happily married to his first wife Phyllis for many years. Later in his life, Fred Astaire got married again. This time to Robyn Smith. A female jockey who was forty-five years younger than Astaire.

Source: Biography Magazine, October 2003

SENTENCE WRITING

Write ten fragments (like the ones in Exercise 5) and then revise them so that they are complete sentences. Or exchange papers with another student and turn your classmate's ten fragments into sentences. Use your own paper, and keep all of your sentence writing results in a folder.

Correcting Run-on Sentences

A word group with a subject and a verb is a clause. As we have seen, the clause may be independent (making a complete statement and able to stand alone as a sentence), or it may be dependent (beginning with a dependent word and unable to stand alone as a sentence). When two *independent* clauses are written together without proper punctuation between them, the result is called a *run-on sentence*. Here are some examples:

> Classical music is soothing I listen to it in the evenings.

> I love the sound of piano therefore, Chopin is one of my favorites.

Run-on sentences can be corrected in one of four ways:

1. Make the two independent clauses into two sentences.

> Classical music is soothing. I listen to it in the evenings.

> I love the sound of piano. Therefore, Chopin is one of my favorites.

2. Connect the two independent clauses with a semicolon.

> Classical music is soothing; I listen to it in the evenings.

> I love the sound of piano; therefore, Chopin is one of my favorites.

When a connecting word (transition) such as

also	however	otherwise
consequently	likewise	then
finally	moreover	therefore
furthermore	nevertheless	thus

is used to join two independent clauses, the semicolon comes before the connecting word, and a comma usually comes after it.

> Mobile phones are convenient; however, they are very expensive.

> Earthquakes scare me; therefore, I don't live in Los Angeles.

> Yasmin traveled to London; then she took the "Chunnel" to Paris.

> The college recently built a large new library; thus we have more study areas.

> **NOTE**—The use of the comma after the connecting word depends on how long the connecting word is. If it is only a short word, like *then* or *thus,* the comma is not necessary.

3. **Connect the two independent clauses with a comma and one of the following seven words (the first letters of which create the word** *fanboys*)**:** *for, and, nor, but, or, yet, so.*

Classical music is soothing, *so* I listen to it in the evenings.

Chopin is one of my favorites, *for* I love the sound of piano.

Each of the *fanboys* has its own meaning. For example, *so* means "as a result," and *for* means "because."

Swans are beautiful birds, *and* they mate for life.

Students may register for classes by phone, *or* they may do so in person.

I applied for financial aid, *but* I am still working.

Brian doesn't know how to use a computer, *nor* does he plan to learn.

Before you put a comma before a *fanboys,* be sure there are two independent clauses. Note that the first sentence that follows has two independent clauses. However, the second sentence contains just one clause with two verbs and therefore needs no comma.

The snow began to fall at dusk, and it continued to fall through the night.

The snow began to fall at dusk and continued to fall through the night.

4. **Make one of the clauses dependent by adding a dependent word, such as** *since, when, as, after, while,* **or** *because.* **See p. 74 for a longer list of these words.**

Since classical music is soothing, I listen to it in the evenings.

Chopin is one of my favorites *because* I love the sound of piano.

Learn these ways to join two clauses, and you'll avoid run-on sentences.

WAYS TO CORRECT RUN-ON SENTENCES

They were learning a new song. They needed to practice. (two sentences)

They were learning a new song; they needed to practice. (semicolon)

They were learning a new song; therefore, they needed to practice. (semicolon + transition)

They were learning a new song, so they needed to practice. (comma + *fanboys*)

Because they were learning a new song, they needed to practice. (dependent clause first)

They needed to practice because they were learning a new song. (dependent clause last)

EXERCISES

Exercises 1 and 2

CORRECTING RUN-ONS WITH PUNCTUATION

Some of the following sentences are run-ons. If the sentence has two independent clauses, separate them with correct punctuation. Use only a period, a semicolon, or a comma to separate the two independent clauses. Remember to capitalize after a period and to insert a comma only when the words *for, and, nor, but, or, yet,* or *so* are already used to join the two independent clauses.

Exercise 1

1. Mary Mallon is a famous name in American history but she is not famous for something good.

2. Most people know Mary Mallon by another name and that is "Typhoid Mary."

3. Mallon lived during the late nineteenth and early twentieth centuries.

4. At that time, there was little knowledge about disease carriers.

5. Mary Mallon was the first famous case of a healthy carrier of disease but she never believed the accusations against her.

6. Mallon, an Irish immigrant, was a cook she was also an infectious carrier of typhoid.

7. By the time the authorities discovered Mallon's problem, she had made many people ill a few of her "victims" actually died from the disease.

8. A health specialist approached Mallon and asked her for a blood sample she was outraged and attacked him with a long cooking fork.

9. Eventually the authorities dragged Mallon into a hospital for testing but she fought them hysterically the entire time.

10. The lab tests proved Mallon's infectious status and health officials forced Mary Mallon to live on an island by herself for twenty-six years.

Sources: Los Angeles Times, September 2, 2002; and *Long Island: Our History Home Page* (*www.lihistory.com*)

Exercise 2

1. Frank Epperson invented something delicious and refreshing and it comes on a stick.

2. In 1905, Epperson was an eleven-year-old boy he lived in San Francisco.

3. On the porch outside his house, he was mixing a fruity drink with a stick and forgot to put his drink away before going to bed.

4. The drink sat outside all night with the stick still in it.

5. There was a record-breaking cold snap that evening and the drink froze.

6. In the morning, Frank Epperson ate his frozen juice creation it made a big impression.

7. Epperson grew up and kept making his frozen "Epsicles" they came in seven varieties.

8. Eighteen years after that cold night, Epperson patented his invention but with a different name.

9. Epperson's kids loved their dad's treat and they always called them "pop's sicles."

10. So Popsicles were born and people have loved them ever since.

Source: Biography Magazine, July 1999

Exercises 3 and 4

CORRECTING RUN-ONS WITH DEPENDENT CLAUSES

Most of the following sentences are run-ons. Correct any run-on sentences by making one or more of the clauses *dependent*. You may rephrase the sentences, but be sure to use dependent words (such as *since, when, as, after, while, because* or the other words listed on p. 74) to begin dependent clauses. Since various words can be used to form dependent clauses, your answers might differ from those suggested at the back of the book.

Exercise 3

1. I went to the orthodontist last month she told me that I needed braces.
2. I was happy I always wanted them.
3. My brother thought that I was crazy for wanting braces.
4. He wore the metal kind for five and a half years, and he hated them.
5. My dentist told me about many types of braces I wanted the invisible kind.
6. The dentist said that the invisible ones were perfect for my case she began the process.
7. She took a casting of my teeth and sent it to the invisible braces company.
8. The company made a series of sets of clear braces I will wear them for several weeks each.
9. The first set fits my teeth perfectly they are almost totally invisible.
10. I am glad that orthodontists offer this new type of braces they are just right for me.

Exercise 4

1. I've been learning about sleep in my psychology class I now know a lot more about it.
2. Sleep has five stages we usually go through all these stages many times during the night.
3. The first stage of sleep begins our muscles relax and mental activity slows down.
4. During stage one, we are still slightly awake.
5. Stage two takes us deeper than stage one we are no longer aware of our surroundings.

6. We spend about half our sleeping time in the second stage.

7. Next is stage three in it we become more and more relaxed and are very hard to awaken.

8. Stage four is the deepest in this stage we don't even hear loud noises.

9. The fifth stage of sleep is called REM (rapid eye movement) sleep our eyes move back and forth quickly behind our eyelids.

10. REM sleep is only about as deep as stage two we do all our dreaming during the REM stage.

Exercise 5

Correct the following run-on sentences using any of the methods studied in this section: adding punctuation or using dependent words to create dependent clauses. See the chart on p. 91 if you need to review the methods.

1. Boston Red Sox fans have a tradition they celebrate it at every home game without question.

2. Very few people know how the tradition began but most people don't care to know.

3. It happens in the eighth inning and everyone looks forward to it.

4. The loud speakers at Fenway Park play the song "Sweet Caroline" all of the fans sing along.

5. There is a problem with the tradition the song has no link to Boston or baseball.

6. Neil Diamond sings the thirty-year-old song but his last name is only a baseball coincidence.

7. In the past, other teams played the song at stadiums but in 2002, Boston started playing it at every game.

8. Some people say that the tradition brought the team good luck.

9. The Red Sox won the 2004 World Series no one really expected that.

10. Players and teams in sports are sometimes superstitious singing "Sweet Caroline" is a lucky charm that the fans, the players, and the management love.

Source: The Boston Globe, May 29, 2005

REVIEW OF FRAGMENTS AND RUN-ON SENTENCES

If you remember that all clauses include a subject and a verb, but only independent clauses can be punctuated as sentences (since only they can stand alone), then you will avoid fragments in your writing. And if you memorize these six rules for the punctuation of clauses, you will be able to avoid most punctuation errors.

PUNCTUATING CLAUSES

I am a student. I am still learning.	(two sentences)
I am a student; I am still learning.	(two independent clauses)
I am a student; therefore, I am still learning.	(two independent clauses connected by a word such as *also, consequently, finally, furthermore, however, likewise, moreover, nevertheless, otherwise, then, therefore, thus*)
I am a student, so I am still learning.	(two independent clauses connected by *for, and, nor, but, or, yet, so*)
Because I am a student, I am still learning.	(dependent clause at beginning of sentence)
I am still learning because I am a student.	(dependent clause at end of sentence) Dependent words include *after, although, as, as if, because, before, even if, even though, ever since, how, if, since, so that, than, that, though, unless, until, what, whatever, when, whenever, where, whereas, wherever, whether, which, whichever, while, who, whom, whose,* and *why.*

It is essential that you learn the italicized words in the previous chart—which ones come between independent clauses and which ones introduce dependent clauses.

PROOFREADING EXERCISE

Rewrite the following paragraph, making the necessary changes so there will be no fragments or run-on sentences.

With all of the attention on cleanliness lately in advertising for soaps and household cleaning products. People are surprised to hear that we may be too clean for our own good. This phenomenon is called the "hygiene hypothesis" and recent studies support its validity. For instance, one study showing the benefits of living with two or more pets. Babies may grow up with healthier immune systems and be less allergic if they live with a dog and a cat or two dogs or two cats. The old thinking was that young children would become more allergic living with many pets but they don't. Somehow the exposure to pets and all their "dirty" habits gives youngsters much-needed defenses. Sometimes as much as a seventy-five percent lower allergy risk, according to this study.

Source: Los Angeles Times, September 2, 2002

SENTENCE WRITING

Write a sample sentence of your own to demonstrate each of the six ways to punctuate two clauses. You may model your sentences on the examples used in the review chart on page 95. Use your own paper, and keep all of your sentence writing results in a folder.

Identifying Verb Phrases

Sometimes a verb is one word, but often the whole verb includes more than one word. These are called verb phrases. Look at several of the many forms of the verb *speak,* for example. Most of them are verb phrases, made up of the main verb (*speak*) and one or more helping verbs.

speak	is speaking	had been speaking
speaks	am speaking	will have been speaking
spoke	are speaking	is spoken
will speak	was speaking	was spoken
has spoken	were speaking	will be spoken
have spoken	will be speaking	can speak
had spoken	has been speaking	must speak
will have spoken	have been speaking	should have spoken

Note that words like the following are never verbs, even though they may be near a verb or in the middle of a verb phrase:

already	ever	not	really
also	finally	now	sometimes
always	just	often	usually
probably	never	only	possibly

Jason has *never* spoken to his instructor before. She *always* talks with other students.

Two forms of *speak*—*speaking* and *to speak*—look like verbs, but neither form can ever be the only verb in a sentence. No *ing* word by itself or *to* _____ form of a verb can be the main verb of a sentence.

Jeanine speaking French. (not a sentence because there is no complete verb phrase)

Jeanine was speaking French. (a sentence with a complete verb phrase)

And no verb with *to* in front of it can ever be the verb of a sentence.

Ted to speak in front of groups. (not a sentence because there is no real verb)

Ted likes to speak in front of groups. (a sentence with *likes* as the verb)

These two forms, *speaking* and *to speak,* may be used as subjects or other parts of a sentence.

adj

Speaking on stage is an art. *To speak* on stage is an art. Ted had a *speaking* part in that play.

E X E R C I S E S

Underline the verbs or verb phrases twice in the following sentences. The sentences may contain independent *and* dependent clauses, so there could be several verbs and verb phrases. (Remember that *ing* verbs alone and the *to* _____ forms of verbs are never real verbs in sentences.)

Exercise 1

1. For the first time, scientists have successfully cloned a dog.

2. Cloning experts had been attempting this accomplishment for many years.

3. They had had success with horses, cats, and even rats before they could clone a dog.

4. The scientists who eventually succeeded were from Seoul National University in South Korea.

5. They named the cloned dog Snuppy as a tribute to the university where the accomplishment was made.

6. Of course, Snuppy can thank his "parent" dog, a three-year-old Afghan hound, for all of his great features.

7. Both dogs have long glossy black fur that is accentuated by identical brown markings on their paws, tails, chests, and eyebrows.

8. Now that a dog has been cloned, everyone anticipates that some pet owners will want a clone of their dogs.

9. The procedure for dogs involves different steps and may always be more difficult.

10. Cloning pets will definitely cost a lot of money and be a gamble at best.

Source: Science News, August 6, 2005

Exercise 2

1. Kris Kliszewicz, a successful businessman in England, has been raising money and interest around the world for a pet project.

2. Kliszewicz wants to build a theme park which will allow people to immerse themselves in the life and times of Shakespeare.

3. Kliszewicz is planning to call the new history-based theme park "Shakespeare's World."

4. He has decided on the perfect location for the first of these parks—on the outskirts of Shakespeare's hometown, Stratford-upon-Avon.

5. At Shakespeare's World, troupes of roaming actors will perform scenes from Shakespeare's plays.

6. According to Kliszewicz, visitors will see the sights and hear the sounds that Shakespeare saw and heard.

7. There will be cobblestoned streets complete with bakeries and butcheries, fields full of animals and farming peasants, and tradespeople who will demonstrate Tudor crafts.

8. Some Shakespeare scholars are not convinced that a Shakespeare theme park is a good idea.

9. But Kliszewicz believes that people might enjoy more exposure to Shakespeare without the purely academic treatment that he is given in classrooms.

10. The idea of Shakespeare's World is also getting some attention in China, Russia, and America, which Kliszewicz plans to make future sites for Shakespeare's World.

Source: London Theatre News, September 8, 2002

Exercise 3

1. I have always wondered how an Etch A Sketch works.

2. This flat TV-shaped toy has been popular since it first arrived in the 1960s.

3. Now I have learned the secrets inside this popular toy.

4. An Etch A Sketch is filled with a combination of metal powder and tiny plastic particles.

5. This mixture clings to the inside of the Etch A Sketch screen.

6. When the pointer that is connected to the two knobs moves, the tip of it "draws" lines in the powder on the back of the screen.

7. The powder at the bottom of the Etch A Sketch does not fill in these lines because it is too far away.

8. But if the Etch A Sketch is turned upside down, the powder clings to the whole underside surface of the screen and "erases" the image again.

9. Although the basic Etch A Sketch has not changed since I was a kid, it now comes in several different sizes.

10. Best of all, these great drawing devices have never needed batteries, and I hope that they never will.

Exercise 4

1. During my last semester of high school, our English teacher assigned a special paper.

2. He said that he was becoming depressed by all the bad news out there, so each of us was asked to find a piece of good news and write a short research paper about it.

3. I must admit that I had no idea how hard that assignment would be.

4. Finally, I found an article while I was reading my favorite magazine.

5. The title of the article was a pun; it was called "Grin Reaper."

6. I knew instantly that it must be just the kind of news my teacher wanted.

7. The article explained that one woman, Pam Johnson, had started a club that she named The Secret Society of Happy People.

8. She had even chosen August 8 as "Admit You're Happy Day" and had already convinced more than fifteen state governors to recognize the holiday.

9. The club and the holiday were created to support people who are happy so that the unhappy, negative people around will not bring the happy people down.

10. As I was writing my essay, I visited the Society of Happy People Web site and, for extra credit, signed my teacher up for their newsletter.

Source: People, August 30, 1999; and *www.sohp.com*

Exercise 5

1. Donald Redelmeier was sitting in front of his television a few years ago, and he was not alone.

2. He was enjoying the Academy Awards along with millions of other TV viewers.

3. Redelmeier focused on the nominees as they were waiting for the announcement of the winners' names.

4. Suddenly, he was struck by the good health and lively mannerisms of them all.

5. Redelmeier's experiences as a doctor of ordinary people did not match what he was seeing on TV.

6. He devised a study that would explore the effects of success and recognition on health.

7. He would use the winners and losers of Academy Awards as the pool of subjects for his data.

8. He wondered if Oscar winners would live longer than losers and those who had never been nominated.

9. The results of his study showed that the winners do live an average of four years longer that the losers.

10. Luckily, nominees who lose also live a few months longer than those who are not nominated, so they do get some benefits.

Source: Current Science, May 6, 2005, and *Forbes.com,* June 19, 2003

REVIEW EXERCISE

To practice finding all of the sentence structures we have studied so far, mark the following excerpt from the vintage science book *The How and Why Book of Weather*. First, put parentheses around prepositional phrases, then underline subjects once and verbs or verb phrases twice. Finally, put a broken line beneath dependent clauses. Begin by marking the first paragraph, then check your answers at the back of the book before marking the rest. (Remember that *ing* verbs alone and the *to* _____ forms of verbs are never real verbs in sentences. We will learn more about them on p. 130.)

There is something that starts in the sky as one thing and lands on earth as something else. It is hail. Hail starts as rain, but before the drops of water can fall very far, the wind blows them high up where the air is colder. They freeze and start to fall again. Over and over they fall and are blown back up again. Each time that they fall, a new layer of water vapor condenses on them. And each time that they are blown up into the freezing layer, this new layer of water turns to ice. Finally, the hailstones become too heavy to be lifted by the wind, and they fall to earth. Some hailstones as large as baseballs have been recorded, but usually hailstones do not grow larger than the size of a pea.

During the next hailstorm, if you pick up a few pieces of hail and cut them in half, you can see the layers that were formed as they fell, collected more moisture, and were swept back up into the freezing air again. If you count the layers, you can record the number of trips that each hailstone made before it finally landed on the ground.

Using Standard English Verbs

The next two discussions are for those who need to practice using Standard English verbs. Many of us grew up doing more speaking than writing. But in college and in the business and professional worlds, knowledge of Standard Written English is essential.

The following charts show the forms of four verbs as they are used in Standard Written English. These forms might differ from the way you use these verbs when you speak. Memorize the Standard English forms of these important verbs. The first verb (*talk*) is one of the regular verbs (verbs that all end the same way according to a pattern); most verbs in English are regular. The other three verbs charted here (*have, be,* and *do*) are irregular and are important because they are used not only as main verbs but also as helping verbs in verb phrases.

Don't go on to the exercises until you have memorized the forms of these Standard English verbs.

REGULAR VERB: TALK

PRESENT TIME		PAST TIME	
I		I	
you		you	
we	talk	we	talked
they		they	
he, she, it	talks	he, she, it	

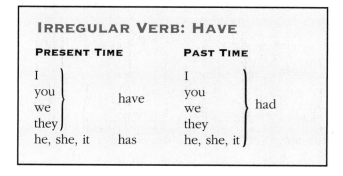

IRREGULAR VERB: HAVE

PRESENT TIME		PAST TIME	
I		I	
you		you	
we	have	we	had
they		they	
he, she, it	has	he, she, it	

IRREGULAR VERB: BE

PRESENT TIME		PAST TIME	
I	am	I	was
you }	are	you }	were
we }		we }	
they }		they }	
he, she, it	is	he, she, it	was

IRREGULAR VERB: DO

PRESENT TIME		PAST TIME	
I }	do	I }	did
you }		you }	
we }		we }	
they }		they }	
he, she, it	does	he, she, it	

Sometimes you may have difficulty with the correct endings of verbs because you don't hear the words correctly. Note carefully the *s* sound and the *ed* sound at the end of words. Occasionally, the *ed* is not clearly pronounced, as in *They tried to help,* but most of the time you can hear it if you listen.

Read the following sentences aloud, making sure that you say every sound:

1. He seems satisfied with his new job.

2. She likes saving money for the future.

3. It takes strength of character to control spending.

4. Todd brings salad to every potluck he attends.

5. I used to know all of their names.

6. They supposed that they were right.

7. He recognized the suspect and excused himself from the jury.

8. The chess club sponsored Dorothy in the school's charity event.

Now read some other sentences aloud from this text, making sure that you say all the *s*'s and *ed*'s. Reading aloud and listening to others will help you use the correct verb endings automatically.

E X E R C I S E S

In these pairs of sentences, use the *present* form of the verb in the first sentence and the *past* form in the second. All the verbs follow the pattern of the regular verb *talk* except the irregular verbs *have, be,* and *do.* Keep referring to the charts if you're not sure which form to use. Check your answers in the back of the book after each set.

Exercise 1

1. (pack) He _____ suitcases very well. He _____ all of our suitcases for the cruise.

2. (be) The twins _____ never late for class in college. In high school, they _____ often late for class, and their grades suffered.

3. (walk) This semester, I _____ to school as often as I can. Last semester, I _____ to school about two times a week.

4. (have) She _____ a class in the gym building at noon. Yesterday, she _____ a cold and missed class.

5. (need) For the speech assignment, we _____ some index cards. For last week's in-class essay, we _____ a large blue book.

6. (do) Helena usually _____ her math homework every night. Last night, she _____ her English homework and fell asleep.

7. (be) Normally, he _____ not a shy person. However, he _____ shy in high school.

8. (like) I _____ that new movie in the trilogy as much as I _____ the one that came out last year.

9. (have) All of my friends _____ new cell phones. They all _____ old phones like mine before they upgraded them.

10. (be) Currently, I _____ a full-time student. I _____ a part-time student last semester.

Exercise 2

1. (do)   You _____ too much homework every night. Last night, you _____ three hours of homework.

2. (be)   We _____ members of the chess club now. Last year, we _____ not members of any clubs.

3. (have)   Tim _____ really short hair. He _____ longer hair before he joined the swim team.

4. (type)   We always _____ our paragraphs and essays in the lab. Last week, we _____ three papers there.

5. (count) The teacher _____ the students before she takes roll. Yesterday, she _____ wrong and thought that everyone was in class.

6. (have)   I always _____ fun in the summer. Last summer, I _____ a great time in Las Vegas.

7. (open)   My little brother _____ his presents very quickly. He _____ his birthday presents so quickly that we couldn't match the cards with the presents.

8. (do)   She _____ the crossword puzzle in the newspaper every Sunday. Last Sunday, she even _____ the bonus puzzle.

9. (plan)   I _____ my class schedules very carefully now that I am in college. I never _____ them carefully before.

10. (be)   I _____ finally as tall as my brother. I _____ the shortest member of my family until recently.

Exercise 3

Circle the correct Standard English verb forms.

1. I (do, does) an exercise routine every morning so that I (don't, doesn't) get out of shape again.

2. A couple of months ago, I (have, had) a bad experience after I (decide, decided) to join some friends for basketball.

3. I (was, were) on my best friend Ana's team, but I (play, played) really badly.

4. Ana (talk, talked) to me after the game.

5. She (ask, asked) me why I (was, were) so slow on the court.

6. I (was, were) really embarrassed.

7. Ana and I (was, were) in high school together, and we (was, were) even in the same P.E. class.

8. We both (enjoy, enjoyed) the track exercises the most and (like, liked) to challenge each other's stamina.

9. Then, after high school, I (start, started) my job as a clerk in an insurance office and (stop, stopped) doing any exercising.

10. Now that I (am, is) back to a good routine, I (plan, planned) to call Ana to set up another game.

Exercise 4

Circle the correct Standard English verb forms.

1. I recently (change, changed) my career plans; now I (want, wants) to be a chef.

2. Last year, I (have, had) my mind set on becoming a kindergarten teacher.

3. I (sign, signed) up for several childhood education classes, and they all (turn, turned) out to be disappointing.

4. The class work (was, were) often too easy, and the reading assignments (was, were) too hard.

5. We (does, did) spend part of the semester working in a real kindergarten class where we (was, were) able to observe just what the teacher (does, did).

6. The teacher that I (observes, observed) (have, had) twenty-seven children to look after.

7. I (watch, watched) her as she (help, helped) them learn their numbers and letters.

8. She (have, had) her students, their parents, and the school's administration to worry about all the time.

9. I never (imagine, imagined) that a kindergarten teacher (have, had) so many responsibilities.

10. A chef (need, needs) to worry about the food and the customers, and those (is, are) responsibilities that I (is, am) ready to take.

Exercise 5

Correct any of following sentences that do not use Standard English verb forms. Use past verb forms for your corrections.

1. Last month, my English teacher assign a narration essay.

2. We have one week to finish a rough draft.

3. Before the assignment, he showed us two sample narration essays.

4. They was about holiday traditions in different families.

5. In one essay, the writer explain the tradition of Thanksgiving at her house.

6. I likes the part about making pies for the adults and candy for the kids.

7. The second essay outline the steps another family went through to prepare for Chinese New Year.

8. That one have even more details about food and gifts for the children.

9. My teacher asked us to write about a family ritual of our own.

10. I finish my rough draft in one night; it describe my dad's obsession with Halloween.

PROOFREADING EXERCISE

In the following paragraph, correct any sentences that do not use Standard English verb forms. Use present verb forms for your corrections.

Most people believe that they has the best pets. I think that we have the cutest pet hamster in the world. Her name is Toots. The name come from the little dog that die in the movie *Lassie Come Home*. Our Toots don't look like that dog, but she have something about her that reminds us of it. The dog in the movie protect her owner from some really mean men. When the men try to beat the man who own her, Toots is so brave. She jump in front of her owner and saves

him. Our hamster is small but fearless too, so her name is Toots.

SENTENCE WRITING

Write ten sentences about a pet that you have (or a friend has). Check your sentences to be sure that they use Standard English verb forms. Try exchanging papers with another student for more practice. Use your own paper, and keep all of your sentence writing results in a folder.

Using Regular and Irregular Verbs

All regular verbs end the same way in the past form and when used with helping verbs. Here is a chart showing all the forms of some *regular* verbs and the various helping verbs with which they are used.

REGULAR VERBS				
BASE FORM	**PRESENT**	**PAST**	**PAST PARTICIPLE**	***ING* FORM**
(Use after *can, may, shall, will, could, might, should, would, must, do, does, did.*)			(Use after *have, has, had.* Some can be used after *forms of be.*)	(Use after *forms of be.*)
ask	ask *(s)*	asked	asked	asking
bake	bake *(s)*	baked	baked	baking
count	count *(s)*	counted	counted	counting
dance	dance *(s)*	danced	danced	dancing
decide	decide *(s)*	decided	decided	deciding
enjoy	enjoy *(s)*	enjoyed	enjoyed	enjoying
finish	finish *(es)*	finished	finished	finishing
happen	happen *(s)*	happened	happened	happening
learn	learn *(s)*	learned	learned	learning
like	like *(s)*	liked	liked	liking
look	look *(s)*	looked	looked	looking
mend	mend *(s)*	mended	mended	mending
need	need *(s)*	needed	needed	needing
open	open *(s)*	opened	opened	opening
start	start *(s)*	started	started	starting
suppose	suppose *(s)*	supposed	supposed	supposing
tap	tap *(s)*	tapped	tapped	tapping
walk	walk *(s)*	walked	walked	walking
want	want *(s)*	wanted	wanted	wanting

> **NOTE**—When there are several helping verbs, the last one determines which form of the main verb should be used: they *should* finish soon; they should *have* finished an hour ago.

When do you write *ask, finish, suppose, use?* And when do you write *asked, finished, supposed, used?* Here are some rules that will help you decide.

Write *ask, finish, suppose, use* (or their *s* forms) when writing about the present time, repeated actions, or facts:

He *ask*s questions whenever he is confused.

They always *finish* their projects on time.

I *suppose* you want me to help you move.

Birds *use* leaves, twigs, and feathers to build their nests.

Write *asked, finished, supposed, used*

1. When writing about the past:

He *asked* the teacher for another explanation.

She *finished* her internship last year.

They *supposed* that there were others bidding on that house.

I *used* to study piano.

2. When some form of *be* (other than the word *be* itself) comes before the word:

He was *asked* the most difficult questions.

She is *finished* with her training now.

They were *supposed* to sign at the bottom of the form.

My essay was *used* as a sample of clear narration.

3. When some form of *have* comes before the word:

The teacher has *asked* us that question before.

She will have *finished* all of her exams by the end of May.

I had *supposed* too much without any proof.

We have *used* many models in my drawing class this semester.

All the verbs in the chart on page 110 are *regular.* That is, they're all formed in the same way—with an *ed* ending on the past form and on the past participle. But many verbs are irregular. Their past and past participle forms change spelling instead of just adding an *ed*. Here's a chart of some *irregular* verbs. Notice that the base, present, and *ing* forms end the same as regular verbs. Refer to this list when you aren't sure which verb form to use. Memorize all the forms you don't know.

IRREGULAR VERBS

BASE FORM	PRESENT	PAST	PAST PARTICIPLE	*ING* FORM
(Use after *can, may, shall, will, could, might, should, would, must, do, does, did.*)			(Use after *have, has, had.* Some can be used after *forms of be.*)	(Use after *forms of be.*)
be	is, am, are	was, were	been	being
become	become *(s)*	became	become	becoming
begin	begin *(s)*	began	begun	beginning
break	break *(s)*	broke	broken	breaking
bring	bring *(s)*	brought	brought	bringing
buy	buy *(s)*	bought	bought	buying
build	build *(s)*	built	built	building
catch	catch *(es)*	caught	caught	catching
choose	choose *(s)*	chose	chosen	choosing
come	come *(s)*	came	come	coming
do	do *(es)*	did	done	doing
draw	draw *(s)*	drew	drawn	drawing
drink	drink *(s)*	drank	drunk	drinking
drive	drive *(s)*	drove	driven	driving
eat	eat *(s)*	ate	eaten	eating
fall	fall *(s)*	fell	fallen	falling
feel	feel *(s)*	felt	felt	feeling
fight	fight *(s)*	fought	fought	fighting
find	find *(s)*	found	found	finding
forget	forget *(s)*	forgot	forgotten	forgetting
forgive	forgive *(s)*	forgave	forgiven	forgiving
freeze	freeze *(s)*	froze	frozen	freezing
get	get *(s)*	got	got *or* gotten	getting
give	give *(s)*	gave	given	giving
go	go *(es)*	went	gone	going
grow	grow *(s)*	grew	grown	growing
have	have *or* has	had	had	having
hear	hear *(s)*	heard	heard	hearing
hold	hold *(s)*	held	held	holding
keep	keep *(s)*	kept	kept	keeping
know	know *(s)*	knew	known	knowing
lay (to put)	lay *(s)*	laid	laid	laying

IRREGULAR VERBS (CONTINUED)

BASE FORM	PRESENT	PAST	PAST PARTICIPLE	*ING* FORM
lead (like "bead")	lead *(s)*	led	led	leading
leave	leave *(s)*	left	left	leaving
lie (to rest)	lie *(s)*	lay	lain	lying
lose	lose *(s)*	lost	lost	losing
make	make *(s)*	made	made	making
meet	meet *(s)*	met	met	meeting
pay	pay *(s)*	paid	paid	paying
read (pron. "reed")	read *(s)*	read (pron. "red")	read (pron. "red")	reading
ride	ride *(s)*	rode	ridden	riding
ring	ring *(s)*	rang	rung	ringing
rise	rise *(s)*	rose	risen	rising
run	run *(s)*	ran	run	running
say	say *(s)*	said	said	saying
see	see *(s)*	saw	seen	seeing
sell	sell *(s)*	sold	sold	selling
shake	shake *(s)*	shook	shaken	shaking
shine (give light)	shine *(s)*	shone	shone	shining
shine (polish)	shine *(s)*	shined	shined	shining
sing	sing *(s)*	sang	sung	singing
sleep	sleep *(s)*	slept	slept	sleeping
speak	speak *(s)*	spoke	spoken	speaking
spend	spend *(s)*	spent	spent	spending
stand	stand *(s)*	stood	stood	standing
steal	steal *(s)*	stole	stolen	stealing
strike	strike *(s)*	struck	struck	striking
swim	swim *(s)*	swam	swum	swimming
swing	swing *(s)*	swung	swung	swinging
take	take *(s)*	took	taken	taking
teach	teach *(es)*	taught	taught	teaching
tear	tear *(s)*	tore	torn	tearing
tell	tell *(s)*	told	told	telling
think	think *(s)*	thought	thought	thinking
throw	throw *(s)*	threw	thrown	throwing
wear	wear *(s)*	wore	worn	wearing
win	win *(s)*	won	won	winning
write	write *(s)*	wrote	written	writing

Sometimes verbs from the past participle column are used after some form of the verb *be* (or verbs that take the place of *be* like *appear, seem, look, feel, get, act, become*) to describe the subject or to say something in a passive, rather than an active, way.

She is contented.

You appear pleased. (You *are* pleased.)

He seems delighted. (He *is* delighted.)

She looked surprised. (She *was* surprised.)

I feel shaken. (I *am* shaken.)

They get bored easily. (They *are* bored easily.)

You acted concerned. (You *were* concerned.)

They were thrown out of the game. (Active: *The referee threw them out of the game.*)

We were disappointed by the news. (Active: *The news disappointed us.*)

Often these verb forms become words that describe the subject; at other times they still act as part of the verb in the sentence. What you call them doesn't matter. The important thing is to be sure you use the correct form from the past participle column.

EXERCISES

Write the correct form of the verbs in the blanks. Refer to the charts and explanations on the preceding pages if you aren't sure which form to use after a certain helping verb. Check your answers after each exercise.

Exercise 1

1. (eat)   People _____ a lot when they go to the movies.

2. (eat)   I can _____ a whole bag of popcorn myself.

3. (eat)   When someone else is _____ popcorn, the crunching sound drives me crazy.

4. (eat)   Once I have _____ my dinner, I stay away from snacks.

5. (eat)   My sister _____ a worm when she was in kindergarten.

6. (eat)   My two-year-old nephew _____ everything; he is not picky.

7. (eat)   He will even _____ sushi when his parents order it at restaurants.

8. (eat)   The meal at the conference was _____ in silence.

9. (eat)   We _____ while we watched a documentary on television.

10. (eat)   If you want to pass the test, you should _____ a good breakfast.

Exercise 2

1. (buy)   My parents should _____ a new television because they _____ their current TV back in the 1980s.

2. (know)   They do not even _____ how outdated their TV is. If I _____ of a way to make it break down, I would do it.

3. (be)   That _____ the only way they would discuss getting a new TV. Unfortunately, old television sets _____ really reliable and well-made.

4. (agree)   Both of my parents _____ that if something isn't broken, it shouldn't be replaced. Obviously, my siblings and I do not _____ with them.

5. (tell)   My brother and I have _____ them all about the great features available on the new sets. We might as well have been _____ them about spaceships.

6. (sit)   Our mom and dad will happily _____ through local broadcast-station shows and would never dream of subscribing to a cable or dish service. Once I house-_____ for my parents while they were on vacation and was extremely bored.

7. (have)   Well, at least my parents are _____ fun together. Maybe I _____ the wrong attitude.

8. (get)   Last year, I _____ a state-of-the-art TV. I may be _____ hundreds of stations now, but I'm still not satisfied.

9. (need)   In fact, I may _____ companionship much more than my parents _____ a new TV.

10. (be)   I _____ sure that my mom and dad _____ the most old-fashioned people I know, but they are also the happiest people I know.

Exercise 3

1. (take, suppose)   My friend Brenda _____ a day off last week even though she was _____ to be working.

2. (do, earn)   She _____ not feel sick exactly; she just felt that she had _____ a day of rest.

3. (call, tell, feel)   So Brenda _____ her office and _____ her boss that she did not _____ well enough to work that day.

4. (think, be)   She never _____ that she would get caught, but she _____ wrong.

5. (leave, drive, see)   Just as Brenda was _____ the house to buy some lunch, her coworker _____ by and _____ her.

6. (feel, know, tell)   She _____ such panic because she _____ that he would _____ their boss that she looked fine.

7. (try, go)   Brenda _____ to explain herself when she _____ back to the office the next day.

8. (be, undo)   The damage had _____ done, however, and nothing could _____ it.

9. (wish, take)   Now Brenda _____ that she could _____ back that day.

10. (use, call, do)   She _____ to have a great relationship with her boss, but since the day she _____ in sick, he _____ not trust her anymore.

Exercise 4

1. (use, put)   Many people _____ a direct deposit system that _____ their salary money directly into their bank accounts.

2. (do, do)   With such a system, the employer _____ not have to issue paychecks, and employees _____ not have to cash or deposit them.

3. (transfer, spend)   The employer's computer just _____ the money to the bank's computer, and the employee can _____ it as usual after that.

4. (be, like, choose)   Direct deposit _____ almost always optional, but so many people _____ the system that most people _____ it.

5. (do, want)   My roommate _____ not trust such systems; he _____ to have complete control over his cash.

6. (trust, be)   He barely even _____ banks to keep his money safe for him, so he _____ definitely suspicious of direct deposit.

7. (imagine, make)   I can _____ him as a pioneer in an old Western movie sleeping on a mattress stuffed with all of the money he has ever _____.

8. (talk, ask, worry)   I was _____ to my roommate about money the other day, and I _____ him why he always _____ about it so much.

9. (look, say, live, understand)   He just _____ at me and _____ , "If you had ever _____ without money, you would _____."

10. (wonder, be)   I _____ about my roommate's past experiences and hope that he _____ never without money again.

Exercise 5

1. (lie, fall)   I was _____ out in the sun last Sunday, and I _____ asleep.

2. (be, do)   That _____ the worst thing I could have _____.

3. (wear, shield)   I was _____ a pair of big dark sunglasses, which _____ my eyes from the light.

4. (lie, wake, realize, happen)   I must have _____ there for over an hour before I _____ up and _____ what had _____.

5. (feel, start)   At first I _____ fine, but then my skin _____ to feel really tight and thin.

6. (pass, turn, begin)   As the minutes _____, my skin _____ bright red, and the pain _____.

7. (describe, experience) I can't even _____ how much pain I _____.

8. (be, feel, see)   Almost worse than the pain _____ the embarrassment I _____ as I _____ my face in the mirror.

9. (look, tape, be, protect, wear) Around my eyes, it _____ as if someone had _____ the shape of white glasses to my face, but that _____ just the skin that had been _____ by the sunglasses I was _____.

10. (have, feel)   The people at work _____ a big laugh the next day at my expense, but then they just _____ sorry for me.

PROGRESS TEST

This test covers everything you've studied so far. One sentence in each pair is correct. The other is incorrect. Read both sentences carefully before you decide. Then write the letter of the incorrect sentence in the blank. Try to name the error and correct it if you can.

1. _____ **A.** I was the only one in the classroom except the teacher.

   B. As soon as I finish the test, the bell rang.

2. _____ **A.** School supplies ordered over the Internet.

   B. They can be less expensive than the ones in stores.

3. _____ **A.** Our assignment required a trip to the museum and I love museums.

   B. I asked the teacher if I could do some extra credit there.

4. _____ **A.** My research paper will probably be late.

   B. I should of gone to the library sooner.

5. _____ **A.** We were suppose to lock the door after class.

   B. We forgot and had to drive back to school.

6. _____ **A.** Adam and Tracy have finished all of their school work.

   B. Their going away for spring break, and I'm staying at home.

7. _____ **A.** The package had no official label, only a handwritten address.

   B. We were surprise that it was delivered on time.

8. _____ **A.** In my math class, we've already took three quizzes.

   B. We'll have six more quizzes before the final exam.

9. _____ **A.** The bus driver tried to start the bus after it stalled.

   B. Nothing worked so we all got off the bus and waited for another one.

10. _____ **A.** Although I don't like the taste of grapefruits and lemons.

    B. I do like cleaning products that smell like grapefruits and lemons.

Maintaining Subject-Verb Agreement

As we have seen, the subject and verb in a sentence work together, so they must always agree. Different subjects need different forms of verbs. When the correct verb follows a subject, we call it subject-verb agreement.

The following sentences illustrate the rule that *s* verbs follow most singular subjects but not plural subjects:

One turtle walks.	Three turtles walk.
The baby cries.	The babies cry.
A democracy listens to the people.	Democracies listen to the people.
One child plays.	Many children play.

The following sentences show how forms of the verb *be* (*is, am, are, was, were*) and helping verbs (*be, have,* and *do*) are made to agree with their subjects. We have labeled only the verbs that must agree with the subjects.

This puzzle is difficult.	These puzzles are difficult.
I am amazed.	You are amazed.
He was sleeping.	They were sleeping.
That class has been canceled.	Those classes have been canceled.
She does not want to participate.	They do not want to participate.

The following words are always singular and take an *s* verb or the irregular equivalent (*is, was, has, does*):

one	anybody	each
anyone	everybody	
everyone	nobody	
no one	somebody	
someone		

Someone feeds my dog in the morning.

Everybody was at the party.

Each does her own homework.

Remember that prepositional phrases often come between subjects and verbs. You should ignore these interrupting phrases, or you may mistake the wrong word for the subject and use a verb form that doesn't agree.

Someone from the apartments feeds my dog in the morning. (*Someone* is the subject, not *apartments*.)

Everybody on the list of celebrities was at the party. (*Everybody* is the subject, not *celebrities*.)

Each of the twins does her own homework. (*Each* is the subject, not *twins*.)

However, the words *some, any, all, none,* and *most* are exceptions to this rule of ignoring prepositional phrases. These words can be singular or plural, depending on the words that follow them in prepositional phrases. Again, we have labeled only the verbs that must agree with the subjects.

Some of the *pie* is gone.

Some of the *cookies* are gone.

Is any of the *paper* still in the supply cabinet?

Are any of the *pencils* still in the supply cabinet?

All of her *work* has been published.

All of her *poems* have been published.

None of the *jewelry* is missing.

None of the *clothes* are missing.

On July 4th, most of the *country* celebrates.

On July 4th, most of the *citizens* celebrate.

When a sentence has more than one subject joined by *and,* the subject is plural:

The teacher *and* the tutors eat lunch at noon.

A glazed doughnut *and* an egg bagel were sitting on the plate.

However, when two subjects are joined by *or,* then the subject *closest* to the verb determines the verb form:

Either the teacher *or* the *tutors* eat lunch at noon.

Either the tutors *or* the *teacher* eats lunch at noon.

A glazed doughnut *or* an egg *bagel* was sitting on the plate.

In most sentences, the subject comes before the verb. However, in some cases, the subject follows the verb, and subject-verb agreement needs special attention. Study the following examples:

Over the building flies a solitary flag. (flag flies)

Over the building fly several flags. (flags fly)

There is a good reason for my actions. (reason is)

There are good reasons for my actions. (reasons are)

E X E R C I S E S

Circle the correct verbs in parentheses to maintain subject-verb agreement in the following sentences. Remember to ignore prepositional phrases, unless the subjects are *some, any, all, none,* or *most.* Check your answers ten at a time.

Exercise 1

1. When most people (think, thinks) of rattlesnakes, they (picture, pictures) them in a desert environment.

2. However, there (is, are) rattlesnakes that (live, lives) in forests.

3. This type of rattlesnake (is, are) called a timber rattlesnake.

4. In wooded areas, timber rattlesnakes (encounter, encounters) chipmunks, squirrels, and birds.

5. When one of these snakes (go, goes) hunting, it (look, looks) for these animals.

6. Scientists (has, have) discovered that chipmunks, squirrels, and birds (defend, defends) themselves in an unusual way.

7. These furry and feathered creatures (tease, teases) and (taunt, taunts) the snake until it (give, gives) up and (leave, leaves).

8. Chipmunks (run, runs) in all directions and (make, makes) loud sounds.

9. A mother squirrel who (is, are) protecting her pups (flick, flicks) its tail and (kick, kicks) dirt at the snake.

10. Two of the birds (work, works) together, (swoop, swoops) down on the snake, and (pounce, pounces) on it.

Source: Science News, August 27, 2005

Exercise 2

1. A group of scientists (is, are) looking into the sensation that we (call, calls) déjà vu.

2. Déjà vu (is, are) the feeling that we (is, are) repeating an exact experience that (has, have) happened before.

3. Part of the odd sensation (is, are) that we (is, are) aware of the illogical part of déjà vu while it (is, are) happening.

4. Scientists (has, have) developed a new profile of a person who (is, are) likely to experience this particular sensation.

5. People who (is, are) most prone to déjà vu (is, are) between fifteen and twenty-five years old.

6. Regardless of age, however, anyone who (experience, experiences) déjà vu probably (has, have) a vivid imagination.

7. Stress and fatigue (is, are) often factors because the mind (function, functions) differently under these conditions.

8. Education level and income also (determine, determines) a person's susceptibility to déjà vu.

9. The phenomenon of déjà vu (seem, seems) to require an open mind.

10. Since political leanings (affect, affects) open-mindedness, liberals (tend, tends) to have more déjà vu experiences than conservatives.

Source: Psychology Today, March/April 2005

Exercise 3

1. Do you know why the skin on our fingertips (wrinkle, wrinkles) after a long shower or bath?

2. The explanation (is, are) simple.

3. All of our skin (absorb, absorbs) water.

4. The bottoms of our hands and feet (absorb, absorbs) the most water.

5. They (soak, soaks) up more water because they (has, have) the thickest layers of skin on our bodies.

6. This thick skin on our fingers (swell, swells) and (expand, expands) from the excess water.

7. Wrinkles (result, results) from the expansion of the skin covering the small surface of our fingertips.

8. The same thing (doesn't, don't) happen as quickly in sea water, however.

9. The salts and other minerals in the sea water (block, blocks) it from being absorbed.

10. So next time you (take, takes) a long bath, you will understand why your fingers and toes (get, gets) so wrinkled.

Exercise 4

1. There (is, are) new risks for kids in this technological age; these risks primarily (involve, involves) their wrists.

2. Many adults already (suffer, suffers) from carpal tunnel syndrome.

3. And now children (is, are) also coming down with similar conditions, called repetitive stress injuries (RSIs).

4. From the use of computers and video games (come, comes) unnatural body positions that (lead, leads) to health problems.

5. The child's wrists, neck, and back (start, starts) to hurt or feel numb after he or she (work, works) or (play, plays) on the computer for a long time.

6. The problem (start, starts) with computer furniture.

7. The chairs, desks, and screens (is, are) usually not at the proper height to be used comfortably by children.

8. Straining and repetition often (cause, causes) reduced circulation and even nerve damage.

9. Often RSI damage to the wrists (is, are) irreversible.

10. Experts in the field of RSI (warn, warns) parents to teach children how to avoid these injuries.

Exercise 5

1. Everyone in my drawing class (is, are) supposed to finish a drawing a week.

2. But each of us (has, have) a different way of beginning.

3. One of my classmates always (start, starts) by humming and rocking back and forth in front of his easel.

4. Another one just (put, puts) dots in the places where she (want, wants) her figures to go.

5. Jennifer, my best friend, (like, likes) to draw really light circles wherever the faces will be.

6. In the past, I (has, have) usually started by drawing a continuous line until it (look, looks) like something.

7. In other words, I (let, lets) the drawing tell me what it (want, wants) to be.

   8. But Jennifer and my other classmates (has, have) taught me something.

   9. It (help, helps) to have a plan; their drawings often (turn, turns) out better than mine.

   10. Either they or I (am, are) right, but I don't know which it (is, are) yet.

PROOFREADING EXERCISE

Find and correct the ten subject-verb agreement errors in the following paragraph.

I exercise in the gardens near my house several times a week. The fresh air and pretty scenery refreshes me and make me happy. There is several paths I can follow each day. One of my favorite walks go up a steep hill and down through a grove of ferns. The droplets of water on the ferns splashes on me as I brush past them. Then the path open into a grassy area that take my breath away sometimes. The late afternoon sunlight shine through the branches of a few large trees, and it create beautiful shadows on top of the grass. Another of the paths goes straight between a row of tall, narrow trees. The trunks of the trees is smooth, but their leafy tops sways in the wind because they are so high. I love my afternoon walks in the gardens.

SENTENCE WRITING

Write ten sentences in which you describe the shoes you are wearing. Use verbs in the present time. Then go back over your sentences—underline your subjects once, underline your verbs twice, and be sure they agree. Exchange papers with another student and check each other's subject-verb agreement. Keep the results in your sentence writing folder.

Avoiding Shifts in Time

People often worry about using different time frames in writing. Let common sense guide you. If you begin writing a paper in past time, don't shift back and forth to the present unnecessarily; and if you begin in the present, don't shift to the past without good reason. In the following paragraph, the writer starts in the present and then shifts to the past, then shifts again to the present:

> In the novel *To Kill a Mockingbird,* Jean Louise Finch is a little girl who lives in the South with her father, Atticus, and her brother, Jem. Everybody in town calls Jean Louise "Scout" as a nickname. When Atticus, a lawyer, chose to defend a black man against the charges of a white woman, some of their neighbors turned against him. Scout protected her father by appealing to the humanity of one member of the angry mob. In this chapter, five-year-old Scout turns out to be stronger than a group of adult men.

All the verbs should be in the present:

> In the novel *To Kill a Mockingbird,* Jean Louise Finch is a little girl who lives in the South with her father, Atticus, and her brother, Jem. Everybody in town calls Jean Louise "Scout" as a nickname. When Atticus, a lawyer, chooses to defend a black man against the charges of a white woman, some of their neighbors turn against him. Scout protects her father by appealing to the humanity of one member of the angry mob. In this chapter, five-year-old Scout turns out to be stronger than a group of adult men.

This sample paragraph discusses only the events that happen within the novel's plot, so it needs to maintain one time frame—the present, which we use to write about literature and repeated actions.

However, sometimes you will write about the present, the past, and even the future together. Then it may be necessary to use these different time frames within the same paragraph, each for its own reason. For example, if you were to give biographical information about Harper Lee, author of *To Kill a Mockingbird,* within a discussion of the novel and its influence, you might need to use all three time frames:

> Harper Lee grew up in Alabama, and she based elements in the book on experiences from her childhood. Like the character Atticus, Lee's father was a lawyer. She wrote the novel in his law offices. *To Kill a Mockingbird* is Harper Lee's most famous work, and it received the Pulitzer Prize for fiction in 1960. Lee's book turned forty years old in the year 2000. It will always remain one of the most moving and compassionate novels in American literature.

The previous paragraph uses past (*grew, based, was, wrote, received, turned*), present (*is*), and future (*will remain*) in the same paragraph without committing the error of shifting. Shifting occurs when the writer changes time frames *inconsistently* or *for no reason,* confusing the reader (as in the first example given).

PROOFREADING EXERCISES

Which of the following student paragraphs shift *unnecessarily* back and forth between time frames? In those that do, change the verbs to maintain one time frame, thus making the entire paragraph read smoothly. One of the paragraphs is correct.

1. Plastic surgery helps many people look better and feel better about themselves. Of course, there were stories of unnecessary surgeries and even heartbreaking mistakes. People could make their own decisions about whether plastic surgery was right for them. Dogs, however, can't communicate what they want. Nevertheless, some people took their dogs in for cosmetic surgeries, such as tummy tucks and face-lifts. Just like humans, dogs sometimes needed surgery to correct painful or unhealthy conditions. A dog with a low-hanging tummy could get an infection from scratches that were caused by rocks on the ground. And another dog may require a face-lift to help it stay clean when it eats. Animal lovers were worried that some canine plastic surgeries were done without good reasons.

Source: Newsweek, March 21, 2005

2. I watched a documentary on the Leaning Tower of Pisa last night. I was amazed to find out that the tower began leaning before it was even finished. Workers over several centuries adjusted their materials as they built the tower to compensate for its increasing angle. That's why the tower is actually shaped a little like a banana. I'm surprised that the famous landmark is still standing after everything people have done to it since it was finished. In the 1930s, for instance, Mussolini thought that it should be straightened. So he had workers drill holes in the foundation and pour tons of concrete beneath it. Others tried digging out the earth around the sunken part. But that just caused flooding because they went below the soil's water table. The narrator of the documentary said that every time anyone tries to correct the tower, it leans a little more to the south. Most recently, scientists have used special drilling techniques to extract enough soil deep beneath the tower to reverse its angle a little. This most recent correction may add as much as three hundred years to the life of the Leaning Tower of Pisa.

3. I really enjoyed my winter break this year. It was too short, of course, but I make the most of the time I had. My extended family had a reunion at my aunt's house in St. Louis. I didn't pack enough coats and sweaters, but the loving atmosphere keeps me warm. Once I'm back in the same room with my cousins, we goofed off just the way we used to when we were kids. One night my four closest cousins and I stay up after everyone else is in bed. We played board games and ate buttery popcorn and got the game pieces all greasy just like the old days. Overall, my trip to St. Louis with its late-night game marathon is the highlight of my winter vacation.

Recognizing Verbal Phrases

We know (from the discussion on p. 97) that a verb phrase is made up of a main verb and at least one helping verb. But sometimes certain forms of verbs are used not as real verbs but as some other part of a sentence. Verbs put to other uses are called *verbals.*

A verbal can be a subject:

Skiing is my favorite Olympic sport. (*Skiing* is the subject, not the verb. The verb is *is.*)

A verbal can be a descriptive word:

His *bruised* ankle healed very quickly. (*Bruised* describes the subject, ankle. *Healed* is the verb.)

A verbal can be an object:

I like *to read* during the summer. (*To read* is the object. *Like* is the verb.)

Verbals link up with other words to form *verbal phrases.* To see the difference between a real verb phrase and a verbal phrase, look at these two sentences:

I was bowling with my best friends. (*Bowling* is the main verb in a verb phrase. Along with the helping verb *was,* it shows the action of the sentence.)

I enjoyed *bowling* with my best friends. (Here the real verb is *enjoyed. Bowling* is not the verb; it is part of a verbal phrase—*bowling with my best friends*—which is what I enjoyed.)

THREE KINDS OF VERBALS

1. *ing* verbs used without helping verbs (*running, thinking, baking . . .*)
2. verb forms that often end in *ed, en,* or *t* (*tossed, spoken, burnt . . .*)
3. verbs that follow *to* _____ (*to walk, to eat, to cause . . .*)

Look at the following sentences using the previous examples in verbal phrases:

Running two miles a day is great exercise. (real verb = is)

She spent two hours *thinking of a title for her essay.* (real verb = spent)

We had such fun *baking those cherry vanilla cupcakes.* (real verb = had)

Tossed in a salad, artichoke hearts add zesty flavor. (real verb = add)

Spoken in Spanish, the dialogue sounds even more beautiful. (real verb = sounds)

The gourmet pizza, *burnt by a careless chef,* shrunk to half its normal size. (real verb = shrunk)

I like *to walk around the zoo by myself.* (real verb = like)

To eat exotic foods takes courage. (real verb = takes)

They actually wanted *to cause an argument.* (real verb = wanted)

E X E R C I S E S

Each of the following sentences contains at least one verbal or verbal phrase. Double underline the real verbs or verb phrases and put brackets around the verbals and verbal phrases. Remember to locate the verbals first (*running, wounded, to sleep* . . .) and include any word(s) that go with them (*running a race, wounded in the fight, to sleep all night*). Real verbs will never be inside verbal phrases. Check your answers after the first set before going on to the next.

Exercise 1

1. Some travelers want to know how to behave in other countries.
2. *Behave Yourself!* is a book written to help such people.
3. It outlines what to do and what not to do in different countries around the world.
4. In Austria, for example, cutting your food with a fork is more polite than cutting it with a knife.

5. In Egypt, nodding the head upward—not shaking the head from side to side—means "no."

6. In the Netherlands, complimenting people about their clothes is not a good idea.

7. An Italian diner will fold lettuce into a bite-size piece with the fork and knife instead of cutting it.

8. A common mistake that people make in many countries is to stand with their hands on their hips.

9. This posture and pointing at anything with the fingers are thought to be very rude and even threatening.

10. Travelers should study any country before visiting it in order to avoid confusing or offending anyone.

Exercise 2

1. Finding the exact origin of the game of poker is probably impossible.

2. Some think that it started as a game played in China around a thousand years ago.

3. Others have a theory placing its origins in an ancient Persian game that involves using twenty-five cards with five suits.

4. Poker also has similarities to the game "poque," played by the French when they colonized New Orleans in the 1700s.

5. Betting and bluffing were both aspects of poque.

6. So was a deck of cards containing the four suits used in modern poker: diamonds, hearts, spades, and clubs.

7. In the 1800s, Jonathan H. Green wrote about a pastime called the "cheating game."

8. He observed that people traveling down the Mississippi river enjoyed this card game.

9. Green used the name "poker" for the first time to identify it.

10. Since human beings have always loved games, tracing the history of one game can be difficult.

Source: Poker (Top That! Publishing, 2004)

Exercise 3

1. The idea of home-schooling children has become more popular recently.

2. Many parents have decided to teach kids themselves instead of sending them to public or private school.

3. There are many different reasons to choose home-schooling.

4. In Hollywood, for instance, child actors often must use home-schooling due to their schedules.

5. The home-schooling option allows for one of their parents, or a special teacher, to continue to instruct them on the set.

6. Other parents simply want to be directly involved in their child's learning.

7. Many school districts have special independent study "schools," offering parents the structure and materials that they need to provide an appropriate curriculum on their own.

8. Children do all of their reading and writing at home, with their parents guiding them along the way.

9. The family meets with the independent study school's teacher regularly to go over the child's work and to clarify any points of confusion.

10. Many parents would like to have the time to home-school their children.

Exercise 4

1. Mixing light of different colors sometimes produces surprising results.

2. It is an entirely different process from mixing colored paints.

3. For example, mixing red and green paints produces a dark brown color.

4. But mixing red and green light produces yellow light.

5. Mixing paints is an example of a process called color subtraction.

6. Mixing colored light is an example of color addition.

7. White light is made up of colored light.

8. When looking at a rainbow, you are seeing sunlight.

9. The band of color in a rainbow is called a spectrum, containing seven basic colors—red, orange, yellow, green, blue, indigo, and violet.

10. Light of these colors can be recombined to form white light.

Source: A modified excerpt from *New Encyclopedia of Science Special Projects Book* (Funk and Wagnalls, 1986)

Exercise 5

1. John Steinbeck, author of *The Grapes of Wrath,* was the first native of California to receive the Nobel Prize for literature.

2. Calling his hometown of Salinas "Lettuceberg," Steinbeck's writing made the area famous.

3. At the time, not everyone liked the attention brought by his portrayals of life in *Cannery Row* and other works.

4. Steinbeck's father was the treasurer of Monterey County for ten years, working also for the Spreckels company.

5. John Steinbeck tried to find satisfaction in his birthplace, enrolling in and quitting his studies at Stanford University many times.

6. Finally, Steinbeck moved to New York, distancing himself from his California roots.

7. Steinbeck won the Nobel Prize in 1962, revealing the literary world's esteem for his work.

8. Not writing anything of the caliber of the Salinas stories while living in New York, Steinbeck did return to California before he died in 1968.

9. In 1972, the Salinas library changed its name, to be known thereafter as the John Steinbeck Library.

10. And the house Steinbeck was born in became a restaurant and then a full-fledged museum chronicling the life of Salinas' most celebrated citizen.

Source: California People (Peregrine Smith, 1982)

PARAGRAPH EXERCISE

Double underline the real verbs or verb phrases and put brackets around the verbals and verbal phrases in the following excerpt about the planet Mars, from the book *The Friendly Guide to the Universe*, by Nancy Hathaway:

Mars glows like a burning ember embedded in the night, and as a result it has long been linked with the color red . . . .

Nonetheless, Mars is not red. It is russet and brown, an autumnal, rust-colored world, as *Viking 1* dramatically showed. The rocky soil is the color of clay, thanks to the presence of iron oxides, and the sky, suffused with large particles of dust, is neither blue, as we might imagine, nor black, as some scientists had expected, but apricot, salmon, and peach.

The air on this coral-colored world is 95 percent carbon dioxide, so it is impossible to breathe . . . .

Mars is beautiful in its way, even though, compared to the blue and verdant Earth, it is a harsh and unlivable steppe. On the other hand, compared to the blistering hell of Venus, it is not half bad.

SENTENCE WRITING

Write ten sentences that contain verbal phrases. Use the ten verbals listed here to begin your verbal phrases: *shopping, earning, giving, wearing, to drive, to sew, to talk, given, baked, built.* The last three are particularly difficult to use as verbals. You will find sample sentences in the Answers section at the back of the book. But first, try to write your own so that you can compare the two. Keep the results in your sentence writing folder.

Correcting Misplaced or Dangling Modifiers

When we modify something, we change whatever it is by adding something to it. We might modify a car, for example, by adding special tires. In English, we call words, phrases, and clauses *modifiers* when they add information to part of a sentence. As we saw on p. 29, to do its job properly, a modifier should be in the right spot—as close to the word it describes as possible. If we put new tires on the roof of the car instead of where they belong, they would be misplaced. In the following sentence, the modifier is too far away from the word it modifies to make sense. It is a misplaced modifier:

Swinging from tree to tree, we watched the monkeys at the zoo.

Was it *we* who were swinging from tree to tree? That's what the sentence says because the modifying phrase *Swinging from tree to tree* is next to *we*. It should be next to *monkeys*.

At the zoo, we watched the monkeys swinging from tree to tree.

The next example has no word at all for the modifier to modify:

At the age of eight, my family finally bought a dog.

Obviously, the family was not eight when it bought a dog. Nor was the dog eight. The modifier *At the age of eight* is dangling there with no word to attach itself to, no word for it to modify. We can get rid of the dangling modifier by turning it into a dependent clause. (See p. 74 for a discussion of dependent clauses.)

When I was eight, my family finally bought a dog.

Here the clause has its own subject and verb—*I was*—and there's no chance of misunderstanding the sentence. Here's another dangling modifier:

After a two-hour nap, the train pulled into the station.

Did the train take a two-hour nap? Who did?

After a two-hour nap, I awoke just as the train pulled into the station.

EXERCISES

Carefully rephrase any of the following sentences that contain misplaced or dangling modifiers. Some sentences are correct.

Exercise 1

1. Lying under the table for a week, they finally found their lost credit card.
2. She located the door to the auditorium walking down the hall.
3. They bought a hammer at the hardware store.
4. After taking an aspirin, my doctor told me to drink extra water.
5. He always brings a calculator to school in his backpack.
6. Our mail carrier tripped and fell on a crack in the sidewalk.
7. Arguing nonstop, the road trip was not as much fun as we hoped it would be.
8. Now that she has finished her math classes, she can focus on her major.
9. Seeing her new granddaughter's picture for the first time, our mother cried.
10. Smiling nicely at everyone, the students immediately liked their substitute teacher.

Exercise 2

1. I found a cell phone walking up the stairs.
2. Full of surprises, we loved that play and want to see it again.
3. The tires need to be replaced on his car.
4. Scribbled quickly, I could not read the phone number.
5. The parking structure on the south side of campus is nearly empty.
6. With outdated functions and styling, I need to upgrade my cell phone.
7. After taking several photographs, the shadows on the trees disappeared.
8. He filled out his application with a ballpoint pen.
9. Finishing his calculations, my accountant told me what my tax refund would be.
10. After talking to the doctor, his ear started to feel better.

Exercise 3

1. Distracted by the crowd, the officer tried to write a report.
2. When I was twelve, I bought my first share of stock.

3. She kicked her mother in the store by accident.

4. The inspector found a few termites searching outside the house.

5. Mixing the paints together, we made the color we wanted.

6. I couldn't wait to taste the food waiting in line at the new restaurant.

7. The garage is too small to hold both of our cars.

8. At the age of sixteen, the State of California offers a test to get out of high school early.

9. As the deadline for admission approached, I gathered all of my transcripts.

10. I have found many unique gift ideas shopping on the Internet.

Exercise 4

1. Getting a headache from the fumes, the ferry finally made it across the river.

2. Full of empty calories, that carnival sold the best cotton candy I'd ever tasted.

3. Two months after moving, our old apartment is still empty.

4. She promised to return the library books in her e-mail message.

5. The students took the notes sitting in small groups.

6. Before saying goodnight, the porch light burned out.

7. Decorated beautifully, our hostess showed us her favorite room.

8. Scampering along the baseboards of the cabin, I saw a tiny gray mouse.

9. Trying to open my car door with a hanger, I stared at the keys dangling from the ignition.

10. All along the highway, volunteers planted trees wearing special T-shirts.

Exercise 5

1. Feeling the excitement of the first day of school, my backpack was left behind.

2. Full of explosions, we saw the new movie that everyone is talking about.

3. My cousins and I always wrapped our gifts in our pajamas on the night before the holiday.

4. Practicing for an hour a day, his tennis has improved.

5. The price of gasoline fluctuates, rising and falling several times a year.

6. Sitting on the beach all day, I made a decision.

7. They discovered a new trail hiking in the nearby mountains.

8. She felt the pressure of trying to get good grades from her parents.

9. I enjoy traveling to new places with my friends and even my family.

10. Written in green ink, the teacher's comments seemed positive even when pointing out a problem.

PROOFREADING EXERCISE

Find and correct any misplaced or dangling modifiers in the following paragraphs.

A man in Edinburgh, Scotland, has invented a device, hoping to become famous and wealthy. The device is a variation on the center-mounted brake light used in the design of many new cars, located just above the trunk and visible from behind. Instead of just a solid red brake light, however, this invention displays words to other drivers written in bold, red-lighted letters.

With simplicity in mind, the vocabulary the inventor gave the machine is limited to three words: "Sorry," "Thanks," and "Help." After making an aggressive lane change, the machine could apologize for us. Or after being allowed to go ahead of someone, the device could offer thanks to the considerate person responsible. Of course, at the sight of the "Help" display, we could summon fellow citizens for assistance.

And there is no need to worry about operating the device while driving. With three easy-to-reach buttons, the messages can be activated without taking our eyes off the road.

SENTENCE WRITING

Write five sentences that contain misplaced or dangling modifiers; then revise those sentences to put the modifiers where they belong. Use the examples in the explanations as models. Keep the results in your sentence writing folder.

Following Sentence Patterns

Sentences are built according to a few basic patterns. For proof, rearrange each of the following sets of words to form a complete statement (not a question):

apples a ate raccoon the

the crashing beach were waves the on

your in am partner I lab the

been she school has to walking

you wonderful in look green

Only one or two combinations are possible for each, due to English sentence patterns. Either *A raccoon ate the apples,* or *The apples ate a raccoon,* and so on. But in each case, the verb or verb phrase makes its way to the middle of the statement, and the nouns and pronouns take their places as subjects and objects.

To understand sentence patterns, you need to know that verbs can do three things. The focus is on the *double* underlined verbs below.

1. Verbs can show actions:

The <u>raccoon</u> <u>ate</u> the apples.

The <u>waves</u> <u>were</u> <u>crashing</u> on the beach.

<u>She</u> <u>has been</u> <u>walking</u> to school.

2. Verbs can link subjects with descriptive words:

<u>I</u> <u>am</u> your partner in the lab.

<u>You</u> <u>look</u> wonderful in green.

3. Verbs can help other verbs form verb phrases:

The <u>waves</u> <u>were</u> <u>crashing</u> on the beach.

<u>She</u> <u>has been</u> <u>walking</u> to school.

Look at these sentences for more examples:

Mel grabbed a slice of pizza. (The verb *grabbed* shows Mel's action.)

His slice was the largest one in the box. (The verb *was* links *slice* with its description as *the largest one.*)

Mel had been craving pizza for a week. (The verbs *had* and *been* help the main verb *craving* in a verb phrase.)

Knowing what a verb does in a clause helps you gain an understanding of the three basic sentence patterns:

SUBJECT + ACTION VERB + OBJECT PATTERN

Some action verbs must be followed by an object (a person, place, thing, or idea) that receives the action.

  S   AV   Obj
Sylvia completed the difficult math test. (*Sylvia completed* makes no sense without being followed by the object that she completed—*test.*)

SUBJECT + ACTION VERB (+ NO OBJECT) PATTERN

At other times, the action verb itself completes the meaning and needs no object after it.

  S   AV
She celebrated at home with her family. (*She celebrated* makes sense alone. The two prepositional phrases—*at home* and *with her family*—are not needed to understand the meaning of the clause.)

SUBJECT + LINKING VERB + DESCRIPTION PATTERN

A special kind of verb that does not show an action but links a subject with a description is called a *linking verb*. It acts like an equal sign in a clause. Learn to recognize the most common linking verbs: *is, am, are, was, were, seem, feel, appear, become, look.*

  S   LV   Desc
Sylvia is an excellent student. (*Sylvia* equals *an excellent student.*)

  S   LV   Desc
Sylvia has become very successful. (*Very successful* describes *Sylvia.*)

> **NOTE**—We learned on page 97 that a verb phrase includes a main verb and its helping verbs. Helping verbs can be used in any of the sentence patterns.

<pre>   S   AV</pre>
Sylvia <u>is going</u> to Seattle for a vacation. (Here the verb *is* helps the main verb *going*, which is an action verb with no object followed by two prepositional phrases—*to Seattle* and *for a vacation.*)

The following chart outlines the patterns using short sentences that you could memorize:

THREE BASIC SENTENCE PATTERNS

S + AV + Obj

<u>Kids</u> <u><u>like</u></u> candy.

S + AV

<u>They</u> <u><u>play</u></u> (with their friends) (on the playground).
                              not objects

S + LV + Desc

<u>They</u> <u><u>are</u></u> fourth-graders.

<u>They</u> <u><u>look</u></u> happy.

These are the basic patterns for most of the clauses used in English sentences. Knowing them can help you control your sentences and improve your use of words.

EXERCISES

First, put parentheses around any prepositional phrases. Next, underline the subjects once and the verbs or verb phrases twice. Then mark the sentence patterns above the words. Remember that the patterns never mix together. For example, unlike an action verb, a linking verb will almost never be used alone (for example, "He seems."), nor will an action verb be followed by a description of the subject (for example, "She took tall."). And if there are two clauses, each one may have a different pattern. Check your answers after the first set of ten.

Exercise 1

1. Horatio Greenough was a sculptor in the 1800s.

2. Greenough created a controversial statue of George Washington.

3. The statue weighed twelve tons, but its weight was not the reason for the controversy.

4. The controversial aspect of the statue involved Washington's clothes.

5. The statue portrayed Washington in a toga-like garment.

6. His stomach, chest, and arms were bare and very muscular.

7. One part of the toga draped over the statue's raised right arm.

8. The bare-chested statue of Washington stood in the rotunda of the Capitol for only three years.

9. Officials moved the statue many times.

10. In 1962, it arrived in its final home at the American History Museum.

Source: *Smithsonian*, February 2005

Exercise 2

1. Many people get migraine headaches.

2. These headaches can be extremely painful.

3. People with migraines may also suffer from nausea and dizziness.

4. Migraine sufferers avoid bright lights and loud sounds.

5. These sensations cause a different kind of discomfort.

6. Some medicines reduce the pain of migraine headaches.

7. Other drugs help with the additional symptoms.

8. No migraine treatment is perfect for everyone.

9. Scientists have been studying migraine headaches for years.

10. A cure for migraines is long overdue.

Exercise 3

1. Sleep is an important part of life.

2. Animals and humans use sleep as a vacation for their brains and bodies.

3. Some facts about sleep might surprise people.

4. Large animals require less sleep than small animals do.

5. A typical cat will sleep for twelve hours in a day.

6. An ordinary elephant will sleep for only three hours.

7. Smaller animals use their brains and bodies at higher rates.

8. Therefore, they need many hours of sleep.

9. The reverse is true for large animals.

10. Humans fall between cats and elephants for their sleep requirements.

Exercise 4

1. Cakes can be plain or fancy.

2. Most grocery stores and almost all bakeries sell cakes.

3. They range in price depending on size, occasion, and amount of decoration.

4. A cake with a "Happy Birthday" inscription will usually cost thirty to fifty dollars.

5. Wedding cakes, however, are often very expensive.

6. An elaborate wedding cake may cost several hundred or even a thousand dollars.

7. The multilayered traditional white wedding cake still seems the most popular kind.

8. These delicate structures need special care during transportation.

9. Some couples order two or more smaller cakes for the occasion.

10. People sometimes save a slice or section of their wedding cake as a memento.

Exercise 5

1. In 1998, Sotheby's auction house sold a piece of 60-year-old wedding cake for an amazing price.

2. It had belonged to the Duke and Duchess of Windsor.

3. On June 3, 1937, the famous couple married in France.

4. On the day of their wedding, they put a piece of cake in a pink box and tied a pink bow around it.

5. They identified its contents as "a piece of our wedding cake"; they initialed and dated the box, and they kept it as a memento for the rest of their lives.

6. This couple's relationship, which began in the 1930s, was one of the most famous love affairs in history.

7. The Duke of Windsor gave up the throne of England to be with Wallis Simpson, the woman that he loved.

8. Unfortunately, she was a divorced American woman and could not, therefore, marry the king of England, so he abdicated.

9. The pre-auction estimate for the box containing the piece of their wedding cake was five hundred to a thousand dollars.

10. When the gavel came down, the high bid by a couple from San Francisco was $29,900.

Sources: http://www.cnn.com/US/9802/21/windsor.auction; and Sotheby's Holdings, Inc. Annual Report 1998

PARAGRAPH EXERCISE

Label the sentence patterns in the following paragraph from a book by Paul Zelanski and Mary Pat Fisher titled, simply, *Color*. It helps to put parentheses around prepositional phrases first to isolate them from the words that make up the sentence patterns—the subjects, the verbs, and any objects after action verbs or any descriptive words after linking verbs (*is, was, were, seem, appear,* and so on).

Color is perhaps the most powerful tool at an artist's disposal. It affects our

emotions beyond thought and can convey any mood, from delight to despair. It can be subtle or dramatic, capture attention or stimulate desire. Used more boldly and freely today than ever before, color bathes our vision with an infinite variety of sensations, from clear, brilliant hues to subtle, elusive mixtures. Color is the province of all artists, from painters and potters to product designers and computer artists.

SENTENCE WRITING

Write ten sentences describing the weather today and your feelings about it. Keep your sentences short and clear. Then go back and label the sentence patterns you have used. Keep the results in your sentence writing folder.

Avoiding Clichés, Awkward Phrasing, and Wordiness

CLICHÉS

A cliché is an expression that has been used so often it has lost its originality and effectiveness. Whoever first said "light as a feather" had thought of an original way to express lightness, but today that expression is worn out. Most of us use an occasional cliché in speaking, but clichés have no place in writing. The good writer thinks up fresh new ways to express ideas.

Here are a few clichés. Add some more to the list.

the bottom line

older but wiser

last but not least

in this day and age

different as night and day

out of this world

white as a ghost

sick as a dog

tried and true

at the top of their lungs

the thrill of victory

one in a million

busy as a bee

easier said than done

better late than never

Clichés lack freshness because the reader always knows what's coming next. Can you complete these expressions?

the agony of . . .

breathe a sigh of . . .

lend a helping . . .

odds and . . .

raining cats and . . .

as American as . . .

been there . . .

worth its weight . . .

Clichés are expressions too many people use. Try to avoid them in your writing.

AWKWARD PHRASING

Another problem—awkward phrasing—comes from using sentence structures that *no one* else would use because they break basic sentence patterns, omit necessary words, or use words incorrectly. Like clichés, awkward sentences might *sound* acceptable when spoken, but as polished writing, they are usually unacceptable.

AWKWARD

There should be great efforts in terms of the communication between teachers and their students.

CORRECTED

Teachers and their students must communicate.

AWKWARD

During the experiment, the use of key principles was essential to ensure the success of it.

CORRECTED

The experiment was a success. *or* We did the experiment carefully.

AWKWARD

My favorite was when the guy with the ball ran the wrong way all the way across the field.

CORRECTED

In my favorite part, the receiver ran across the field in the wrong direction.

WORDINESS

Good writing is concise writing. Don't use ten words if you can say it better in five. "In today's society" isn't as effective as "today," and it's a cliché. "At this point in time" could be "presently" or "now."

Another kind of wordiness comes from saying something twice. There's no need to write "in the month of August" or "9 a.m. in the morning" or "my personal opinion." August *is* a month, 9 a.m. *is* morning, and anyone's opinion *is* personal. All you need to write is "in August," "9 a.m.," and "my opinion."

Still another kind of wordiness comes from using expressions that add nothing to the meaning of the sentence. "The point is that we can't afford it" says no more than "We can't afford it."

Here is a sample wordy sentence:

The construction company actually worked on that particular building for a period of six months.

And here it is after eliminating wordiness:

The construction company worked on that building for six months.

For more examples, compare the two columns below:

WORDY WRITING	CONCISE WRITING
advance planning	planning
an unexpected surprise	a surprise
ask a question	ask
at a later date	later
basic fundamentals	fundamentals
green in color	green
but nevertheless	but (or nevertheless)
combine together	combine
completely empty	empty
down below	below
each and every	each (or every)
end result	result
fewer in number	fewer
free gift	gift
in order to	to
in spite of the fact that	although
just exactly	exactly
large in size	large
new innovation	innovation
on a regular basis	regularly
past history	history
rectangular in shape	rectangular
refer back	refer
repeat again	repeat
serious crisis	crisis
sufficient enough	sufficient (or enough)
there in person	there
two different kinds	two kinds
very unique	unique

PROOFREADING EXERCISES

The following student paragraphs contain examples of clichés, awkward phrasing, and wordiness. Revise the paragraphs so that they are concise examples of Standard Written English. When you're done, compare your revisions with the sample answers at the back of the book.

1. If I had to tell about my favorite class from high school, I would have to say that it was the cooking class that I took in tenth grade. The really great part of the class was that it was an independent study, and I got to choose my own meals to learn to cook and then eat. The assignments were all the same: do some research on a meal from a particular country or culture. Then buy all the ingredients for that meal, and learn to cook that meal. In order to get a grade for the assignments, I had to bring in a plate full of that food to my teacher, and then I would be graded on the meal and on my report about making it.

2. *While You Were Sleeping* is one of my favorite movies. It comes on TV at the holidays because it takes place in the snow, and there are a lot of holiday parties and celebrations in it. The whole story revolves around a case of mistaken identity when Sandra Bullock's character saves a man's life who gets injured at the train station where she works. He goes into a coma, and she pretends to be his fiancée for about a week while he is unconscious. After she becomes close to his whole family, and especially his brother, the man that she thought she liked suddenly wakes up from his coma. Eventually, everybody realizes that her character really should be with the brother, and it all ends up happily ever after.

3. Full-grown people weren't the only things that ancient civilizations made mummies out of. They also made mummies out of children who died and out of animals, too. Making mummies was a way of helping them enter into the next world, and it was done to show respect. One mummy of an Eskimo baby was found in Greenland. It dated back to the 1400s, and it was wrapped up in beautiful fur to protect it from the cold. In Egypt, archeologists discovered the mummies of everything from cats to crocodiles, cows, baboons, and birds. In Alaska, a mummy was found of a huge bison that the experts thought was over 35,000 years old. The bison was perfectly preserved, and it still had a big lion's tooth in its neck, which showed how it probably died.

Source: *Kids Discover*, June 2005

Correcting for Parallel Structure

Your writing will be clearer and more memorable if you use parallel structure. That is, when you write two pieces of information or any kind of list, put the items in similar form. Look at this sentence, for example:

My favorite movies are comic, romantic, or the ones about outer space.

The sentence lacks parallel structure. The third item in the list doesn't match the other two. Now look at this sentence:

My favorite movies are comedies, love stories, and sci-fi fantasies.

Here the items are parallel; they are all plural nouns. Or you could write the following:

I like movies that make me laugh, that make me cry, and that make me think.

Again the sentence has parallel structure because all three items in the list are dependent clauses. Here are some more examples. Note how much easier it is to read the sentences with parallel structure.

WITHOUT PARALLEL STRUCTURE	**WITH PARALLEL STRUCTURE**
I like to hike, to ski, and going sailing.	I like to hike, to ski, and to sail. (all "to _____" verbs)
The office has run out of pens, paper, ink cartridges, and we need more toner, too.	The office needs more pens, paper, ink cartridges, and toner. (all nouns)
They decided that they needed a change, that they could afford a new house, and wanted to move to Arizona.	They decided that they needed a change, that they could afford a new house, and that they wanted to move to Arizona. (all dependent clauses)

The parts of an outline should always be parallel. Following are two brief outlines about food irradiation. The parts of the outline on the *left* are not parallel. The first subtopic (I.) is a question; the other (II.) is just a noun. And the supporting points (A., B., C.) are written as nouns, verbs, and even clauses. The parts of the outline on the *right* are parallel. Both subtopics (I. and II.) are plural nouns, and all details (A., B., C.) are action verbs followed by objects.

NOT PARALLEL	PARALLEL
Food Irradiation	Food Irradiation
I. How is it good?	I. Benefits
A. Longer shelf life	A. Extends shelf life
B. Using fewer pesticides	B. Requires fewer pesticides
C. Kills bacteria	C. Kills bacteria
II. Concerns	II. Concerns
A. Nutritional value	A. Lowers nutritional value
B. Consumers are worried	B. Alarms consumers
C. Workers' safety	C. Endangers workers

Using parallel structure will make your writing more effective. Note the parallelism in these well-known quotations:

A place for everything and everything in its place.

Isabella Mary Beeton

Ask not what your country can do for you; ask what you can do for your country.

John F. Kennedy

We hold these truths to be self-evident, that all men are created equal, that they are endowed by their creator with certain unalienable rights, that among these are Life, Liberty, and the pursuit of Happiness.

Thomas Jefferson

EXERCISES

In the following exercises, rephrase any sentences that do not contain parallel structures.

Exercise 1

1. I have read about many foods that can help people stay healthy, and a longer life may result from eating them.

2. Eating whole wheat bread benefits the brain, and energy can increase, too.

3. Apples contain ingredients to aid memory, keeping lungs healthy, and preventing cancer.

4. Kidney beans can reduce cholesterol, give someone more energy, and make moods more stable.

5. Oranges fight inflammation and the losing of eyesight.

6. Substances found in fish can prevent heart problems and depression, as well as high cholesterol.

7. Milk boosts the nervous system and also helps to postpone aging.

8. Antioxidants in red grapes benefit the heart, protect the brain, and can keep people from getting cancer.

9. Red peppers can decrease the risk of strokes or heart attacks.

10. By eating these foods, people can live longer, stay stronger, and they can be very happy.

Source: Psychology Today, July/August 2005

Exercise 2

1. Preparing for emergencies is not as complicated as it seems.

2. The process involves two steps: planning and to gather certain supplies.

3. When planning for emergencies, ask yourself the following questions.

4. What kinds of emergencies have occurred before or could occur someday?

5. Where would you go, and what method of transportation would you use?

6. Make a list of phone contacts within the area and outside the area.

7. The adults, teenagers, and even the children in a family should carry those phone numbers with them.

8. The most important supplies for emergencies include water, food, a flashlight, a radio, and don't forget batteries.

9. First-aid kits can be made or by purchasing them.

10. Reading, understanding, and to update insurance policies is the final step in the process.

Source: Westways, September/October 2005

Exercise 3

1. I like coffee, and I sort of like tea.

2. I've heard that coffee is bad for you, but drinking tea is good.

3. It must not be the caffeine that's bad because coffee has caffeine and so does tea.

4. I heard one expert say that it's the other chemicals in the coffee and tea that make the difference in health benefits.

5. All teas are supposed to be healthy, but the healthiest is supposed to be green tea.

6. Unfortunately, green tea is the only type of tea I don't like.

7. I love orange pekoe tea with tons of milk and a ton of sugar too.

8. I was really surprised to find out that all tea leaves come from the same plant.

9. I know that all coffee comes from coffee beans, but it shocked me to find out that green tea and orange pekoe are both made with leaves from the *Camellia sinensis* plant.

10. Maybe I'll give green tea another try since it could improve my health.

Exercise 4

1. I was washing my car two weeks ago, and that's when I noticed a few bees buzzing around the roof of my garage.

2. I didn't worry about it at the time, but it was something that I should have worried about.

3. As I drove into my driveway a week later, a whole swarm of bees flew up and down in front of my windshield.

4. The swarm wasn't that big, but the bees flying tightly together looked really frightening.

5. They flew in a pattern as if they were riding on a roller coaster or almost like waves.

6. I was glad that my wife and kids were away for the weekend.

7. There was nothing I could do but to wait in my car until they went away.

8. Finally, the bees flew straight up into the air and then disappeared.

9. Once inside my house, I opened the phone book and started to call a bee expert.

10. The bees had made a hive out of part of my garage roof, the expert said, but once I replace the lumber in that area, I should not be bothered with bees anymore.

Exercise 5

Make the following sentences into a list of clear suggestions using parallel structures. You may want to add transitions like *first* and *finally* to help make the steps clear.

1. Experts give the following tips to those who want to get the most out of a visit to the doctor.

2. Avoid getting frustrated in the waiting room or if you have to wait a long time in the exam room.

3. You should always answer the doctor's questions first then asking the doctor a few of your own might be a good idea.

4. It's smart to inquire about a referral to a specialist if you think you need one.

5. Finding out if there are other treatments besides the one the doctor first recommends can't hurt.

6. Ask about any tests that the doctor orders and you might wonder what the results mean, so you probably want to get in touch with the doctor after the results come back.

7. Prescriptions are often given hastily and with little explanation, so ask about side effects and optional medicines if one doesn't work.

8. Discussing these things should not make a good doctor nervous, but try not to be too aggressive in your approach.

9. Get prepared to wait in a long line at the pharmacy.

10. If you follow these suggestions when visiting a doctor, you will be more informed and also you can feel involved in your own treatment.

PROOFREADING EXERCISE

Proofread the following paragraph about Shirley Temple, the famous child star of the 1930s, and revise it to correct any errors in parallel structure.

Shirley Temple was born in 1928. In 1931, when she was just three years old, someone discovered her natural talent at a dance lesson, and she was asked to be in movies. She starred in many films that are still popular today. Among them are *Heidi, Rebecca of Sunnybrook Farm,* and *Curly Top* was one of her earliest. Directors loved Shirley's acting style and the fact that she was able to do a scene in only one take, but not everyone trusted Shirley Temple. Graham Greene was sued when he claimed that Shirley was about thirty years old and in reality was a dwarf. Little Shirley's parents helped with her career, and they also earned money for their efforts. In the early days, the studios paid her mother several hundred dollars a week to put fifty-six curlers in Shirley's hair each night. That way, her famous ringlets would always be perfect, and her hair looked the same each time. Shirley's father managed her money, so much money that at one point Shirley Temple was among the ten highest paid people in America. It was 1938, and she was only ten years old.

Source: California People (Peregrine Smith, 1982)

SENTENCE WRITING

Write ten sentences that use parallel structure in a list or a pair of objects, actions, locations, or ideas. You may choose your own subject or describe a process that involves several steps to complete. Keep the results in your sentence writing folder.

Using Pronouns

Nouns name people, places, things, and ideas—such as *students, school, computers,* and *cyberspace.* Pronouns take the place of nouns to avoid repetition and to clarify meaning. Look at the following two sentences:

> Naomi's father worried that the children at the party were too loud, so Naomi's father told the children that the party would have to end if the children didn't calm down.

> Naomi's father worried that the children at the party were too loud, so *he* told *them* that *it* would have to end if *they* didn't calm down.

Nouns are needlessly repeated in the first sentence. The second sentence uses pronouns in their place. *He* replaces *father,* *they* and *them* replace *children,* and *it* takes the place of *party.*

Of the many kinds of pronouns, the following cause the most difficulty because they include two ways of identifying the same person (or people), but only one form is correct in a given situation:

SUBJECT GROUP	OBJECT GROUP
I	me
he	him
she	her
we	us
they	them

Use a pronoun from the Subject Group in two instances:

1. Before a verb as a subject:

> *He* is my cousin. (*He* is the subject of the verb *is.*)

> *He* is taller than *I.* (The sentence is not written out in full. It means "*He* is taller than *I* am." *I* is the subject of the verb *am.*)

Whenever you see *than* in a sentence, ask yourself whether a verb has been left off the end of the sentence. Add the verb, and then you'll automatically use the correct pronoun. In both speaking and writing, always add the verb. Instead of saying, "She's smarter than (I, me)," say, "She's smarter than I *am.*" Then you will use the correct pronoun.

2. After a linking verb (*is, am, are, was, were*) as a pronoun that renames the subject:

> The one who should apologize is *he*. (*He* is *the one who should apologize.* Therefore, the pronoun from the Subject Group is used.)

> The winner of the lottery was *she*. (*She* was *the winner of the lottery.* Therefore, the pronoun from the Subject Group is used.)

Modern usage allows some exceptions to this rule, however. For example, *It's me* or *It is her* (instead of the grammatically correct *It is I* and *It is she*) may be common in spoken English.

Use pronouns from the Object Group for all other purposes. In the following sentence, *me* is not the subject, nor does it rename the subject. It follows a preposition; therefore, it comes from the Object Group.

> My boss went to lunch with Jenny and *me*.

A good way to tell whether to use a pronoun from the Subject Group or the Object Group is to leave out any extra name (and the word *and*). By leaving out *Jenny and,* you will say, *My boss went to lunch with me.* You would never say, *My boss went to lunch with I.*

> My father and *I* play chess on Sundays. (*I* play chess on Sundays.)

> *She* and her friends rented a video. (*She* rented a video.)

> We saw Kevin and *them* last night. (We saw *them* last night.)

> The teacher gave *us* students certificates. (Teacher gave *us* certificates.)

> The coach asked Craig and *me* to wash the benches. (Coach asked *me* to wash the benches.)

PRONOUN AGREEMENT

Just as subjects and verbs must agree, pronouns should agree with the words they refer to. If the word referred to is singular, the pronoun should be singular. If the noun referred to is plural, the pronoun should be plural.

> Each classroom has its own chalkboard.

The pronoun *its* refers to the singular noun *classroom* and therefore is singular.

> Both classrooms have their own chalkboards.

The pronoun *their* refers to the plural noun *classrooms* and therefore is plural.

The same rules that we use to maintain the agreement of subjects and verbs also apply to pronoun agreement. For instance, ignore any prepositional phrases that come between the word and the pronoun that takes its place.

The *box* of chocolates has lost *its* label.

Boxes of chocolates often lose *their* labels.

A *player* with the best concentration usually beats *her or his* opponent.

Players with the best concentration usually beat *their* opponents.

When a pronoun refers to more than one word joined by *and,* the pronoun is plural:

The *teacher* and the *tutors* eat *their* lunches at noon.

The *salt* and *pepper* were in *their* usual spots on the table.

However, when a pronoun refers to more than one word joined by *or,* then the word closest to the pronoun determines its form:

Either the teacher or the *tutors* eat *their* lunches in the classroom.

Either the tutors or the *teacher* eats *her* lunch in the classroom.

Today many people try to avoid gender bias by writing sentences like the following:

If anyone wants help with the assignment, he or she can visit me in my office.

If anybody calls, tell him or her that I'll be back soon.

Somebody has left his or her pager in the classroom.

But those sentences are wordy and awkward. Therefore some people, especially in conversation, turn them into sentences that are not grammatically correct:

If anyone wants help with the assignment, they can visit me in my office.

If anybody calls, tell them that I'll be back soon.

Somebody has left their pager in the classroom.

Such ungrammatical sentences, however, are not necessary. It takes just a little thought to revise each sentence so that it avoids gender bias and is also grammatically correct:

Anyone who wants help with the assignment can visit me in my office.

Tell anybody who calls that I'll be back soon.

Somebody has left a pager in the classroom.

Probably the best way to avoid the awkward *he or she* and *him or her* is to make the words plural. Instead of writing, "Each actor was in his or her proper place on stage," write, "All the actors were in their proper places on stage," thus avoiding gender bias and still having a grammatically correct sentence.

PRONOUN REFERENCE

A pronoun replaces a noun to avoid repetition, but sometimes the pronoun sounds as if it refers to the wrong word in a sentence, causing confusion. Be aware that when you write a sentence, *you* know what it means, but your reader may not. What does this sentence mean?

> The students tried to use the school's computers to access the Internet, but they were too slow, so they decided to go home.

Who or what was too slow, and who or what decided to go home? We don't know whether the two pronouns (both *they*) refer to the students or to the computers. One way to correct such a faulty reference is to use singular and plural nouns:

> The students tried to use a school computer to access the Internet, but it was too slow, so they decided to go home.

Here's another sentence with a faulty reference:

> Calvin told his father that he needed a haircut.

Who needed the haircut—Calvin or his father? One way to correct such a faulty reference is to use a direct quotation:

> Calvin told his father, "You need a haircut."
>
> Calvin said, "Dad, I need a haircut."

Or you could always rephrase the sentence completely:

> Calvin noticed his father's hair was sticking out in odd places, so he told his father to get a haircut.

Another kind of faulty reference is a *which* clause that appears to refer to a specific word, but it doesn't really.

> I wasn't able to finish all the problems on the exam, which makes me worried.

The word *which* seems to replace *exam,* but it isn't the exam that makes me worried. The sentence should read as follows:

I am worried because I wasn't able to finish all the problems on the exam.

The pronoun *it* causes its own reference problems. Look at this sentence, for example:

When replacing the ink cartridge in my printer, it broke, and I had to call the technician to come and fix it.

Did the printer or the cartridge break? Here is one possible correction:

The new ink cartridge broke when I was putting it in my printer, and I had to call the technician for help.

E X E R C I S E S

Exercise 1

Circle the correct pronoun. Remember the trick of leaving out the extra name to help you decide which pronoun to use. Use the correct grammatical form even though an alternate form may be acceptable in conversation.

1. My stepmother and (I, me) went to the opera last night.

2. She usually enjoys the opera more than (I, me).

3. This time, however, (she and I, her and me) both enjoyed it.

4. Since I am less familiar with opera than (she, her), I usually don't like it as much.

5. Every time (she and I, her and me) have seen an opera before, she has chosen what to see and where to sit.

6. The one who made the choices this time was (I, me).

7. I may not know as much about opera as (she, her), but I sure picked a winner.

8. The singers seemed to be performing especially for (she and I, her and me).

9. Opera may never mean as much to me as it does to (she, her), but I am learning to appreciate it.

10. In the future, perhaps my stepmother will leave all the decisions of what to see and where to sit up to the box office and (I, me).

Exercise 2

Circle the pronoun that agrees with the word the pronoun replaces. If the correct answer is *his or her/her or his,* revise the sentence to eliminate the need for this awkward expression. Check your answers as you go through the exercise.

1. I live a long way from the city center and don't own a car, so I use public transportation and rely on (its, their) stability.

2. Based on my experiences, I'd say the city's system of buses has (its, their) problems.

3. Each of the bus routes that I travel on my way to work falls behind (its, their) own schedule.

4. Many of the other passengers also transfer on (his or her, their) way to work.

5. One day last week, each of the passengers had to gather (his or her, their) belongings and leave the bus, even though it had not reached a scheduled stop.

6. Both the driver and the mechanic who came to fix the bus offered (his, their) apologies for making us late.

7. Once the bus was fixed, the passengers were allowed to bring (his or her, their) things back on board.

8. Everyone did (his or her, their) best to hide (his or her, their) annoyance from the driver because he had been so nice.

9. As every passenger stepped off the bus at the end of the line, the driver thanked (him or her, them) for (his or her, their) patience and understanding.

10. Sometimes it is the people within a system that makes (it, them) work after all.

Exercise 3

Circle the correct pronoun. Again, if the correct answer is *his or her/her or his,* revise the sentence to eliminate the need for this awkward expression.

1. A car insurance company must be very competitive in (its, their) rates.

2. The one who received the reward money was (he, him).

   3. Each of the students will buy (his or her, their) own materials for the sculpture class.

   4. Players in the poker tournament have completed (its, their) first round of competition.

   5. When it comes to lizards, no one knows more than (she, her).

   6. Everyone in the class was allowed to turn (his or her, their) essay in late thanks to the extended deadline.

   7. The university representative gave my friend and (I, me) great advice.

   8. (You and me, You and I) drive the same kind of car, but mine is green.

   9. According to (they, them), we aren't permitted in the employee's lounge.

   10. It was (I, me) who loaned them the money for their vacation.

Exercise 4

Most—but not all—of the sentences in the next two sets aren't clear because we don't know what word the pronoun refers to. Revise such sentences, making the meaning clear. Since there are more ways than one to rewrite each sentence, yours may be as good as the ones at the back of the book. Just ask yourself whether the meaning is clear.

   1. As I was cooking my burrito in the microwave, it exploded.

   2. The student told the librarian that she didn't understand her.

   3. While we were putting the decorations on the tables, they blew away.

   4. Our cat sleeps all the time, which is boring.

   5. Samantha asked her friend why she wasn't invited to join the debate team.

   6. I shuffled the cards and asked Josh to pick one.

   7. He finished printing his book report, turned off the printer, and put it in his folder.

   8. Max told his brother that his bike had a flat tire.

   9. I bought my parking pass early, which gave me one less thing to worry about.

   10. Irene's mom lets her take her cell phone to school even though it's against the rules.

Exercise 5

1. As the raccoon was walking across the tree limb, it fell.

2. When children play in groups, they can be hard to manage.

3. I signed the application with a pen and put it in an envelope.

4. When I placed the bowls on top of the plates, they broke.

5. Sheila told her friend Helen that she had made a mistake.

6. We studied hard for the test, which didn't guarantee we would get a good grade.

7. Students who carry their campus ID cards receive discounts on food and books.

8. Luke's tutor asked him to sharpen his pencil.

9. We take a lot of tests in that class, which is exhausting.

10. They typed all of their essays in the computer lab.

PROOFREADING EXERCISE

The following paragraph contains errors in the use of pronouns. Find and correct the errors.

My daughter and me drove up the coast to visit a little zoo I had heard about. It was a hundred miles and took about two hours. Once her and I arrived, we saw the petting zoo area and wanted to pet the baby animals, but they wouldn't let us. They said that it was the baby animals' resting time, so we couldn't pet them. Then we got to the farm animals. There was a prize-winning hog that was as big as a couch when it was lying down. My daughter liked the hog best of all, and as she and I drove home in the car, it was all she could talk about.

SENTENCE WRITING

Write ten sentences in which you describe similarities and/or differences between you and someone else. Then check that your pronouns are grammatically correct, that they agree with the words they replace, and that references to specific nouns are clear. Keep the results in your sentence writing folder.

Avoiding Shifts in Person

To understand what "person" means when using pronouns, imagine a conversation between two people about a third person. The first person speaks using "I, me, my . . ."; the second person would be called "you"; and when the two of them talked of a third person, they would say "he, she, they . . . ." You'll never forget the idea of "person" if you remember it as a three-part conversation.

First person—*I, me, my, we, us, our*

Second person—*you, your*

Third person—*he, him, his, she, her, hers, they, them, their, one, anyone*

You may use all three of these groups of pronouns in a paper, but don't shift from one group to another without good reason.

Wrong: Few people know how to manage *their* time. *One* need not be an efficiency expert to realize that *one* could get a lot more done if *he* budgeted *his* time. Nor do *you* need to work very hard to get more organized.

Better: *Everyone* should know how to manage *his or her* time. *One* need not be an efficiency expert to realize that *a person* could get a lot more done if *one* budgeted *one's* time. Nor does *one* need to work very hard to get more organized. (Too many *one*'s in a paragraph make it sound overly formal, and they lead to the necessity of avoiding sexism by using *s/he* or *he or she,* etc. Sentences can be revised to avoid using either *you* or *one.*)

Best: Many of *us* don't know how to manage *our* time. *We* need not be efficiency experts to realize that *we* could get a lot more done if *we* budgeted *our* time. Nor do *we* need to work very hard to get more organized.

Often students write *you* in a paper when they don't really mean *you, the reader.*

You wouldn't believe how many times I saw that movie.

Such sentences are always improved by getting rid of the *you.*

I saw that movie many times.

PROOFREADING EXERCISES

Which of the following student paragraphs shift *unnecessarily* between first-, second-, and third-person pronouns? In those that do, revise the sentences to eliminate such shifting, thus making the entire paragraph read smoothly. One of the paragraphs is correct.

1. Americans have always had more than we actually need. Americans have gotten used to having as much food, water, and clothes as they want. Our restaurants throw away plates and plates of food every day. If you don't want something, you throw it in the trash. But a lot of people have started to think differently. Recycling doesn't just involve aluminum cans and plastic bottles. Americans can recycle food, water, and clothes if we think more creatively and responsibly than they've been doing in the past. You can change the society's view of recycling by just doing it.

2. My friends took me out to dinner for my birthday last week. We went to the new restaurant on the corner that allows its customers to grill their own food right at the table. As soon as we sat down, one of the servers came to our table and asked us if we had been there before. We told her that it was our first time, and she explained the process. It was all new to us. The servers kept bringing out plates of raw chicken, beef, and vegetables, and we kept throwing the food on our little grill and eating it as fast as we could. The dipping sauces were especially delicious, and the atmosphere at the new restaurant was exciting and unique.

3. If I had a choice to live in the city or the country, I would choose the city. I would choose the city because you are surrounded by other people there, and it feels friendly. The country is too quiet. There is dirt everywhere, flies flying around in the sky, bugs—which I hate—crawling on the floor inside and out. The city is a place where the lights are always on. Yes, you deal with pollution, smog, and crowds, but it just feels like home to me. A city house can be any size, shape, and color. All the houses in the country look the same to me. No matter who you are, you have a white house and a big red barn. I have to admit that I have only been to the country a couple of times to visit my relatives, but the city would have to be the place for me.

REVIEW OF SENTENCE STRUCTURE ERRORS

One sentence in each pair contains an error. Read both sentences carefully before you decide. Then write the letter of the *incorrect* sentence in the blank. Try to name the error and correct it if you can. You may find any of these errors:

awk	awkward phrasing
cliché	overused expression
dm	dangling modifier
frag	fragment
mm	misplaced modifier
pro	incorrect pronoun
pro agr	pronoun agreement error
pro ref	pronoun reference error
ro	run-on sentence
shift	shift in time or person
s-v agr	subject-verb agreement error
wordy	wordiness
//	not parallel

1. _____ **A.** We had a great time on our first trip to New York City.

   B. We saw a play on Broadway, walked down Fifth Avenue, and we visited the Statue of Liberty.

2. _____ **A.** There is a problem, and that is that the ATM machine sometimes runs out of cash.

   B. Once, the ATM machine recorded my withdrawal but didn't dispense the money.

3. _____ **A.** I planned to go on the field trip to the museum but my car broke down.

   B. The students who went said that the paintings and drawings were beautiful.

4. _____ **A.** The teacher's assistant in our biology lab is very helpful.

   B. She stayed with my lab partner and I during our whole experiment.

5. _____ **A.** Everyone in the graduation ceremony received their own fake diploma.

   B. The real diplomas arrived later in the mail.

6. _____ **A.** I finished my summary paragraph, printed it, and ran to class.

   B. I knew that it was better late than never.

7. _____ **A.** Each of the reference books I needed were checked out.

   B. The reference librarian told me that I could do some research online.

8. _____ **A.** I am planning to major in business.

   B. I do well in math classes I also love to read the biographies of entrepreneurs.

9. _____ **A.** I had a conference with my fencing teacher in his office.

   B. Me and him agreed that I needed to improve my footwork.

10. _____ **A.** The construction company who will build the new auditorium.

   B. They came to campus for the groundbreaking ceremony.

11. _____ **A.** A person who quits smoking can recover from lung damage.

   B. The tissues in your lungs slowly repair themselves.

12. _____ **A.** My car has a mind of its own.

   B. I can never tell when it is going to break down.

13. _____ **A.** Last night's dinner was a disaster.

   B. Cold mashed potatoes, overcooked broccoli, and tough pork chops.

14. _____ **A.** Some kind of chemical came through the vents in the classroom yesterday.

   B. Everyone's eyes are watering, and they were coughing.

15. _____ **A.** At the age of four, a brick fell on his right foot.

   B. He has had a scar on that foot ever since.

PROOFREADING EXERCISE

Find and correct the sentence structure errors in the following essay.

Mother Tells All

The most memorable lessons I have learned about myself have come from my own children. A mother is always on display she has nowhere to hide. And children are like parrots. Whatever they hear her say will be repeated again. If I change my mind about anything, you can be sure they will repeat back every word I uttered out of my mouth.

For example, last summer I told my kids that I was going to go to an exercise class and lose about forty pounds. Well, I lost some of the weight, and I did go to that exercise class. But as soon as I lost weight, I felt empty like a balloon losing air. I felt that I did not want to lose any more weight or do exercise anymore. I thought that my children would accept what I had decided.

When I stopped, the first thing one of my sons said was, "Mom, you need to go back to exercise class." Then they all started telling me what to eat all the time and I felt horrible about it. I had given up these things because I wanted to, but my words were still being repeated to me like an alarm clock going off without stopping. Finally, my kids ran out of steam and got bored with the idea of my losing weight. Once in a while, one of them still make a joke about my "attempt" to lose weight it hurts me that they don't understand.

The lesson that I have learned from this experience is that, if I am not planning on finishing something, I won't tell my children about it. They will never let me forget.

Punctuation and Capital Letters

Period, Question Mark, Exclamation Point, Semicolon, Colon, Dash

Every mark of punctuation should help the reader. Here are the rules for six marks of punctuation. The first three you have known for a long time and probably have no trouble with. The one about semicolons you learned when you studied independent clauses (p. 89). The ones about the colon and the dash may be less familiar.

Put a period (.) at the end of a sentence and after most abbreviations.

> The students elected Ms. Daniels to represent the class.

> Sept.   Mon.   in.   sq.   ft.   lbs.

Put a question mark (?) after a direct question but not after an indirect one.

> Will we be able to use our notes during the test? (direct)

> I wonder if we will be able to use our notes during the test. (indirect)

Put an exclamation point (!) after an expression that shows strong emotion. This mark is used mostly in dialogue or informal correspondence.

> I can't believe I did so well on my first exam!

Put a semicolon (;) between two independent clauses in a sentence unless they are joined by one of the connecting words *for, and, nor, but, or, yet, so*.

> My mother cosigned for a loan; now I have my own car.

> Some careers go in and out of fashion; however, people will always need teachers.

To be sure that you are using a semicolon correctly, see if a period and capital letter can be used in its place. If they can, you are putting the semicolon in the right spot.

My mother cosigned for a loan. Now I have my own car.

Some careers go in and out of fashion. However, people will always need teachers.

Put a colon (:) after a complete statement that introduces one of the following elements: a name, a list, a quotation, or an explanation.

The company announced its Employee-of-the-Month: Lee Jones. (The sentence before the colon introduces the name that follows it.)

That truck comes in the following colors: red, black, blue, and silver. (The complete statement before the colon introduces the list that follows it.)

That truck comes in red, black, blue, and silver. (Here the list is simply part of the sentence. There is no complete statement used to introduce the list, so it does not need a colon.)

Thoreau had this to say about time: "Time is but the stream I go a-fishin in." (The writer introduces the quotation with a complete statement. Therefore, a colon comes between them.)

Thoreau said, "Time is but the stream I go a-fishin in." (Here the writer leads directly into the quotation; therefore, no colon—just a comma—comes between them.)

Use dashes (—) to isolate inserted information, to signal an abrupt change of thought, or to emphasize what follows.

Lee Jones—March's Employee-of-the-Month—received his own special parking space.

I found out today—or was it yesterday?—that I have inherited a fortune.

We have exciting news for you—we're moving!

E X E R C I S E S

Exercises 1 and 2

Add to these sentences the necessary end punctuation (periods, question marks, and exclamation points). The semicolons, colons, dashes, and commas used within the sentences are correct and do not need to be changed. Pay close attention to them, however, to help with further exercises.

Exercise 1

1. Have you heard of the phenomenon known as a "milky sea"

2. Sailors throughout history have described this eerie condition

3. A milky sea occurs when ocean water turns almost completely white

4. What accounts for this milky color

5. It is due to huge amounts of bacteria that glow with white light

6. Until recently, no one had photographs or other visual proof of this condition

7. In 1995, however, people took the first pictures of a milky sea off the coast of Somalia

8. Scientists later reviewed satellite images from the same period and discovered their own startling documentation that milky seas exist

9. The satellite photos clearly showed a long glowing white stretch of ocean water

10. It was the size of the state of Connecticut

Source: Science News, October 1, 2005

Exercise 2

1. Wasn't the company's holiday party nice this year

2. At first, I wasn't sure that I wanted to go; now I'm glad I did

3. The music—especially the harp music—made everyone so calm and contented

4. The twinkling lights in the trees on the patio gave off a beautiful light

5. Even the cubicles around our desks looked festive

6. The boss announced our new Employee of the Year: Ted Haynes

7. With so many of us doing the same job, there is a lot a competition; however, all that was put aside for the party

8. The boss's husband is nicer than I thought he would be; I enjoyed meeting him

   9. I talked with coworkers that I haven't had any fun with in a long time—
      even Charlie

   10. I hope that everyone will still be in a holiday spirit once we get back to
      work on Monday

Exercises 3 and 4

Add any necessary semicolons, colons, and dashes to these sentences. The
commas and end punctuation are correct and do not need to be changed. Some
sentences do not need any more punctuation.

Exercise 3

   1. People can learn foreign languages in several new ways these days by
      practicing with a partner, by studying on long plane flights, and by listen-
      ing to foreign news on the radio or watching movies in other languages.

   2. The Internet allows people especially those who want to learn a
      language to correspond easily with people from other countries.

   3. The exchange goes something like this one person wants to know
      French he contacts a person in France who wants to learn English.

   4. The two exchange emails then, as they correct each other's phrasing,
      they learn more about the other's language.

   5. Certain audio programs and books have been designed for one purpose
      to offer airline passengers a quick course in a foreign language.

   6. Portable music devices usually hold book-length works therefore, these
      in-flight language programs are easy to use.

   7. The third new way to become more fluent in a foreign language with
      the help of new technology is to listen to radio and film programs in
      another language.

   8. It's easy to find foreign news sites on the Internet these radio programs
      feature reporters who speak clearly and use many common phrases.

   9. There is a variation that anyone with a DVD player can use most DVD
      menus include the option of listening to the movie dubbed in another
      language.

   10. In this way, movies can be even more entertaining they can also be
      more educational.

Exercise 4

1. Nancy Cartwright is a well-known actress on television however, we never see her when she is acting.

2. Cartwright is famous for playing one part the voice of Bart Simpson.

3. Besides her career as the most mischievous Simpson, Cartwright is married and has children of her own a boy and a girl.

4. Wouldn't it be strange if your mother had Bart Simpson's voice?

5. Cartwright admits that she made her own share of trouble in school.

6. But the similarities between her and her famous character end there.

7. Bart is perpetually ten years old Cartwright is in her forties.

8. Bart is a boy Cartwright is obviously a woman.

9. It's no surprise that Cartwright is very popular with her children's friends.

10. When they yell for her to "Do Bart! Do Bart!" she declines with Bart's favorite saying "No way, man!"

Source: People, December 14, 1998

Exercise 5

Add the necessary periods, question marks, exclamation points, semicolons, colons, and dashes. Any commas are correct and do not need to be changed.

1. What do math and origami Japanese paper folding have to do with each other

2. Erik Demaine and other origami mathematicians would answer, "Everything"

3. If you have never heard of the field of origami mathematics, you're not alone

4. Origami math is a relatively new field back in 2003, Demaine won a "genius" award partly due to his work with origami and its applications in many fields

5. The MacArthur Foundation awarded Demaine more than just the title "genius" it awarded him half a million dollars

6. At twenty, Demaine was hired as a professor by the Massachusetts Institute of Technology he became the youngest professor MIT has ever had

7. Erik Demaine has his father to thank for much of his education Martin Demaine home-schooled Erik as the two of them traveled around North America

8. Erik was always intensely interested in academic subjects during his travels, he and his father would consult university professors whenever Erik had questions that no one else could answer

9. Erik Demaine continues to investigate one area in particular the single-cut problem

10. This problem involves folding a piece of paper then making one cut the result can be anything from a swan to a star, a unicorn, or any letter of the alphabet

Source: New York Times, February 15, 2005

PROOFREADING EXERCISE

Find the punctuation errors in this student paragraph. They all involve periods, question marks, exclamation points, semicolons, colons, and dashes. Any commas used within the sentences are correct and should not be changed.

The ingredients you will need for a lemon meringue pie are: lemon juice, eggs, sugar, cornstarch, flour, butter, water, and salt. First, you combine flour, salt, butter, and water for the crust and bake until lightly brown then you mix and cook the lemon juice, egg yolks, sugar, cornstarch, butter, and water for the filling. Once the filling is poured into the cooked crust; you whip the meringue. Meringue is made of egg whites and sugar! Pile the meringue on top of the lemon filling; place the pie in the hot oven for a few minutes, and you'll have the best lemon meringue pie you've ever tasted.

SENTENCE WRITING

Write ten sentences of your own that use periods, question marks, exclamation points, semicolons, colons, and dashes correctly. Imitate the examples used in the explanations if necessary. Write about a success you had at school, at home, or at work and explain how you felt as a result.

Comma Rules 1, 2, and 3

Commas and other pieces of punctuation guide the reader through your sentence structures in the same way that signs guide drivers on the highway. Imagine what effects misplaced or incorrect road signs would have. Yet students often randomly place commas in their sentences. Try not to use a comma unless you know there is a need for it. Memorize this rhyme about comma use: *When in doubt, leave it out.*

Among all of the comma rules, six are most important. Learn these six rules, and your writing will be easier to read. You have already studied the first rule on pages 90–91.

1. **Put a comma before** *for, and, nor, but, or, yet, so* **(remember these seven words as the** *fanboys***) when they connect two independent clauses.**

    The neighbors recently bought a minivan, and now they take short trips every weekend.

    We wrote our paragraphs in class today, but the teacher forgot to collect them.

    She was recently promoted, so she has moved to a better office.

If you use a comma alone between two independent clauses, the result is an error called a ***comma splice.***

    The cake looked delicious, it tasted good too. (comma splice)

    The cake looked delicious, and it tasted good too. (correct)

Before using a comma, be sure such words do connect two independent clauses. The following sentence is merely one independent clause with one subject and two verbs. Therefore, no comma should be used.

    The ice cream looked delicious and tasted good too.

2. **Use a comma to separate three or more items in a series.**

    Students in literature classes are reading short stories, poems, and plays.

    Today I did my laundry, washed my car, and cleaned my room.

Occasionally, writers leave out the comma before the *and* connecting the last two items in a series, but it is more common to use it to separate all of the items equally. Some words work together and don't need commas between them even though they do make up a kind of series.

    The team members wanted to wear their brand new green uniforms.

    The bright white sunlight made the room glow.

To see whether a comma is needed between words in a series, ask yourself whether *and* could be used naturally between them. It would sound all right to say *short stories and poems and plays;* therefore, commas are used. But it would not sound right to say *brand and new and green uniforms* or *bright and white sunlight;* therefore, no commas are used.

If an address or date is used in a sentence, put a comma after every item, including the last.

> My father was born on August 19, 1941, in Mesa, Arizona, and grew up there.

> Shelby lived in St. Louis, Missouri, for two years.

When only the month and year are used in a date, no commas are needed.

> My aunt graduated from Yale in May 1985.

3. Put a comma after an introductory expression (a word, a phrase, or a dependent clause) or before a comment or question tagged onto the end.

> Finally, he was able to get through to his insurance company.

> During her last performance, the actress fell and broke her foot.

> Once I have finished my homework, I will call you.

> He said he needed to ruminate, whatever that means.

> The new chairs aren't very comfortable, are they?

E X E R C I S E S

Add commas to the following sentences according to the first three comma rules. Any other punctuation already in the sentences is correct. Check your answers after the first set.

Exercise 1

Add commas according to Comma Rule 1. Put a comma before a *fanboys* when it connects two independent clauses. Some sentences may be correct.

1. My cousins and I used to go fishing with our grandfather but we rarely enjoyed it.

2. He told long stories about his old friends and we rolled our eyes.

3. We sat through lectures about baiting our hooks and flinging our lines.

4. Sometimes he asked us about our friends or he told us stories about our parents when they were children.

5. Then we became interested for the stories about our moms and dads were very funny.

6. One time my cousin Joey threw a whole can of bait in the water and my grandfather chased him all around the edge of the lake.

7. Now I know how special those times were and I wish I could go fishing with him again.

8. I would be nicer to my grandfather and would pay attention to all his stories.

9. My cousins remember those fishing trips too and we feel bad about how we acted sometimes.

10. Our grandfather isn't with us anymore but we think about him all the time.

Exercise 2

Add commas according to Comma Rule 2. Use a comma to separate three or more items in a series. If an address or date is used, put a comma after each item, including the last. Some sentences may not need any commas.

1. I graduated from high school on June 25 2002 in San Antonio Texas.

2. I was lucky to have an English teacher in high school who was young enthusiastic and highly motivated.

3. We read essays stories poems and research articles in her class.

4. One time we read a short play chose parts to memorize and gave a performance of it in front of the whole school.

5. One of my favorite of Ms. Kern's assignments was the complaint letter that she asked us to write.

6. She was trying to teach us how to follow directions how to explain something clearly and how to think about what she called our "tone of voice" when we wrote.

7. We had to write a real letter of complaint about a product a service or an experience that was unsatisfactory to us.

8. Then we sent a copy of our letter to the company's business address to our home address and to Ms. Kern's school address.

9. Ms. Kern assured us that we would receive a response from the company if we explained our complaint well asked for a reasonable solution and used an appropriate tone.

10. In the big envelope from my company was a letter of apology a bumper sticker and an impressive discount coupon to use at any of the company's stores.

Exercise 3

Add commas according to Comma Rule 3. Put a comma after introductory expressions and before any tag comments or questions.

1. Most people don't know how coffee is decaffeinated do you?

2. Although there are three methods used to decaffeinate coffee one of them is the most popular.

3. The most popular method is called water processing drawing the caffeine from the coffee beans into a water solution and removing most of it.

4. After going through the natural water processing method the coffee may be a little less flavorful.

5. To decaffeinate coffee another way manufacturers add a chemical solution to the beans and then steam them to remove the leftover chemicals.

6. Compared to the water processing method the chemical method is more "scientific" and removes more of the caffeine.

7. Finally there is the method that infuses coffee beans with carbon dioxide gas to get rid of the caffeine.

8. Since carbon dioxide is plentiful and nontoxic this process is also popular.

9. Even though the carbon dioxide method is the most expensive of the three ways to decaffeinate coffee it also removes the most caffeine.

10. Whenever I drink a cup of decaf in the future I'll wonder which method was used to remove the caffeine.

Source: Scientific American, October 2002

Exercise 4

Add commas according to the first three comma rules.

1. When the government issued the Susan B. Anthony dollar coin on July 2 1979 it met with some disapproval.

2. People didn't dislike the person on the coin but they did dislike the size and color of the coin.

3. It was nearly the same size as a quarter had a rough edge like a quarter's and was the same color as a quarter.

4. It differed from a quarter in that it was faceted around the face was lighter in weight and was worth four times as much.

5. Due to these problems the Susan B. Anthony dollar was discontinued and in January 2000 the government issued a new golden dollar.

6. Like the Anthony dollar the new coin portrayed the image of a famous American woman.

7. She was the young Native American guide and interpreter for the Lewis and Clark expedition and her name was Sacagawea.

8. Although the Sacagawea dollar was roughly the same size as the Anthony dollar it had a smooth wide edge and its gold color made it easy to distinguish from a quarter.

9. Sacagawea's journey included hardship suffering and illness but it also revealed her incredible knowledge courage and strength.

10. While the men on the expedition had only themselves to worry about Sacagawea made the treacherous journey to the Pacific with her baby strapped to her back.

Exercise 5

Add commas according to the first three comma rules.

1. In the past people believed that emeralds held magical powers.

2. They were supposed to cure disease lengthen life and protect innocence.

3. Part of their appeal was their rarity for emeralds are even rarer than diamonds.

4. Geologists have been mystified by emeralds because they are produced through a unique process the blending of chromium vanadium and beryllium.

5. These substances almost never occur together except in emeralds.

6. In South Africa Pakistan and Brazil emeralds were created by intrusions of granite millions of years ago.

7. These areas are known for their beautiful gems but emeralds from Colombia are the largest greenest and most sparkling of all.

8. In Colombia the makeup of the sedimentary rock accounts for the difference.

9. Instead of the granite found in other emerald-rich countries the predominant substance in Colombia is black shale.

10. Even though emeralds can be synthesized a real one always contains a trapped bit of fluid and jewelers call this tiny imperfection a "garden."

PROOFREADING EXERCISE

Apply the first three comma rules to the following paragraph:

I couldn't believe it but there I was in the pilot's seat of an airplane. I had casually signed up for a course in flying at the aviation school and hadn't expected to start flying right away. The instructor told me what to do and I did it. When I turned the stick to the right the plane turned right. When I turned it to the left the plane went left. Actually it was very similar to driving a car. Most of my practice involved landing bringing the plane in softly and safely. After many hours of supervised flying my time to solo came and I was really excited. I covered the checklist on the ground took off without any problems and landed like a professional. On May 8 2005 I became a licensed pilot so now I can pursue my dream of being a private pilot for a rock star.

SENTENCE WRITING

Combine the following sets of sentences in different ways using all of the first three comma rules. You may need to reorder the details and change the phrasing. Sample responses are provided in the Answers section.

I take ski trips in the winter.

I go hiking in the summer.

I like hiking better.

Tutors will not correct a student's paper.

They will explain how to clarify ideas.

They will explain how to add stronger details.

They will explain how to improve organization.

Charles bought his first car.

He bought a big car.

The dealer gave Charles a good price.

Charles should have thought more about gas mileage.

Now he spends over a hundred dollars a month on gas.

Comma Rules 4, 5, and 6

The next three comma rules all involve using pairs of commas to enclose what we like to call "scoopable" elements. Scoopable elements are certain words, phrases, and clauses that can be taken out of the middle of a sentence without affecting its meaning. Notice that the comma **(,)** is shaped somewhat like the tip of an ice cream scoop? Let this similarity help you remember to use commas to enclose *scoopable* elements. Two commas are used**,** one before and one after**,** to show where scoopable elements begin and where they end.

4. Put commas around the name of a person spoken to.

Did you know, Danielle, that you left your backpack at the library?

We regret to inform you, Mr. Davis, that your policy has been canceled.

5. Put commas around expressions that interrupt the flow of the sentence (such as *however, moreover, therefore, of course, by the way, on the other hand, I believe, I think*).

I know, of course, that I have missed the deadline.

They will try, therefore, to use the rest of their time wisely.

Today's exam, I think, was only a practice test.

Read the previous examples *aloud,* and you'll hear how these expressions surrounded by commas interrupt the flow of the sentence. Sometimes such expressions flow smoothly into the sentence and don't need commas around them.

Of course he checked to see if there were any rooms available.

We therefore decided to stay out of it.

I think you made the right decision.

Remember that when a word like *however* comes between two independent clauses, that word needs a semicolon before it. It may also have a comma after it, especially if there seems to be a pause between the word and the rest of the sentence. (See p. 89.)

The bus was late; *however,* we still made it to the museum before it closed.

I am improving my study habits; *furthermore,* I am getting better grades.

She was interested in journalism; *therefore,* she took a job at a local newspaper.

I spent hours studying for the test; *finally,* I felt prepared.

Thus, you've seen a word like *however* or *therefore* used in three ways:

1. as a "scoopable" word that interrupts the flow of the sentence (needs commas around it)

2. as a word that flows into the sentence (no commas needed)

3. as a connecting word between two independent clauses (semicolon before and often a comma after)

6. Put commas around additional information that is not needed in a sentence.

Certain additional information is "scoopable" and should be surrounded by commas whenever the meaning would be clear without it. Look at the following sentence:

Maxine Taylor, who organized the fund-raiser, will introduce the candidates.

The clause *who organized the fund-raiser* is not needed in the sentence. Without it, we still know exactly who the sentence is about and what she is going to do: "Maxine Taylor will introduce the candidates." Therefore, the additional information is surrounded by commas to show that it is scoopable. Now read the following sentence:

The woman who organized the fund-raiser will introduce the candidates.

The clause *who organized the fund-raiser* is necessary in this sentence. Without it, the sentence would read as follows: "The woman will introduce the candidates." The reader would have no idea *which woman*. The clause *who organized the fund-raiser* cannot be left out because it identifies which woman. Therefore, the clause is not scoopable, and no commas are used around it. Here is another sample sentence:

Hamlet, Shakespeare's famous play, has been made into a movie many times.

The additional information *Shakespeare's famous play* is scoopable. It could be left out, and we would still understand the meaning of the sentence: "*Hamlet* has been made into a movie many times." Therefore, the commas surround the scoopable information to show that it could be taken out. Here is the same sentence with the information reversed:

Shakespeare's famous play *Hamlet* has been made into a movie many times.

Here the title of the play is necessary. Without it, the sentence would read as follows: "Shakespeare's famous play has been made into a movie many times." The reader would have no idea which of Shakespeare's famous plays has been made into a movie many times. Therefore, the title is not scoopable, and commas should not be used around it.

The trick in deciding whether additional information is scoopable or not is to remember, "If I can scoop it out and still understand the sentence, I'll put commas around it."

E X E R C I S E S

Surround any "scoopable" elements with commas according to Comma Rules 4, 5, and 6. Any commas already in the sentences follow Comma Rules 1, 2, and 3. Some sentences may be correct. Check your answers after the first set.

Exercise 1

1. This year's Feast of Lanterns in Pacific Grove I think was better than last year's.

2. I think this year's Feast of Lanterns in Pacific Grove was better than last year's.

3. The weather was certainly perfect this year.

4. Certainly the weather was perfect this year.

5. The people who decorated their houses with lanterns were the unsung heroes of the weeklong festival.

6. Laurie and Jane who decorated their houses were among the unsung heroes of the weeklong festival.

7. The people who organized the Pet Parade did a great job; there were plenty of costumes and animals, and the children had lots of fun.

8. Adrienne and Andrea two volunteers at the Pet Parade were also dancers in the ballet.

9. The salads at the Feast of Salads I have to say were better last year.

10. I have to say that the salads at the Feast of Salads were better last year.

Exercise 2

1. We trust of course that people who get their driver's licenses know how to drive.

2. Of course we trust that people who get their driver's licenses know how to drive.

3. The people who test drivers for their licenses make the streets safer for all of us.

4. Mr. Kraft who tests drivers for their licenses makes the streets safer for all of us.

5. We may therefore understand when we fail the driving test ourselves.

6. Therefore we may understand when we fail the driving test ourselves.

7. The driver's seat we know is a place of tremendous responsibility.

8. We know that the driver's seat is a place of tremendous responsibility.

9. We believe that no one should take that responsibility lightly.

10. No one we believe should take that responsibility lightly.

Exercise 3

1. The writing teacher Ms. Gonzales has published several of her own short stories.

2. The Ms. Gonzales who teaches writing is not the Ms. Gonzales who teaches history.

3. My daughter's friend Harry doesn't get along with her best friend Jenny.

4. My daughter's best friend Jenny doesn't get along with one of her other friends Harry.

5. The tiger which is a beautiful and powerful animal symbolizes freedom.

6. The tiger that was born in September is already on display at the zoo.

7. The students who helped set up the chairs were allowed to sit in the front row.

8. Kim and Teresa who helped set up the chairs were allowed to sit in the front row.

9. My car which had a tracking device was easy to find when it was stolen.

10. A car that has a tracking device is easier to find if it's stolen.

Exercise 4

1. Arthur S. Heineman a California architect designed and built the world's first motel in the mid-1920s.

2. He chose the perfect location the city of San Luis Obispo which was midway between Los Angeles and San Francisco.

3. Heineman an insightful man of business understood the need for inexpensive drive-in accommodations on long motor vehicle trips.

4. Hotels which required reservations and offered only high-priced rooms within one large structure just didn't fulfill the needs of motorists.

5. Heineman envisioned his "Motor Hotel" or Mo-Tel as a place where the parking spaces for the cars were right next to separate bungalow-style apartments for the passengers.

6. Heineman's idea was so new that when he put up his "Motel" sign several residents of the area told him to fire the sign's painter who couldn't even spell the word *hotel.*

7. Heineman had the sign painter place a hyphen between *Mo* and *Tel* to inform the public of a new kind of resting place.

8. Heineman's Milestone Mo-Tel the world's first motel opened in San Luis Obispo in 1925.

9. Before Heineman's company the Milestone Interstate Corporation could successfully trademark the name "Mo-Tel," other builders adopted the style and made *motel* a generic term.

10. Much of the original Milestone Mo-Tel building now called the Motel Inn still stands on the road between L.A. and San Francisco.

Source: Westways, May/June 2000

Exercise 5

1. I bought a book *The Story of the "Titanic"* because I am interested in famous events in history.

2. This book written by Frank O. Braynard is a collection of postcards about the ill-fated ocean liner.

3. The book's postcards four on each page can be pulled apart and mailed like regular ones.

4. The postcards have images of *Titanic*-related people, places, and events on one side.

5. The blank sides where messages and addresses go include brief captions of the images on the front of the cards.

6. The book's actual content the part written by Braynard offers a brief history of each image relating to the *Titanic*.

7. One of my favorite cards shows the ship's captain Edward Smith and its builder Lord Pirrie standing on the deck of the *Titanic* before it set sail.

8. Another card is a photograph of *Titanic* passengers on board the *Carpathia* the ship that rescued many survivors.

9. There is also picture of two small children survivors themselves who lost their father in the disaster but were later reunited with their mother.

10. The most interesting card a photo of the ship's gymnasium shows that one of the pieces of exercise equipment for the passengers was a rowing machine.

PROOFREADING EXERCISE

Surround any "scoopable" elements in the following paragraph with commas according to Comma Rules 4, 5, and 6.

Do you know Ryan that there is a one-unit library class that begins next week? It's called Library 1 Introduction to the Library and we have to sign up for it before Friday. The librarians who teach it will give us an orientation and a series of assignment sheets. Then as we finish the assignments at our own pace we will turn them in to the librarians for credit. Ms. Kim the librarian that I spoke with said that we will learn really valuable library skills. These skills such as finding books or articles in our library and using the Internet to access other databases are the ones universities will expect us to know. I therefore plan to take this class, and you I hope will take it with me.

SENTENCE WRITING

Combine the following sets of sentences in different ways according to Comma Rules 4, 5, and 6. Try to combine each set in a way that needs commas and in a way that doesn't need commas. In other words, try to make an element "scoopable" in one sentence and not "scoopable" in another. You may reorder the details and change the phrasing as you wish. Sample responses are provided in the Answers section.

Soup tastes best when it's hot.

Chicken noodle soup is especially good when it's hot.

I believe.

We should start a savings account.

A savings account will help us prepare for financial emergencies.

My roommate got a job in the bookstore.

Her name is Leslie.

The job allows her to get good discounts on books.

REVIEW OF THE COMMA

SIX COMMA RULES

1. Put a comma before *for, and, nor, but, or, yet, so* when they connect two independent clauses.

2. Put a comma between three or more items in a series.

3. Put a comma after an introductory expression or before a tag comment or question.

4. Put commas around the name of a person spoken to.

5. Put commas around words like *however* or *therefore* when they interrupt a sentence.

6. Put commas around unnecessary additional ("scoopable") information.

COMMA REVIEW EXERCISE

Add the missing commas, and identify which one of the six comma rules applies in the brackets at the *end* of each sentence. Each of the six sentences illustrates a different rule.

I'm writing you this reminder Lisa so that you won't forget our date to go to the museum this Saturday. [   ] I know we're still friends but lately some of our plans have slipped your mind. [   ] After we decided to meet in the library last weekend you forgot all about it. [   ] I'm taking this opportunity therefore to refresh your memory. [   ] I know that you're busy with work with school and with family. [   ] I've made a reservation to have lunch in The Greenhouse an expensive little restaurant at the museum as a special treat. [   ] I know that you'll love it. See you Saturday!

SENTENCE WRITING

Write at least one sentence of your own to demonstrate each of the six comma rules.

Quotation Marks and Underlining/*Italics*

Put quotation marks around a direct quotation (the exact words of a speaker) but not around an indirect quotation.

> The officer said, "Please show me your driver's license." (a direct quotation)

> The officer asked to see my driver's license. (an indirect quotation)

If the speaker says more than one sentence, quotation marks are used before and after the entire speech.

> She said, "One of your brake lights is out. You need to take care of the problem right away."

If the quotation begins the sentence, the words telling who is speaking are set off with a comma unless the quotation ends with a question mark or an exclamation point.

> "I didn't even know it was broken," I said.

> "Do you have any questions?" she asked.

> "You mean I can go!" I shouted.

> "Yes, consider this just a warning," she said.

Notice that each of the previous quotations begins with a capital letter. But when a quotation is interrupted by an identifying phrase, the second part doesn't begin with a capital letter unless the second part is a new sentence.

> "If you knew how much time I spent on the essay," the student said, "you would give me an A."

> "A chef might work on a meal for days," the teacher replied. "That doesn't mean the results will taste good."

Put quotation marks around the titles of short stories, poems, songs, essays, TV program episodes, or other short works.

> I couldn't sleep after I read "The Lottery," a short story by Shirley Jackson.

> My favorite Woodie Guthrie song is "This Land Is Your Land."

> We had to read George Orwell's essay "A Hanging" for my speech class.

> Jerry Seinfeld's troubles in "The Puffy Shirt" episode are some of the funniest moments in TV history.

Underline titles of longer works such as books, newspapers, magazines, plays, record albums or CDs, movies, or the titles of TV or radio series.

<u>The Color Purple</u> is a novel by Alice Walker.

I read about the latest discovery of dinosaur footprints in <u>Newsweek</u>.

<u>Gone with the Wind</u> was re-released in movie theaters in 1998.

My mother listens to <u>The Writer's Almanac</u> on the radio every morning.

You may choose to *italicize* instead of underlining if your word processor gives you the option. Just be consistent throughout any paper in which you use underlining or italics.

The Color Purple is a novel by Alice Walker.

I read about the latest discovery of dinosaur footprints in *Newsweek*.

Gone with the Wind was re-released in movie theaters in 1998.

My mother listens to *The Writer's Almanac* on the radio every morning.

EXERCISES

Correctly punctuate quotations and titles in the following sentences by adding quotation marks or underlining (*italics*). Check your answers often.

Exercise 1

1. Do you need any help with your homework? my father asked.

2. In William Zinsser's book On Writing Well, he explains that Readers want the person who is talking to them to sound genuine.

3. Sigmund Freud had this to say about the intensity of a particular dream: The dream is far shorter than the thoughts which it replaces.

4. Cat People and The Curse of the Cat People are two movies about people who turn into panther-like cats.

5. All for love, and nothing for reward is a famous quotation by Edmund Spenser.

6. Forrest Gump made many sayings famous, but Life is like a box of chocolates is the most memorable.

7. My teacher wrote Well done! at the top of my essay.

8. Poker expert Phil Gordon admits that Everyone makes mistakes. A bad poker player, he adds, will make the same mistake over and over again.

9. Donna asked, What time is the meeting?

10. My family subscribes to The New Yorker, and we all enjoy reading it.

Exercise 2

1. Emilie Buchwald once noted, Children are made readers on the laps of their parents.

2. Have you read Mark Twain's book The Adventures of Tom Sawyer?

3. I took a deep breath when my counselor asked, How many math classes have you had?

4. Let's start that again! shouted the dance teacher.

5. Last night we watched the Beatles' movie Help! on DVD.

6. Books, wrote Jonathan Swift, are the children of the brain.

7. Voltaire stated in A Philosophical Dictionary that Tears are the silent language of grief.

8. Why do dentists ask questions like How are you? as soon as they start working on your teeth?

9. Time is the only incorruptible judge is just one translation of Creon's line from the Greek play Oedipus Rex.

10. My favorite essay that we have read this semester has to be The Pie by Gary Soto.

Exercise 3

1. Marks is the title of a poem by Linda Pastan.

2. I'll never understand what No news is good news means.

3. The student asked the librarian, Can you help me find an article on spontaneous human combustion?

4. Whatever happened to The Book of Lists?

5. My Antonia is the title of one of Willa Cather's most famous novels.

6. Let's begin, the relaxation expert said, by closing our eyes and imagining ourselves in an empty theater.

7. Television series like Frontier House and Colonial House have made PBS a real competitor for reality-TV-hungry audiences.

8. I can't keep this a secret anymore, my neighbor told me. Your son has a tattoo that he hasn't shown you yet.

9. Phil Gordon's Little Green Book is the whole title of his book, and the subtitle is Lessons and Teachings in No Limit Texas Hold'em.

10. I was shocked when my high school English teacher told us, Most of Shakespeare's stories came from other sources; he just dramatized them better than anyone else did.

Exercise 4

1. Alfred Tonnelle defined art this way: The artist does not see things as they are, but as he is.

2. I found a vintage children's book called Baby Island at the thrift store; it was a fascinating story.

3. A Russian proverb says, When money speaks, the truth is silent.

4. When someone suggested that Walt Disney run for mayor of Los Angeles following the success of Disneyland, Disney declined, saying, I'm already king.

5. About trying new foods, Swift said, It was a bold man who first ate an oyster.

6. Mark Twain noted about California, It's a great place to live, but I wouldn't want to visit there.

7. There is a French expression *L'amour est aveugle; l'amitié ferme les yeux*, which translates as follows: Love is blind; friendship closes its eyes.

8. Let's keep our voices down, the librarian said as we left the study room.

9. One of Emily Dickinson's shortest poems begins, A word is dead/When it is said/Some say.

10. Dickinson's poem ends like this: I say it just/Begins to live/That day.

Exercise 5

1. In Booker T. Washington's autobiography Up from Slavery, he describes his early dream of going to school.

2. I had no schooling whatever while I was a slave, he explains.

3. He continues, I remember on several occasions I went as far as the schoolhouse door with one of my young mistresses to carry her books.

4. Washington was incredibly attracted by what he saw from the doorway: several dozen boys and girls engaged in study.

5. The picture, he adds, made a deep impression upon me.

6. Washington cherished this glimpse of boys and girls engaged in study.

7. It contrasted directly with his own situation: My life had its beginning in the midst of the most miserable, desolate, and discouraging surroundings.

8. I was born, he says, in a typical log cabin, about fourteen by sixteen feet square.

9. He explains, In this cabin I lived with my mother and a brother and sister till after the Civil War, when we were all declared free.

10. As a slave at the door of his young mistress's schoolhouse, Booker T. Washington remembers, I had the feeling that to get into a schoolhouse and study in this way would be about the same as getting into paradise.

Source: Great Americans in Their Own Words (Mallard Press, 1990)

PARAGRAPH EXERCISE

Correctly punctuate quotations and titles in the following paragraph by adding quotation marks or underlining (*italics*).

I've been reading the book How Children Fail by John Holt. I checked it out to use in a research paper I'm doing on education in America. Holt's book was published in the early 1960s, but his experiences and advice are still relevant today. In one of his chapters, Fear and Failure, Holt describes intelligent children this way: Intelligent children act as if they thought the universe made some sense. They check their answers and their thoughts against common sense, while other children, not expecting answers to make sense, not knowing what is sense, see no point in checking, no way of checking. Holt and others stress the child's self-confidence as one key to success.

SENTENCE WRITING

Write ten sentences that list and discuss your favorite songs, TV shows, characters' expressions, movies, books, and so on. Be sure to punctuate quotations and titles correctly. Refer to the rules at the beginning of this section if necessary.

Capital Letters

1. Capitalize the first word of every sentence.

Peaches taste best when they are cold.

A piece of fruit is an amazing object.

2. Capitalize the first word of every direct quotation.

She said, "I've never worked so hard before."

"I have finished most of my homework," she said, "but I still have a lot to do." (The *but* is not capitalized because it does not begin a new sentence.)

"I love my speech class," she said. "Maybe I'll change my major." (*Maybe* is capitalized because it begins a new sentence.)

3. Capitalize the first, last, and every important word in a title. Don't capitalize prepositions (such as *in, of, at, with*), short connecting words, the *to* in front of a verb, or *a, an,* or *the*.

I saw a copy of Darwin's *The Origin of Species* at a yard sale.

The class enjoyed the essay "How to Write a Rotten Poem with Almost No Effort."

Shakespeare in Love is a film based on Shakespeare's writing of the play *Romeo and Juliet.*

4. Capitalize specific names of people, places, languages, races, and nationalities.

English	China	Cesar Chavez
Ireland	Spanish	Japanese
Ryan White	Philadelphia	Main Street

5. Capitalize names of months, days of the week, and special days, but not the seasons.

March	Fourth of July	spring
Tuesday	Earth Day	winter
Valentine's Day	Labor Day	fall

6. Capitalize a title of relationship if it takes the place of the person's name. If *my* (or *your, her, his, our, their*) is in front of the word, a capital is not used.

I think Mom wrote to him.	*but*	I think my mom wrote to him.
We visited Aunt Sophie.	*but*	We visited our aunt.
They spoke with Grandpa.	*but*	They spoke with their grandpa.

7. Capitalize names of particular people or things, but not general terms.

I admire Professor Washborne.	*but*	I admire my professor.
We saw the famous Potomac River.	*but*	We saw the famous river.
Are you from the South?	*but*	Is your house south of the mountains?
I will take Philosophy 4 and English 100.	*but*	I will take philosophy and English.
She graduated from Sutter High School.	*but*	She graduated from high school.
They live at 119 Forest St.	*but*	They live on a beautiful street.
We enjoyed the Monterey Bay Aquarium.	*but*	We enjoyed the aquarium.

E X E R C I S E S

Add all of the necessary capital letters to the sentences that follow. Check your answers after the first set

Exercise 1

1. j.k. rowling is a very famous british writer.

2. her harry potter novels are among the most popular books ever written.

3. the series begins with the book *harry potter and the sorcerer's stone.*

4. in england, the first book is called *harry potter and the philosopher's stone.*

5. next comes *harry potter and the chamber of secrets,* which introduces the character of tom riddle.

6. in *harry potter and the prisoner of azkaban,* everyone is trying to catch the supposed criminal named sirius black.

7. the fourth book in the series is *harry potter and the goblet of fire.*

8. harry's friends ron and hermione aggravate him in *harry potter and the order of the phoenix.*

9. readers learn more about harry's nemesis, voldemort, in *harry potter and the half-blood prince.*

10. rowling's seventh and final book will no doubt pair harry with another fabulous subtitle.

Exercise 2

1. now that dvds are more popular than vhs tapes, i am updating my movie library.

2. my friends say that i shouldn't waste my money on repeat titles.

3. but my friend jake is on my side because he and i are usually the ones who watch movies together.

4. even though I have good vhs copies of famous films such as *chinatown, jaws,* and *blade runner,* the dvd versions offer behind-the-scenes footage and original trailers that vhs tapes don't include.

5. of course, i'm aware that another technology will replace dvds before too long.

6. then i guess i'll just have to commit to that new format.

7. there are always collectors who want the old stuff.

8. in fact, i know someone who has a collection of video discs and 8-track cassette tapes.

9. i may be leaning that way myself.

10. i haven't disposed of my vhs duplicates yet, and i've been buying old record albums at thrift stores.

Exercise 3

1. when my art teacher asked the class to do research on frida kahlo, i knew that the name sounded familiar.

2. then i remembered that the actress salma hayek starred in the movie *frida,* which was about this mexican-born artist's life.

3. frida kahlo's paintings are all very colorful and seem extremely personal.

4. she painted mostly self-portraits, and each one makes a unique statement.

5. one of these portraits is called *my grandparents, my parents, and i.*

6. kahlo gave another one the title *the two fridas.*

7. but my favorite of kahlo's works is *self-portrait on the borderline between mexico and the united states.*

8. in an article i read in *smithsonian* magazine, kahlo's mother explains that after frida was severely injured in a bus accident, she started painting.

9. kahlo's mother set up a mirror near her daughter's bed so that frida could use herself as a model.

10. in the *smithsonian* article from the november 2002 issue, kahlo is quoted as saying, "i never painted dreams. i painted my own reality."

Exercise 4

1. hidden beneath the church of st. martin-in-the-fields in london is a great little place to have lunch.

2. it's called the café in the crypt, and you enter it down a small staircase just off trafalgar square.

3. the café is literally in a crypt, the church's resting place for the departed.

4. the food is served cafeteria-style: soups, stews, sandwiches, and salads.

5. you grab a tray at the end of the counter and load it up with food as you slide it toward the cash register.

6. although the café is dark, the vaulted ceilings make it comfortable, and you can just make out the messages carved into the flat tombstones that cover the floor beneath your table.

7. one of london's newspapers ranked the café in the crypt high on its list of the "50 best places to meet in london."

8. the café in the crypt can even be reserved for private parties.

9. the café has its own gallery, called—what else?—the gallery in the crypt.

10. so if you're ever in london visiting historic trafalgar square, don't forget to look for that little stairway and grab a bite at the café in the crypt.

Source: www.stmartin-in-the-fields.org

Exercise 5

1. my mom and dad love old movie musicals.

2. that makes it easy to shop for them at christmas and other gift-giving occasions.

3. for mom's birthday last year, i gave her the video of gilbert and sullivan's comic opera *the pirates of penzance.*

4. it isn't even that old; it has kevin kline in it as the character called the pirate king.

5. i watched the movie with her, and i enjoyed the story of a band of pirates who are too nice for their own good.

6. actually, it is funnier than i thought it would be, and kevin kline sings and dances really well!

7. dad likes musicals, too, and i bought him tickets to see the revival of *chicago* on stage a few years ago.

8. he loves all those big production numbers and the bob fosse choreography.

9. thanks to baz luhrmann and others, movie musicals are making a comeback.

10. *moulin rouge* and the film version of *chicago* are just two recent examples.

REVIEW OF PUNCTUATION AND CAPITAL LETTERS

Punctuate these sentences. They include all the rules for punctuation and capitalization you have learned. Compare your answers carefully with those at the back of the book. Sentences may require several pieces of punctuation or capital letters.

1. the alamo is a famous historical site in texas

2. have you ever seen the first episode of the simpsons

3. theyve remodeled their garage and now their daughter uses it as an apartment

4. how much will the midterm affect our grades the nervous student asked

5. we have refunded your money ms jones and will be sending you a confirmation letter

6. one of the teachers who visited the library left a textbook on the checkout counter

7. the united parcel service better known as ups was hiring on campus yesterday

8. even though i am enjoying my latin class i should have taken spanish instead

9. you always remember the date of my birthday march 20 but you forget your own

10. pink is a calming color but not if its hot pink

11. pam martha justin and luke left class early to practice their presentation in the hallway

12. finding a good deal for a new car online takes time patience and luck

13. my friend is reading a shakespeare play in her womens studies class

14. i wonder how much my history of textiles book will cost

15. steve jobs is ceo of apple computer he deserves a lot of credit for the success of the ipod products

COMPREHENSIVE TEST

In these sentences you'll find all the errors that have been discussed in the entire text. Try to name the error in the blank before each sentence, and then correct the error if you can. You may find any of the following errors:

adj	incorrect adjective
adv	incorrect adverb
apos	apostrophe
awk	awkward phrasing
c	comma needed
cap	capitalization
cliché	overused expression
cs	comma splice
dm	dangling modifier
frag	fragment
mm	misplaced modifier
p	punctuation
pro	incorrect pronoun
pro agr	pronoun agreement
pro ref	pronoun reference
ro	run-on sentence
shift	shift in time or person
sp	misspelled word
s-v agr	subject-verb agreement
wordy	wordiness
ww	wrong word
//	not parallel

A perfect—or almost perfect—score will mean you've mastered the first part of the text.

1. _____ When you step inside a greenhouse the air feels so refreshing.

2. _____ People should check their online accounts regularly because you never know whether there has been a breach in security.

3. _____ We all feel badly about the way we treated the substitute.

4. _____ Either the title or the main points needs to be changed.

5. _____ She was getting the most highest grades in the class.

6. _____ The twins spent there summer vacation in Canada.

7. _____ There are one or two questions that I have about the return policy.

8. _____ I love Fall and Spring; they are my favorite seasons.

9. _____ The cadet gave my friend and I a ticket for parking without our permits.

10. _____ Campers can have fun or they can be miserable.

11. _____ My counselors advice has served me well.

12. _____ I consider myself creative, however, I have no interest in becoming an artist.

13. _____ Under the lid of the bottle, my friend found a sticker that said "Winner."

14. _____ We read the essay called "Once More To The Lake," by E.B. White.

15. _____ Everyone on the jury was able to express their own opinions.

16. _____ I took their comments about my essay as complements.

17. _____ His research paper is more developed then mine, but mine has a better title.

18. _____ Its not easy to take two final exams in one day.

19. _____ The end result of my petition was that the school allowed me to take the class again.

20. _____ The students broke into groups and starts discussing the poem.

P A R T 4

Writing

Aside from the basics of word choice, spelling, sentence structure, and punctuation, what else do you need to understand to write better? Just as sentences are built according to accepted patterns, so are other "structures" of English—paragraphs and essays, for example.

Think of writing as including levels of structures, beginning small with words connecting to form phrases, clauses, and sentences. Then sentences connect to form paragraphs and essays. Each level has its own set of "blueprints." To communicate clearly in writing, words must be chosen and spelled correctly. Sentences must have a subject, a verb, and a complete thought. Paragraphs must be indented and should contain a main idea supported with sufficient detail. Essays explore a valuable topic in several coherent paragraphs, usually including an introduction, a body, and a conclusion.

Not everyone approaches writing as structure, however. It is possible to write better without thinking about structure at all. A good place to start might be to write what you care about and care about what you write. You can make an amazing amount of progress by simply being *genuine,* being who you are naturally. No one has to tell you to be yourself when you speak, but you might need encouragement to be yourself in your writing.

Writing is almost never done without a reason. The reason may come from an experience, such as receiving an unfair parking ticket, or from a requirement in a class. And when you are asked to write, you often receive guidance in the form of an assignment: tell a story to prove a point, paint a picture with your words, summarize an article, compare two subjects, share what you know about something, explain why you agree with or disagree with a statement or an idea.

Learning to write well is important, one of the most important things you will do in your education. Confidence is the key. The Writing sections will help you build confidence, whether you are expressing your own ideas or summarizing and responding to the ideas of others. Like the Sentence Structure sections, the Writing sections are best taken in order. However, each one discusses an aspect of writing that you can review on its own at any time.

What Is the Least You Should Know about Writing?

"Unlike medicine or the other sciences," William Zinsser points out, "writing has no new discoveries to spring on us. We're in no danger of reading in our morning newspaper that a breakthrough has been made in how to write [clearly]. . . . We may be given new technologies like the word processor to ease the burdens of composition, but on the whole we know what we need to know."

One thing that's certain is that you learn to write by *writing*—not by reading long discussions about writing. Therefore, the explanations and instructions in these sections are as brief as they can be, followed by samples from student and professional writers.

Understanding the basic structures and learning the essential skills covered in these sections will help you become a better writer.

BASIC STRUCTURES

I. The Paragraph

II. The Essay

WRITING SKILLS

III. Writing in Your Own Voice

IV. Finding a Topic

V. Organizing Ideas

VI. Supporting with Details

VII. Revising Your Papers

VIII. Presenting Your Work

IX. Writing about What You Read

Basic Structures

I. THE PARAGRAPH

A paragraph is unlike any other structure in English. Visually, it has its own profile: the first line is indented about five spaces, and sentences continue to fill the space between both margins until the paragraph ends (which may be in the middle of the line):

_____

_____

_____

_____

_____

As a beginning writer, you may forget to indent your paragraphs, or you may break off in the middle of a line within a paragraph, especially when writing in class. You must remember to indent whenever you begin a new paragraph and fill the space between the margins until it ends. (Note: In business writing, paragraphs are not indented but double-spaced in between.)

Defining a Paragraph

A typical paragraph develops one idea, usually phrased in a topic sentence from which all the other sentences in the paragraph radiate. The topic sentence does not need to begin the paragraph, but it most often does, and the other sentences support it with specific details. (For more on topic sentences and organizing paragraphs, see p. 226.) Paragraphs usually contain several sentences, though no set number is required. A paragraph can stand alone, but more commonly paragraphs are part of a larger composition, an essay. There are different kinds of paragraphs, based on the jobs they are supposed to do.

Types of Paragraphs

SAMPLE PARAGRAPHS IN AN ESSAY

Introductory paragraphs begin essays. They provide background information about the essay's topic and usually include the thesis statement or main idea of the essay. (See p. 223 for information on how to write a thesis statement.) Here is the introductory paragraph of a student essay entitled "Really Understanding":

> I was so excited when my parents told me that I could join them in America. Four years earlier, they left China to open a Chinese fast food

restaurant in Los Angeles. After my parents asked me to help them in the restaurant, I started to worry about my English because I knew only a few words that I learned in China. They told me not to worry, that I would quickly grasp the language once I heard it every day. Soon after I joined them, I made a big mistake because of my lack of English skills and my conceit. From this experience, I learned the importance of really understanding.

In this opening paragraph, the student leads up to the main idea—"the importance of really understanding"—with background information about her family's restaurant and "a big mistake" that she made.

Body paragraphs are those in the middle of essays. Each body paragraph contains a topic sentence and presents detailed information about one subtopic or idea that relates directly to the essay's thesis. (See p. 226 for more information on organizing body paragraphs.) Here are the body paragraphs of the same essay:

My mistake happened during my second week at the restaurant. Usually my mom and I stayed in front, dishing out the food and keeping the tables clean while my father cooked in the kitchen. If I needed any help or if someone asked a question in English, my mom took care of it. However, that day my mom was sick, so she stayed home. My father and I went to work. He went straight to the kitchen, and I wiped those six square tables. By noon, my father had put big steaming trays of food on the counter. There was orange chicken, chicken with mushrooms, sweet and sour pork, kong bao chicken, and B.B.Q. pork. People came in, ordering their favorite foods.

After I took care of the lunch rush, it was 2:00, but my favorite customer had not arrived. He was an old, kind, educated man who came in almost every day at 12:00. Why hadn't he come for the last two days? Was he sick? I looked at his favorite dish and started to worry about him. As I was wondering, he walked through the door. I smiled to see him. He ordered "the usual"—chicken with mushrooms and steamed rice—and sat down at the table in the left corner. I wanted to ask him why he came late to show that I cared about him, but more customers came in, and I had to serve them. They ordered all the chicken with mushrooms left in the tray, so I called to my father to cook more. The old man finished his food and walked toward me. He looked at that tray of newly cooked chicken with mushrooms for a second, and then he asked me something. I only understood the word *yesterday*. Since he had not been in yesterday, I guessed that he said "Were you open yesterday?" I quickly answered, "Oh, yes!" He looked at me, and I could see that he didn't believe my answer, so I said "Yes" again. He just turned and walked away.

I did not understand what had happened. Two days passed, and he did not return. I thought about what he could have asked me and stared at the chicken and mushrooms for a minute. Suddenly, I realized what must have happened. He had come in two hours later than usual, at 2:00 that day, but the dish had been cooked at 12:00. Fast food cooked two hours earlier would not taste as fresh as if it were just prepared. He must have asked me "Was this *cooked* yesterday?" How could I have answered "Yes" not once but twice? He must have felt so bad about us. "He will never come back," I told myself.

Notice that each of the three body paragraphs discusses a single stage of the experience that taught her the value of really understanding.

Concluding paragraphs are the final paragraphs in essays. They bring the discussion to a close and share the writer's final thoughts on the subject. (See p. 225 for more about concluding paragraphs.) Here is the conclusion of the sample essay:

> Four years have passed since then, and my favorite customer has not come back. It still bothers me. Why didn't I ask him to say the question again? If I had not been so conceited, I would have risked looking foolish for a moment. Now I am so repentant. I will never answer a question or do anything before I really understand what it means.

In this concluding paragraph, the student describes the effects of her experience—the regret and the lesson she learned.

SAMPLE OF A PARAGRAPH ALONE

Single-paragraph writing assignments may be given in class or as homework. They test your understanding of the unique structure of a paragraph. They may ask you to answer a single question, perhaps following a reading, or to provide details about a limited topic. Look at this student paragraph, the result of a homework assignment asking students to report on a technological development in the news:

> I just read that soon there will be self-serve pet washing machines shaped like clothes washing machines. These machines will be located inside pet laundromats called Lavacans. The article states that a dirty dog or cat can be placed in one of these machines, which are controlled by computers, and then about forty nozzles will spray water and air onto the pet's fur. The makers of Lavacans say that the pets enjoy the massaging feeling of the spray. The three-cycle process of washing, rinsing, and drying takes about half an hour to complete. According to the article, these machines have already become popular in other countries, Spain for example, where the Lavacan originated. Pet laundromats seem to be a good idea, as long as the pets are safe and happy.

Source: Current Science, September 27, 2002

These shorter writing assignments help students practice presenting information within the limited structure of a paragraph.

The assignments in the upcoming Writing Skills section will sometimes ask you to write paragraphs. Remember that you may review the previous pages as often as you wish until you understand the unique structure of the paragraph.

II. THE ESSAY

Like the paragraph, an essay has its own profile, usually including a title and several paragraphs.

Title

_____

_____

_____

_____

_____

_____.

_____

_____

_____

_____

_____

_____.

_____

_____

_____

_____

_____.

_____

_____

_____

_____

_____

_____.

_____

_____

_____

_____.

While the paragraph is the single building block of text used in almost all forms of writing (in essays, magazine articles, letters, novels, newspaper stories, and so on), an essay is a larger, more complex structure.

The Five-Paragraph Essay and Beyond

The student essay analyzed on pages 208–210 illustrates the different kinds of paragraphs within essays. Many people like to include five paragraphs in an essay: an introductory paragraph, three body paragraphs, and a concluding paragraph. Three is a comfortable number of body paragraphs—it is not two, which makes an essay seem like a comparison even when it isn't; and it is not four, which may be too many subtopics for the beginning writer to organize clearly.

However, an essay can include any number of paragraphs. As you become more comfortable with the flow of your ideas and gain confidence in your ability to express yourself, you are free to create essays of different shapes and lengths. As with many skills, learning about writing begins with structure and then expands to include all possibilities.

Defining an Essay

There is no such thing as a typical essay. Essays may be serious or humorous, but the best of them are thought-provoking and—of course—informative. Try looking up the word *essay* in a dictionary right now. Some words used to define an essay might need to be explained themselves:

An essay is *prose* (meaning it is written in the ordinary language of sentences and paragraphs).

An essay is *nonfiction* (meaning it deals with real people, factual information, actual opinions and events).

An essay is a *composition* (meaning it is created in parts that make up the whole, several paragraphs that explore a single topic).

An essay is *personal* (meaning it shares the writer's unique perspective, even if only in the choice of topic, method of analysis, and details).

An essay is *analytical* and *instructive* (meaning it examines the workings of a subject and shares the results with the reader).

A SAMPLE ESSAY

For an example of a piece of writing that fits the above definition, read the following essay, in which professional writer Joanne Kaufman explains how hard it is to share her most valuable possessions—her *books*.

Neither a Borrower nor a Lender Be

If you need a place to stay, come on by; the pullout couch is yours. The Subaru? Keys are under the sun visor. The shirt off my back? Let me iron it first. One of my four copies of *Sense and Sensibility*? Park yourself in the wing chair and read away. But those books—and every other volume in the joint—stay on the premises. And don't make me call security.

It used to be that if I loved a particular book, I wanted the people I cared about to care about it too. In fact, I used certain books as a litmus test. Could I truly have a deep friendship or a serious romance with someone who couldn't get through *Jane Eyre*? But I enacted a policy change after lending a number of books, some out of print, and never seeing them again. Friends who wouldn't dream of borrowing a lawn mower or any item of clothing without promptly returning it seem to assume that a book comes with a long lease. The assumption, no doubt, is that if I'm lending it, I've already read it and won't have any immediate need for it. At times, I've imagined posting a most-wanted list of sticky-fingered readers on the bulletin board of my local bookstore. Public enemy number one: the woman who borrowed my hardcover copy of a favorite biography, and who, after more than a year—and considerable hectoring—mailed back the book, postage-due, *in paperback*.

Now, I know what you may be thinking: Just when do I honestly think I'm going to reread those gossipy Hollywood memoirs or those 18th-century British masterpieces I've collected for a rainy day? But I can't shake the belief that just as soon as I stamp their exit visa, I'll suddenly decide I want them. Now. Further, I do read cherished sections of cherished books over and over again—like the moment Anne of Green Gables realizes life would be utterly meaningless without Gilbert Blythe, or when Elizabeth Bennett comes to the same conclusion at the end of *Pride and Prejudice*. So I want to know those volumes are within easy reach.

I'm aware that, by coldly taking this stance, I'm blowing my reputation as a generous sort. But better to be viewed as selfish than as someone who learns nothing from experience. In any case, I am not a hypocrite: I wouldn't dream of borrowing books. It's like taking care of someone else's kids: The responsibility is too overwhelming.

Essayist Anne Fadiman—whose collection, *Ex Libris*, is staying on my shelf—notes, "The longer you own a book, the more it differs from other copies." Certain beloved texts of my childhood—I'm thinking of *A Little Princess* and *Daddy Long Legs*—are liberally annotated with mustard and chocolate milk; markers of those special occasions when I was permitted to read at the dinner table. These books, some immaculate in their dust jackets, others broken-spined, are part of my personal landscape. They say that this place is my home in much the same way a particular arrangement of pots and pans and spices might say it about a cook.

Literature is full of characters moved by desperation to scheme and cheat and lie. I've learned from them. Last week, when someone wanted to borrow an early Alison Lurie novel, I said I was reading it. When it comes up again, I'll say I've lent it out. Then I'll mention a place that does this sort of thing quite often: the public library.

Source: Reprinted with permission of the author. Originally appeared in *Good Housekeeping* (January 2004).

Now that you have learned more about the basic structures of the paragraph and the essay, you are ready to practice the skills necessary to write them.

Writing Skills

III. Writing in Your Own Voice

All writing "speaks" on paper. And the person "listening" is the reader. Some beginning writers forget that writing and reading are two-way methods of communication, just like spoken conversations between two people. When you write, your reader "hears" you; when you read, you also listen.

When speaking, you express a personality in your choice of phrases, your movements, your tone of voice. Family and friends probably recognize your voice messages on their answering machines without your having to identify yourself. Would they also be able to recognize your writing? They would if you extended your "voice" into your writing.

Writing should not sound like talking, necessarily, but it should have a *personality* that comes from the way you decide to approach a topic, to develop it with details, to say it your way.

The beginning of this book discusses the difference between spoken English, which follows the looser patterns of *speaking,* and Standard Written English, which follows accepted patterns of writing. Don't think that the only way to add "voice" to your writing is to use the patterns of spoken English. Remember that Standard Written English does not have to be dull or sound academic. Look at this example of Standard Written English that has a distinct voice, from the book *100 Birds and How They Got Their Names* by Diana Wells:

> The roadrunner, as well as being a cartoon character, is a type of cuckoo. Less surprisingly, roadrunners avoid flying, preferring to run (along roads!). They can reach speeds of fifteen miles per hour.
>
> Roadrunners are about two feet in length, with long tails and zygodactyl feet, like other cuckoos. This means that two toes point forward and two back, making it hard to tell from their tracks whether they were going forward or backward. Pueblo Indians used to surround the houses of their dead with a scratched pattern of roadrunner tracks, to confuse any evil spirits that might be lurking around.

Wells' description of the roadrunner illustrates Standard Written English at its best—from its solid sentence structures to its precise use of words. But more importantly, Wells' clear voice speaks to us and informs us about the impact this bird has had on human lives.

You can involve your reader, too, by writing in your own voice. Here is an example of a student response to a brief assignment to write about a memorable school experience.

I remember in high school, our life skills teacher had us take a test to evaluate our learning abilities. My test results said that I was a "kinesthetic learner." That was supposed to mean that I learned best by seeing and doing. After thinking about the results, I realized that I have always been interested in how things work. I used to open up all of the electronic or mechanical things I was given—from clocks to toys—to see what made them "tick." When I was ten, my brother and I constructed a tree house out of scrap wood we gathered from around our neighborhood. Surprisingly enough, that tree house still stands today. There are also many things that I have just figured out on my own over the years. Many people have a hard time with even simple things, such as changing their car's oil or putting on a spare tire. I have never taken an auto-repair class, yet I can change my car's brakes, oil, alternator, starter, and fuel filter—just to name a few. I guess that test back in high school helped me discover what makes me "tick," too.

Notice that both the professional and the student writers tell stories (narration) and paint pictures (description) in the sample paragraphs. Narration and description require practice, but once you master them, you will gain a stronger voice and will be able to add interest and clarity to even the most challenging academic writing assignments.

Narration

Narrative writing tells the reader a story, and since most of us like to tell stories, it is a good place to begin writing in your own voice. An effective narration allows readers to experience an event with the writer. Since we all see the world differently and feel unique emotions, the purpose of narration is to take readers with us through an experience. As a result, the writer gains a better understanding of what happened, and readers get to live other lives momentarily. Listen to the "voice" of this student writer sharing her experience of living near a canal as a child.

The Canal

I don't remember much about the first five years of my life. Maybe that's because I lived in Mexico, and I was too young. However, I still remember the canal down our street—well, our dirt road is more like it—and many times our mud road. I remember this canal being about twenty feet deep, but have recently been told that it was more like five or six. Small bridges along the canal allowed people to cross to the other side. Living near this canal was one of the most satisfying stages of my life.

Early in the morning, the water would be clear and cold. It flowed slowly at first as if it had just gotten up and didn't quite have the strength to run any faster. It would just jog in place for a while until it warmed up. Once it was warmer, the children would come out and start playing along the edges. I remember the red dirt that would fall in as we got down on our stomachs and dipped our faces gently into its fresh surface. By afternoon, the canal would turn rusty brown from so much churning, and we could no longer see our reflections in it.

The water made a sound that I wouldn't be able to describe because I was too young then and took for granted that beautiful noise as it rushed "home" in the late evening. Swish-swashing back and forth against the narrow banks and stumbling over ridges in little waves, it carried twigs and all sorts of little nothings down its path. At times the current carried a message on paper two or three houses down. Then morning would come again, and it was time for the daily jog that switched to a faster speed throughout the day.

As a daily "chore," my mother would send my older sister, my older brother, and me to the canal to bring the morning's supply of water. She would make us buckets

out of tin cans and wire or rope. It was a big deal for
me to go down for water because I was only three or four
when I started. However, no matter how confident I felt
or how sure of myself I was, I would always lose my
bucket. Down the river it would go, and my brother would
have to run it after it and only sometimes catch it
before it was too late. I can remember my mom making a
new bucket for me nearly every other day. I didn't fear
the canal, but I did have a deep respect for it. It was
the first or earliest challenge that I can remember
having. At times, it made me angry because I felt it was
mocking me by grabbing my bucket. I swear at times I
heard it saying, "Nah, nah, nah, nah, nah." Other times,
it was my buddy and would give me a break.

At five years old, I was too young to find a real, deep
meaning in my experience with the canal. Now, however,
living in L.A. and having no more experiences with
rivers or streams, I just wish there could be more
because they are very peaceful and represent nature at
its most beautiful. To think that I had a canal all to
myself for five years just seems like a dream to me now.
I know that I could go visit the canal again, but our
relationship would not be the same. We wouldn't be
buddies anymore, and it would all be very impersonal. It
probably wouldn't remember me—that I had lived there once
before, just like the kids it's challenging now.

Description

Descriptive writing paints word pictures with details that appeal to the reader's five
senses—sight, sound, touch, taste, and smell. The writer of description often uses
comparisons to help readers picture one thing by imagining something else, just as
the writer of "The Canal" compares the movement of the water to that of a person
waking up: "It would just jog in place for a while until it warmed up." In the following paragraph, a student uses vivid details to bring the place she loves best
to life:

Fort Baker is located across the bay from San Francisco, almost under
the Golden Gate Bridge. When I lived there as a child, nature was all I saw.

Deer came onto our porch and nibbled the plants; raccoons dumped the trash cans over; skunks sprayed my brother because he poked them with a stick, and little field mice jumped out of the bread drawer at my sister when she opened it. Behind the house was a small forest of strong green trees; the dirt actually felt soft, and tall grassy plants with bright yellow flowers grew all around. I don't know the plants' real name, but my friend and I called it "sour grass." When we chewed the stems, we got a mouth full of sour juice that made our faces crinkle and our eyes water.

Here is another example of a descriptive paragraph. In it, the student describes her car door's remote control device by comparing it to a robot. The robot comparison helps her incorporate vivid details in order to bring the description to life.

My Robot

My car door's remote control looks like a small robot's head. The front of it resembles a human face to me. It has two droopy eyes, a nose, and a mouth—eyes that cannot see, a nose that cannot smell, and a mouth that cannot open. It is wrapped in old shiny clear tape because its connector for a key ring is broken. The tape covers its face like an uncomfortable mask and secures the "robot" to a flat piece of leather, shaped like a bottle, which has a small chain attached to it. The chain holds my little robot like a prisoner on my key ring. My robot has a mind of its own. Like a small child, it can be capricious. Sometimes it does what I want it to do, but other times it does what it wants to do. Its brain shows that it's working by blinking a red light on its forehead. And even though my little robot looks old and tired, it usually works when I need it the most.

You may have noticed that many of the examples in this section use both narration and description. In fact, most effective writing—even a good resume or biology lab report—calls for clear storytelling and the creation of vivid word pictures for the reader.

Writing Assignments

The following two assignments will help you develop your voice as a writer. For now, don't worry about topic sentences or thesis statements or any of the things we'll consider later. Narration and description have their own logical structures. A story has a beginning, a middle, and an end. And we describe things from top to bottom, side to side, and so on.

Assignment 1

NARRATION: FAMOUS SAYINGS

The following is a list of well-known expressions. No doubt you have had an experience that proves at least one of these to be true. Write a short essay that tells a story from your own life that relates to one of these sayings. (See if you can tell which of the sayings fit the experiences narrated in the essays "Neither a Borrower nor a Lender Be" on p. 213 and "The Canal" on p. 217.) You might want to identify the expression you have chosen in your introductory paragraph. Then tell the beginning, middle, and end of the story. Be sure to use vivid details to bring the story to life. Finish with a brief concluding paragraph in which you share your final thoughts on the experience.

> Time flies when you're having fun.
>
> Experience is the best teacher.
>
> No good deed goes unpunished.
>
> Absence makes the heart grow fonder.
>
> When you have your health, you have everything.

Assignment 2

DESCRIPTION: A VALUABLE OBJECT

Describe an object that means a lot to you. It could be a gift that you received, an object you purchased for yourself, an heirloom in your family, a memento from your childhood, or just something you carry around with you every day. Your goal is to make the reader visualize the object. Try to use details and comparisons that appeal to the reader's senses in some way. Look back at the examples for inspiration. Be sure the reader knows—from your choice of details—what the object means to you.

IV. Finding a Topic

You will most often be given a topic to write about, perhaps based on a reading assignment. However, when the assignment of a paper calls for you to choose your own topic without any further assistance, try to go immediately to your interests.

Look to Your Interests

If the topic of your paper is something you know about and—more important— something you *care* about, then the whole process of writing will be smoother and more enjoyable for you. If you ski, if you are a musician, or even if you just enjoy watching a lot of television, bring that knowledge and enthusiasm into your papers.

Take a moment to think about and jot down a few of your interests now (no matter how unrelated to school they may seem), and then save the list for use later when deciding what to write about. One student's list of interests might look like this:

buying and selling on eBay

playing video games with friends

boogie boarding in summer

collecting baseball cards

Another student's list might be very different:

playing the violin

going to concerts

watching old musicals on video

drawing caricatures of my friends

While still another student might list the following interests:

going to the horse races

reading for my book club

traveling in the summer

buying lottery tickets

These students have listed several worthy topics for papers. And because they are personal interests, the students have the details needed to support them. With a general topic to start with, you can use several ways to gather the details you will need to support it in a paragraph or an essay.

Focused Free Writing (or Brainstorming)

Free writing is a good way to begin. When you are assigned a paper, try writing for ten minutes putting down all your thoughts on one subject—traveling in the summer, for example. Don't stop to think about organization, sentence structures, capitalization, or spelling—just let details flow onto the page. Free writing will help you see what material you have and will help you figure out what aspects of the subject to write about.

Here is an example:

> When my friends and I went to Sea World in San Diego last summer, we saw an amazing bird show. The birds weren't in cages or tied to perches. Instead they flew freely down out of the sky and out of windows in a phony town that surrounded the stage. And they didn't just have parrots and cockatoos like all the other bird shows I've ever seen before. In those shows the birds just did tricks for treats. But Sea World's show had eagles and falcons and really tall cranes with feathers that looked like ladies' hats on their heads. It was really amazing.

Now the result of this free writing session is certainly not ready to be typed and turned in as a paragraph. But what did become clear in it was that the student could probably compare the two types of bird shows she has seen—the species of birds used and how they were presented.

Clustering

Clustering is another way of putting ideas on paper before you begin to write an actual draft. A cluster is more visual than free writing. You could cluster the topic of "flea markets," for instance, by putting it in a circle in the center of a piece of paper and then drawing lines to new circles as ideas or details occur to you. The idea is to free your mind from the limits of sentences and paragraphs to generate pure details and ideas. When you are finished clustering, you can see where you want to go with a topic.

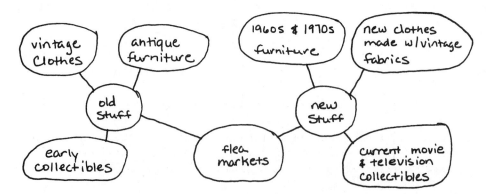

This cluster shows that the student has found two main categories of merchandise at flea markets. This cluster might lead to another where the student chooses one subcategory—early collectibles, for instance—and thinks of more details about them.

Talking with Other Students

It may help to talk to others when deciding on a topic. Many teachers break their classes up into groups at the beginning of an assignment. Talking with other students helps you realize that you see things just a little differently. Value the difference—it will help your written voice that we discussed earlier emerge.

Assignment 3
LIST YOUR INTERESTS

Make a list of four or five of your own interests. Be sure that they are as specific as the examples listed on p. 221. Keep the list for later assignments.

Assignment 4
DO SOME FREE WRITING

Choose one of your interests, and do some focused free writing about it. Write for ten minutes with that topic in mind but without stopping. Don't worry about anything such as spelling or sentence structures while you are free writing. The results are meant to help you find out what you have to say about the topic *before* you start to write a paper about it. Save the results for a later assignment.

Assignment 5
TRY CLUSTERING IDEAS

Choose another of your interests. Put it in the center of a piece of paper, and draw a cluster of details and ideas relating to it following the sample shown above. Take the cluster as far as it will go. Then choose one aspect to cluster again on its own. This way you will arrive at specific, interesting details and ideas—not just the first ones that come to mind. Save the results of all your efforts.

V. ORGANIZING IDEAS

Most important to keep in mind, no matter what you are writing, is the idea you want to get across to the reader. Whether you are writing a paragraph or an essay, you must have in mind a single idea that you want to express. In a paragraph, such an idea is called a *topic sentence;* in an essay it's called a *thesis statement,* but they mean the same thing—an idea you want to get across. We will begin with a discussion of thesis statements.

Thesis Statements

Let's choose one of the students' interests listed on p. 221 as a general topic. "Buying and selling on eBay" by itself doesn't make any point. What about it? What does it do for you? What point about buying and selling on eBay would you like to present to your reader? You might write

> Buying and selling on eBay is fun and educational.

But this is a vague statement, not worth developing. You might move into more specific territory and write

> I have learned about business and geography by buying and selling items on eBay.

Now you have said something specific. *When you write in one sentence the point you want to present to your reader, you have written a thesis statement.*

All good writers have a thesis in mind when they begin to write, or the thesis may well evolve as they write. Whether they are writing essays, novels, poems, or plays, they eventually have in mind an idea they want to present to the reader. They may develop it in various ways, but behind whatever they write is their ruling thought, their reason for writing, their thesis.

For any writing assignment, after you have done some free writing or clustering to explore your topic, the next step is to write a thesis statement. As you write your thesis statement, keep two things in mind:

1. A thesis statement must be a sentence *with a subject and a verb* (not merely a topic).

2. A thesis statement must be *an idea that you can explain or defend* (not simply a statement of fact).

Exercise 1

THESIS OR FACT?

Which of the following are merely topics or facts, and which are thesis statements that you could explain or defend? In front of each one that could be a thesis statement, write THESIS. In front of each one that is just a fact, write FACT. Check your answers with those at the back of the book.

1. _____ I have a friend who never lets me drive her car.

2. _____ Most people do not drink enough water.

3. _____ I am a college student because my parents want me to be.

4. _____ The word *happiness* is difficult to define.

5. _____ My life changed for the better when I got divorced.

6. _____ Most Americans see several movies a month.

7. _____ I woke up to find graffiti on my fence again.

8. _____ People should be allowed to use cell phones in cars.

9. _____ I would rather read a science fiction story than a love story.

10. _____ Prequels are more of a fad than a step forward in moviemaking.

Assignment 6
WRITE A THESIS STATEMENT

Use your free-writing or clustering results from Assignments 4 and 5 (p. 223) and write at least one thesis statement based on one of your interests. Be sure that the thesis you write is phrased as a complete thought that can be defended or explained in an essay.

Organizing an Essay

Once you have written a good thesis and explored your topic through discussion with others or by free writing and clustering, you are ready to organize your essay.

First, you need an introductory paragraph. It should catch your reader's interest, provide necessary background information, and either include or suggest your thesis statement. (See p. 208 and p. 217 for two examples of student writers' introductory paragraphs.) In your introductory paragraph, you may also list supporting points, but a more effective way is to let them unfold paragraph by paragraph rather than to give them all away in the beginning of the essay. Even if your supporting points don't appear in your introduction, your reader will easily spot them later if your paper is clearly organized.

Your second paragraph will present your *first* supporting point—everything about it and nothing more.

Your next paragraph will be about your *second* supporting point—all about it and nothing more.

Each additional paragraph will develop *another* supporting point.

Finally, you'll need a concluding paragraph. In a short paper, it isn't necessary to restate your points. Your conclusion may be brief; even a single sentence to round out the paper may do the job. Remember that the main purpose of a concluding paragraph is to bring the paper to a close by sharing your final thoughts on the subject. (See p. 209 and p. 218 for two examples of concluding paragraphs.)

Learning to write a brief organized essay of this kind will help you to distinguish between the parts of an essay. Then when you're ready to write a longer paper, you'll be able to organize it clearly and elaborate on its design and content.

Topic Sentences

A topic sentence does for a paragraph what a thesis statement does for an essay—it states the main idea. Like thesis statements, topic sentences must be phrased as complete thoughts to be proven or developed through the presentation of details. But the topic sentence introduces an idea or subtopic that is the right size to cover in a paragraph. The topic sentence doesn't have to be the first sentence in a paragraph. It may come at the end or even in the middle, but putting it first is most common.

Each body paragraph should contain only one main idea, and no detail or example should be in a paragraph if it doesn't support the topic sentence or help to transition from one paragraph to another. (See p. 209, p. 210, and p. 217 for more examples of effective body paragraphs within essays and of paragraphs alone.)

Organizing Body Paragraphs (or Single Paragraphs)

A single paragraph or a body paragraph within an essay is organized in the same way as an entire essay only on a smaller scale. Here's the way you learned to organize an essay:

Thesis: stated or suggested in introductory paragraph

First supporting paragraph

Second supporting paragraph

Additional supporting paragraphs

Concluding paragraph

And here's the way to organize a paragraph:

Topic sentence

First supporting detail or example

Second supporting detail or example

Additional supporting details or examples

Concluding or transitional sentence

You should have several details to support each topic sentence. If you find that you have little to say after writing the topic sentence, ask yourself what details or examples will make your reader believe that the topic sentence is true for you.

Transitional Expressions

Transitional expressions within a paragraph and between paragraphs in an essay help the reader move from one detail or example to the next and from one supporting point to the next. When first learning to organize an essay, you might start each supporting paragraph in a paper with a transitional expression. Later, if they sound too repetitious, take these expressions out and replace them with more detailed prepositional phrases or dependent clauses, thereby improving your sentence variety.

Here are some transitions that show sequence:

First	Next	One (example, point, step, etc. . . .)
Second	Then	Another (example, point, step, etc. . . .)
Third . . .	Finally	In conclusion

Here are a few to show addition:

Also

Furthermore

In addition

Here are several that show comparison or contrast:

Similarly	In the same way	In comparison
However	On the other hand	In contrast

Here are those that show consequence:

Therefore	Consequently
As a result	In other words

Exercise 2

ADDING TRANSITIONAL EXPRESSIONS

Using transitional expressions from the lists above, fill in the blanks in the following paragraph to make it read smoothly. More than one answer is possible for some of the sentences. Compare your choices with the answers at the back of the book.

Whenever I plan a trip that involves driving long distances, I go through the following routine. _____, I make sure that I have a recent map of the highways so that if I get lost along the way, I won't panic. _____, even if I do have a map to the city of my destination, I go online to get specific driving directions to the hotel from the highway. _____ way that I prepare is to check my car's tires and get its engine serviced, if necessary. I know how impor-

tant cell phones are on long drives; _____, I never forget to bring mine.

_____, before I leave my house on the day of the trip, I call the Highway

Patrol hotline to see if there are any highway closures. This routine has always

worked for me. _____, I would give it up for a car with its own computer-

ized navigation system.

Assignment 7
LET'S GET ORGANIZED!

To practice using transitions, write a paragraph about the steps you would take to reorganize an area at home or at work. It could be a small task, such as re-organizing your CDs or DVDs at home, or a larger task, such reorganizing your desk or work station at work. What area would you organize in a different way if you could? What materials would you need? How would you proceed? Report the steps in order, one by one, using transitional expressions from the list on p. 227 wherever you see fit. Sometimes it's helpful to add humor to a "how-to" paragraph or essay to avoid sounding like an instruction manual.

VI. Supporting with Details

Now you're ready to support your main ideas with subtopics and specific details. That is, you'll think of ways to convince your reader that what you say in your the-sis is true. How could you convince your reader that buying and selling on eBay has taught you about business and geography? You might write

> I have learned a great deal about business and geography by buying and selling items on eBay. (because)

1. I must be honest in my dealings with other buyers and sellers.
2. I have to keep good records and be very organized.
3. I learn about places I have never heard of before by shipping packages all over the world.

NOTE—Sometimes if you imagine a *because* at the end of your thesis statement, it will help you write your reasons or subtopics clearly and in parallel form.

Types of Support

The subtopics developing a thesis and the details presented in a paragraph are not always *reasons*. Supporting points may take many forms based on the purpose of the essay or paragraph. They may be

examples (in an illustration)

steps (in a how-to or process paper)

types or kinds (in a classification)

meanings (in a definition)

similarities and/or differences (in a comparison/contrast)

causes or effects (in a cause-and-effect analysis).

Whatever they are, supporting points should develop the main idea expressed in the thesis or topic sentence and prove it to be true.

Here is the final draft of a student essay about a challenging assignment. Notice how the body paragraphs map out the stages of the assignment. And all of the details within the body paragraphs bring the experience to life.

Drawing a Blank

On the day my drawing class started to learn about self-portraits last year, each of us had to bring a mirror to class. In backpacks and purses were make-up mirrors, dressing table mirrors—large and small mirrors of every shape and kind. I was nervous about drawing a self-portrait, so I brought only a tiny plastic pocket mirror. That way if I didn't do a good job, it would be my mirror's fault. I should have known I could do it if I tried.

I had never done well on human figure drawing. First our teacher, Ms. Newman, demonstrated the proportion of a human figure; she explained that a human body measures about seven times a human head. She used a tiny piece of chalk to draw on the board while she was talking. Then she showed how to sketch the face, from eyebrows to eyes, nose, mouth, and ears. After her lecture, she told us to begin drawing our self-portraits.

We all set up our mirrors. The ceiling danced with the reflections they made as we got to work. I looked down at my little square of scratched-up plastic and started to draw gingerly on my paper. I tried to put the eyes, nose, and mouth I had seen on the paper. When I finished, I wondered, "Who the heck is this?" The drawing didn't look anything like me. I was frustrated and sank down in my chair. After a minute, I told myself, "Try again." I drew another one, and it was a little better. But I could not really call it a self-portrait because it didn't look exactly like me.

I asked Ms. Newman for help. She glanced at my previous attempts and said, "A good self-portrait doesn't just look like you, it also shows your personality and your feelings." She did not see any of these in my other drawings. So I tried again. I borrowed my friend's big glass mirror and stared into it; I was not only looking at my face, but also deep inside my face. This time, I freely sketched the shape of my face. Then I roughly placed my eyebrows, eyes, nose, mouth, and ears. I looked into the mirror again and drew the expression I saw there.

When my portrait was finished, I wondered at the amazing work I had done. Even though it did not perfectly look like me, it really showed my personality and emotions through the contrast of light and dark. When Ms. Newman saw it, she applauded. Not only did I get an A on this project, it also became one of the strongest pieces in my portfolio. I realized that few things can be done successfully the first time. If I had given up after my first try, I would never have captured the real me.

(Note: See p. 231 for a rough draft of the above essay, before its final revisions.)

Learning to support your main ideas with vivid details is perhaps the most important goal you can accomplish in this course. Many writing problems are not really *writing* problems but *thinking* problems. Whether you're writing a term paper or merely an answer to a test question, if you take enough time to think, you'll be able to write a clear thesis statement and support it with paragraphs full of meaningful details.

Assignment 8

WRITE AN ESSAY ON ONE OF YOUR INTERESTS

Return to the thesis statement you wrote about one of your interests for Assignment 6 on p. 225. Now write a short essay to support it. You can explain the allure of your interest, its drawbacks, or its benefits (such as the one about eBay teaching the student about business and geography). Don't forget to use any free writing or clustering you may have done on the topic beforehand and to use transitional expressions.

Assignment 9

A MISTAKE

Like the student writer of the essay "Really Understanding" (p. 208), we all make mistakes. And these mistakes often affect other people. Write an essay about a mistake you have made or a mistake someone else made that had an effect on you.

VII. REVISING YOUR PAPERS

Great writers don't just sit down and write a final draft. They write and revise. You may have heard the expression "Easy writing makes hard reading." True, it is *easier* to turn in a piece of writing the first time it lands on paper. But you and your reader will probably be disappointed by the results. Try to think of revision as an opportunity instead of a chore, as a necessity instead of a choice.

Whenever possible, you should write the paper several days before the first draft is due. Let it sit for a while. When you reread it, you'll see ways to improve the organization or to add more details to a weak paragraph. After revising the paper, put it away for another day, and try again to improve it. Save all of your drafts along the way to see the progress that you've made or possibly to return to an area left out in later drafts but that fits in again after revision.

Don't call any paper finished until you have worked it through several times. Revising is one of the best ways to improve your writing.

Take a look at an early draft of the student essay you read on page 229 on the assignment to draw a self-portrait. Notice that the student has revised her rough draft by crossing out some parts, correcting word forms, and adding new phrasing or reminders for later improvement.

Drawing a Blank

~~If at First You Don't Succeed . . . Try, Try Again~~

On the day ~~that~~ my drawing class started to learn

about self portraits last year, each of us had to bring a

In backpacks and purses

mirror to class. ~~There~~ were make-up mirrors, dressing

table mirrors—large and small mirrors of every shape and
kind. I was nervous about drawing a self portrait, so I
brought [only] a tiny plastic pocket mirror. That way if I
didn't do a good job, it would be my mirror's fault. [*Add a thesis]

I had never done well on human figure drawing. ~~Anyway,~~ [First]
, Ms. Newman, demonstrated our teacher ~~showed us how to do~~ the proportion of a human
figure; ~~something like~~ [she explained that] a human body measures about seven
times a human head. She used a tiny piece of chalk to
draw on the board while she was talking. Then she ~~also~~
showed how to sketch ~~out~~ the face, from eyebrows to eyes,
nose, mouth and ears. After ~~all that~~ [her lecture], she ~~led~~ [told] us to ~~start~~ [begin]
~~our~~ drawing [our self-portraits.]

[We all] ~~Everyone in the class~~ set up ~~their~~ [our] mirrors, and ~~t~~[T]he
ceiling danced with ~~all of~~ the reflections they made [as we got to work.]
~~Then we started to draw~~ I looked down at my little
square [of] scratched-up ~~mirror~~ [plastic] and started to draw gingerly
on my ~~drawing~~ paper. ~~I looked at my face, eyebrows, eyes,
nose, mouth, and ears~~ [the eyes, nose, and mouth]. I tried to put ~~what~~ I had seen on
the paper. ~~Then~~ [When] I finished, I ~~was like~~ [wondered,] "Who the heck is
this?" The drawing [didn't look anything] ~~was totally bad. Nothing looked~~ like
me. I was ~~so~~ frustrated and sank down in my chair. After
a minute, I told myself, "Try again[,"] ~~the next one will be
better~~ I drew another one, and it was a little better.
~~It looked a little like me. Nevertheless,~~ [But] I could not
really ~~say that~~ [call] it ~~was~~ a self-portrait because it did not
look exactly like me.

I asked [Ms. Newman for help.] ~~my teacher to come over and help me out~~ She
[glanced at] ~~saw~~ my previous ~~drawings~~ [attempts] and said, "A good self-portrait
doesn't just look like you, it also shows your personal-
ity and ~~characteristics."~~ [your feelings."] ~~From my drawing~~ [in my other drawings.] she did not see
any of these. So I tried again. I borrowed my friend's
big glass mirror and stared into it; I was not only looking

at my face, but also deep inside my face. This time,
I freely sketched ~~out~~ *the shape of* my face~~, shape first.~~ Then, roughly
I placed my eyebrows, eyes, nose, mouth, and ears. ~~And~~ I
looked ~~at~~ *into* the mirror *again and* ~~, seeing my reflection closely. I~~
drew ~~what I felt to be like in the mirror.~~ *the expression I saw there.*
When my ~~drawing~~ *portrait* was finished, I wondered at ~~what an~~ *the*
amazing work I had done. Even though it did not perfectly
look like me, it really showed my ~~characteristics~~ *personality and emotions* through
the *contrast of* light and dark. When ~~my teacher~~ *Ms. Newman* saw it, she applauded.
~~my drawing and she really liked it.~~ Not only did I get an
A ~~in~~ *on* this project; it also became one of the strongest
pieces in my portfolio. I ~~recognized~~ *realized* that ~~nothing could~~ *few things can*
be done successfully the first time. If I ~~gave~~ *had given* up after
my first try, I would never have ~~known I could have done~~ *captured the real me.*
~~such a great job. Now I know I will succeed no matter how~~
~~many times I must try.~~

Can you see why each change was made? Analyzing the reasons for the changes will help you improve your own revision skills.

Assignment 10

TO SHARE OR NOT TO SHARE?

In her essay "Neither a Borrower nor a Lender Be" on page 213, Joanne Kaufman writes about how upsetting it is to share her books with anyone else. She confesses that she might even lie to avoid lending a friend a prized volume from her shelves. Write about your own habits of sharing (or *not* sharing) something of your own—your car, your money, your time. . . . What are the reasons for your choices to share or not to share? How do your habits affect the other people in your life? Would you change your sharing habits if you could?

Write a rough draft of the paper and then set it aside. When you finish writing about your sharing habits, reread your paper to see what improvements you can make to your rough draft. Use the following checklist to help guide you through this or any other revision.

REVISION CHECKLIST

Here's a checklist of revision questions. If the answer to any of these questions is no, revise that part of your paper until you're satisfied that the answer is yes.

1. Does the introductory paragraph introduce the topic clearly and suggest or include a thesis statement that the paper will explain or defend?

2. Does each of the other paragraphs support the thesis statement?

3. Does each body paragraph contain a clear topic sentence and focus on only one supporting point?

4. Do the body paragraphs contain enough details, and are transitional expressions well used?

5. Do the final thoughts expressed in the concluding paragraph bring the paper to a smooth close?

6. Does your (the writer's) voice come through?

7. Do the sentences read smoothly and appear to be correct?

8. Are words well-chosen and are spelling and punctuation consistent and correct?

Exchanging Papers

This checklist could also be used when you exchange papers with another student in your class. Since you both have written a response to the same assignment, you will understand what the other writer went through and learn from the differences between the two papers.

Proofreading Aloud

Finally, read your finished paper *aloud.* If you read it silently, you will see what you *think* is there, but you are sure to miss some errors. Read your paper aloud slowly, pointing to each word as you read it to catch omissions and errors in spelling and punctuation. Reading a paper to yourself this way may take fifteen minutes to half an hour, but it will be time well spent. There are even word processing programs that will "speak" your text in a computer's voice. Using your computer to read your paper to you can be fun as well as helpful. If you don't like the way something sounds, don't be afraid to change it! Make it a rule to read each of your papers *aloud* before handing it in.

Here are four additional writing assignments to help you practice the skills of writing and revising.

Assignment 11

"HEY, MAN, GIVE ME SOME SPACE!"

Some people need almost no "personal space" and feel comfortable even when in crowded situations. Others need lots of physical space around them to be happy. How much "personal space" do you need? Make sure you answer the question, offer the reasons for your answer, and give a few examples in your discussion. Organize your results into the structure of a brief essay.

Assignment 12

WHAT IS HOME?

"Home is where the heart is" is just one of many old sayings that try to define the meaning of the word *home.* It is an abstract word—like *love*—that means different things to different people. How do you define the word *home?* Is it the building you live in or another place altogether? Do you consider yourself "home*less*"—if so, why? Write a brief essay in which you help the reader understand what you mean by "home." Be sure to use plenty of details to bring your definition to life.

Assignment 13

THE BEST ADVICE

What was the best advice you ever received? What prompted the advice? Who gave it to you, and why was it so valuable? Organize your responses to these questions into the structure of a brief essay.

Assignment 14

"LOVE IS BLIND; FRIENDSHIP CLOSES ITS EYES"

"Love is blind; friendship closes its eyes" is a quotation from Exercise 4 on p. 195. Write a short essay in which you react to this quotation and support your reaction or explanation with examples from your own experiences.

VIII. PRESENTING YOUR WORK

Part of the success of a paper could depend on how it looks. The same paper written sloppily or typed neatly might even receive different grades. It is human nature to respond positively when a paper has been presented with care. Here are some general guidelines to follow.

Paper Formats

Your paper should be typed or written on a computer, double-spaced, or copied neatly in ink on 8½-by-11-inch paper on one side only. A one-inch margin should be left around the text on all sides for your instructor's comments. The beginning of each paragraph should be indented five spaces.

Most instructors have a particular format for presenting your name and the course material on your papers. Always follow such instructions carefully.

Titles

Finally, spend some time thinking of a good title. Just as you're more likely to read a magazine article with an interesting title, so your readers will be more eager to read your paper if you give it a good title. Which of these titles from student papers would make you want to read further?

An Embarrassing Experience	Super Salad?
Falling into The Gap	Buying Clothes Can Be Depressing
Hunting: The Best Sport of All?	Got Elk?

Remember these three rules about titles:

1. Only the first letter of the important words in a title should be capitalized.

   A Night at the Races

2. Don't put quotation marks around your own titles unless they include a quotation or title of an article, short story, or poem within them.

   "To Be or Not to Be" Is Not for Me

3. Don't underline (or *italicize*) your own titles unless they include the title of a book, play, movie, or magazine within them.

   Still Stuck on *Titanic*

A wise person once said, "Haste is the assassin of elegance." Instead of rushing to finish a paper and turn it in, take the time to give your writing the polish it deserves.

IX. WRITING ABOUT WHAT YOU READ

Reading and writing are related skills. The more you read, the better you will write. When you are asked to prepare for a writing assignment by reading a newspaper story, a magazine article, a professional essay, or part of a book, there are many ways to respond in writing. Among them, you may be asked to write your reaction to a reading assignment or a summary of a reading assignment.

Writing a Reaction

Reading assignments become writing assignments when your teacher asks you to share your opinion about the subject matter or to relate the topic to your own experiences. In a paragraph, you would have enough space to offer only the most immediate impressions about the topic. However, in an essay you could share your personal reactions, as well as your opinions on the value of the writer's ideas and support. Of course, the first step is always to read the selection carefully, looking up unfamiliar words in a dictionary.

SAMPLE REACTION PARAGRAPH

Here is a sample paragraph-length response following the class's reading of an excerpt from the book *Everything but Money,* by Sam Levenson. In the excerpt, Levenson explains that his family stressed the importance of books and ideas above all else while he was growing up, and it had a profound effect on him. This student shares his own experiences in reaction to reading about Levenson's. Notice that the student titled his reaction paragraph—and that the title makes reference to Levenson's book.

Everything for Love

My family was different from Sam Levenson's in some ways, but they had the same respect for learning. My parents did not have much of a formal "education." They were busy taking care of everything at home: money, food, clothes, etc. However, they wanted us—my four brothers and me—to get a real education. They provided us with all the necessities and encouraged us to learn. Even though my parents did not read much, my brothers and I did. We had the time, and they bought or borrowed the books. The five of us kids used to play "*la escuelita*" and gave each other homework that we assigned ourselves. Reading was one of my favorite "activities." I knew my parents were sacrificing for us, and that made me try harder in real school. They said encouraging things like, "An education is forever. No one can take it away from you once you get it." Now that I'm in college, it is obvious that my parents were as smart as anyone else's—even Levenson's.

If this had been an essay-length response, the student could have included more details about his parents' backgrounds and their methods of encouragement, in contrast to Levenson's. He could have described his four brothers and a few of their mock-homework assignments.

Assignment 15

WRITE A REACTION PARAGRAPH

The following is an excerpt from *Talking with Your Child about a Troubled World* by Lynn S. Dumas, in which she discusses ways to help children deal with disasters that they might see on the news or that might affect them personally. Write a paragraph in which you respond thoughtfully to Dumas' advice and to the details she uses to support it.

How to Talk with Your Child about Disasters

Encourage empathy. As awful as they are, disasters can offer us a chance to teach children that while the world can be troubling, it is also a place where people care about one another and, in times of distress, help each other out. Keep in mind, though, that this lesson can't be taught with words alone; actions do speak louder here. So if you and your child are watching a newscast about an earthquake in Mexico, you might say, "Isn't this terrible? I bet those people will need lots of food and clothing and toys. Why don't we call the Red Cross and see what we can send? Then, maybe you can pick out one or two of your toys and sweaters and we can send them to the children in Mexico." Not only does such action encourage empathy, but it gives them a sense of power. They learn that they have the ability to make a difference in someone else's life.

Stress the positives. So many negatives surround disasters that it's important to offer children a little balance by pointing out the positives. Of course, survivors will always say, "Aren't we lucky that we survived," and that's important to note. But you can go a step further; you can stress that not only do people weather a disaster but they rebuild after one. . . . You can point out to your nine-year-old, "You know, this flood was pretty awful. But look at how we learned to help each other, and to help our neighbors since it happened. Not only that, but we've made lots of new friends [give examples]. Also, we've learned how to share our feelings a little more. We know that we can cry in front of each other and that no one will make fun of us. Sometimes even bad events can make good things happen. And that's nice to know."

Before starting your reaction paragraph, *read the selection again carefully*. Be sure to use a dictionary to look up any words you don't know. You can also use the free writing and clustering techniques explained on page 222. Or your instructor may want you to discuss the reading in groups.

Coming to Your Own Conclusions

Often you will be asked to come to your own conclusions based on a reading that requires interpretation. In other words, you will have to think about and write about what it might mean based only on the details that the writer provides. Such a reading might be a poem, a short story, or even an advertisement.

Here is a poem by Michael Stephans that may not look like a poem at first glance. In it, Stephans gives step-by-step "instructions" on how to read a poem.

Instructions

First, take this poem and hold it over your head, poetical side down; next, shake poem vigorously until words disengage themselves from page and float downward. Upon contact, some of them will sting like tiny summer wasps, but most will feel morning-mirror cool and pleasant to the touch. Some may even be absorbed beneath the skin and carried by the blood directly to the heart. Once the page is blank, empty, wordless, verb and vowel vacant, discard it. And when you are so moved, pick up another poem and start over again.

Source: "Instructions," by Michael Stephans, from *The Color of Stones.* © 1997.

Assignment 16

WHAT ARE YOUR CONCLUSIONS?

Consider the poem "Instructions" above. Be sure to read the poem out loud at least once, and listen to it closely. Then write a page that shares your conclusions about Stephans' poem. Explain why you think he has chosen to present it as a series of directions that look more like a regular paragraph than a poem. Does he really want the reader to follow all of the directions?

Here are two tips for reading and writing about poetry: first, have fun with it; and second, look for words and phrases that might hint at more than one meaning.

As an alternate or additional assignment, write a page that tells "how to" do something that you know well, using short descriptive commands that you don't necessarily want the reader to follow literally. If you choose to imitate the structure of Stephans' poem, remember not to copy his exact phrasing, but to write your own set of "instructions."

Writing 100-Word Summaries

One of the best ways to learn to read carefully and to write concisely is to write 100-word summaries. Writing 100 words sounds easy, but actually it isn't. Writing 200- or 300- or 500-word summaries isn't too difficult, but condensing all the main ideas of an essay or article into 100 words is a time-consuming task—not to be undertaken in the last hour before class.

A summary presents only the main ideas of a reading, *without including any reactions to it.* A summary tests your ability to read, understand, and *rephrase* the ideas contained in an essay, article, or book.

If you work at writing summaries conscientiously, you'll improve both your reading and your writing. You'll improve your reading by learning to spot main ideas and your writing by learning to construct a concise, clear, smooth paragraph. Furthermore, your skills will carry over into your reading and writing for other courses.

Sample 100-Word Summary

First, read the following excerpt from the book *Eccentrics: A Study of Sanity and Strangeness,* by Dr. David Weeks and Jamie James. It will be followed by a student's 100-word summary.

Franz Anton Mesmer

Today medicine is closely associated with chemistry, but in the past there were healers who looked to physics for the causes of illness, and for cures. Franz Anton Mesmer (1734–1815) thought he found a link between health and magnetism, and like other eccentric scientists, once he had found the connection, he devoted his lifetime to . . . his great discovery. . . .

Mesmer brought current theories of astronomy and Newton's law of gravitation into his biological model of animal magnetism. His theory assumed that there was an ethereal fluid present in all living things, similar to the chi of Chinese medicine. . . . Good health, he concluded, results when this inner magnetic fluid is in balance with the magnetic fluid that fills the universe. If the equilibrium got out of whack, order could be restored by pulling the fluids back into alignment with magnets.

At first Mesmer simply fitted small magnets onto various parts of his patients' bodies. . . . Soon he progressed to group healing at his lavishly appointed clinic, where patients sat around a tub filled with water and iron powder, and held tight to iron bars. . . .

Mesmer was widely criticized by the medical establishment, and he didn't help his case by the increasing theatricality of his performances. Before long, the group treatments resembled séances . . . which he presided over wearing a lilac cloak and waving an iron wand. He finally abandoned the use of magnets and began channeling the cosmic fluid through his own body and, via the iron wand, into his patients.

While Mesmer's theory of animal magnetism was, of course, without any foundation in fact, he did make a lasting contribution to science with the invention of hypnotism, which used to be known as mesmerism. . . . [H]is hypnotic technique is still in use today in legitimate medicine, with a multitude of practical applications.

Here is a student's 100-word summary of the article:

> Franz Anton Mesmer was born in the mid-1700s. He was an unconventional scientist who got stuck on an idea and built his life around it. Mesmer believed that people became sick when their magnetic juices were unbalanced. He thought he could cure them by putting their juices in balance again. At first, he treated patients with magnets but eventually started zapping them with his magic wand. Mesmer made quite a production out of these curing sessions. People under his spell were said to be "mesmerized." Even though many scientists did not take him seriously back then, Mesmer actually invented hypnosis.

Assignment 17

WRITE A 100-WORD SUMMARY

Your aim in writing your summary should be to give someone who has not read the article a clear idea of it. First, read the following excerpt from the book *The Films of Elvis Presley* by Susan Doll and then follow the instructions given after it.

Elvis on Celluloid

No actor has been less appreciated than Elvis Presley; no group of films has been more belittled than Elvis's musical comedies. In countless Presley biographies and career overviews and in most rock 'n' roll histories and analyses, Elvis's films have been written off as mindless, unrealistic, formulaic, and trite. Yet, no Presley picture ever lost money, and through the benefit of cable television and video, audiences still enjoy his 31 features and two concert films, as well as the many documentaries and TV shows and miniseries about his life. This contradiction points to the narrowness of the standard view concerning Elvis's Hollywood career while simultaneously calling for a reevaluation of his films by placing them in context.

Much of the rationale for the usual negative view of Presley's films derives from Elvis himself. Elvis became disillusioned with his film career when he was prevented from reaching his goal. From the moment he took his screen test with producer Hal Wallis in April 1956, the young singer had wanted to be a serious actor. Interviews with Elvis from this early period indicate his desire to work hard, learn from the veteran performers who costarred in his films, and become a dramatic actor—just as singers Frank Sinatra and Bing Crosby had done before him. . . .

Elvis quickly became disappointed with what he termed the "Presley Travelogues," complaining about their unrealistic storylines and repetitive nature. He also found the tendency for his character to burst into song at any time to be particularly offensive. Friends, relatives, and acquaintances have all testified to his bitterness at having been thrust into so many musical comedies.

A good way to begin the summary of an article is to figure out the thesis statement, the main idea the author wants to get across to the reader. Write that idea down now *before reading further.*

How honest are you with yourself? Did you write that thesis statement? If you didn't, *write it now* before you read further.

You probably wrote something like this:

Elvis Presley's film career disappointed many people but none more than Elvis himself.

Using that main idea as your first sentence, summarize the article by choosing the most important points. *Be sure to put them in your own words.* Your rough draft may be 150 words or more.

Now cut it down by including only essential points and by getting rid of wordiness. Keep within the 100-word limit. You may have a few words less but not one word more. (And every word counts—even *a, an,* and *the.*) By forcing yourself to keep within 100 words, you'll get to the kernel of the author's thought and understand the article better.

When you have written the best summary you can, then and only then compare it with the summary in the answers. If you look at the model sooner, you'll cheat yourself of the opportunity to learn to write summaries because, once you read the model, it will be almost impossible not to make yours similar. So do your own thinking and writing, and then compare.

SUMMARY CHECKLIST

Even though your summary is different from the model, it may be just as good. If you're not sure how yours compares, answer these questions:

1. Did you include the same main ideas *without* adding your own reactions or opinions?

2. Did you leave out all unnecessary words and examples?

3. Did you rephrase the writer's ideas, not just recopy them?

4. Does the summary read smoothly?

5. Would someone who had not read the article get a clear idea of it from your summary?

Assignment 18

WRITE A REACTION OR A 100-WORD SUMMARY

Respond to Carolyn Wyman's article "Tarts and Sciences" in any of the three ways we've discussed–in a reaction paragraph, an essay, or a 100-word summary. If you plan to respond with an essay, briefly summarize Wyman's information about the history of toaster pastries in your introductory paragraph. Then write about your reactions to the events involved in that history in your body paragraphs. Save your final thoughts for your concluding paragraph.

Tarts and Sciences

A Lot of Technology Goes into Your Toaster—Literally

In the mid-1950s, Charles Mortimer, President of General Foods Corporation, urged the company's Post division to think outside the cereal box. Mortimer's push to diversify Post's breakfast-food offerings led to a number of culinary milestones: Brim, a breakfast-in-milk product that is now remembered mostly as the inspiration for Carnation Instant Breakfast; Tang, the powdered orange drink that the astronauts drank; and, most important, the world's first toaster pastries.

The pastries needed to have less moisture than most fresh foods (to prevent decay at room temperature and keep the crust from getting soggy) but more than most dried ones (to make them palatable). Fortunately, General Foods had recently developed a dog food called Gaines Burgers. These could be kept on the pantry shelf indefinitely, yet they still looked and tasted plausibly like real hamburgers (to a dog, anyway). Post engineers adapted this technology for human consumption in their toaster pastries and, in so doing, helped establish intermediate-moisture foods as a new category. The dog-food-inspired technology was soon applied to military rations, and it is found in today's supermarkets in such products as granola bars, pie crust, canned frosting, meat snack sticks, and thin-rolled fruit snacks.

In August 1963, Post began testing its toaster pastries in Seattle, Indianapolis, and Portland, and on February 16, 1964, Post Country Squares were introduced nationwide. The new product alarmed Post's archrival, Kellogg. "My first thought was that it would be highly unlikely any youngster who had one of those for breakfast would be eating a bowl of cereal too," recalls Bill LaMothe, then Kellogg's vice president for product development. So Kellogg decided to make its own.

Not knowing much about pastry, Kellogg sought help from a Keebler plant with experience making fig bars. Development went fast, and on September 14, 1964, Kellogg had a competitive toaster pastry called Pop-Tarts in stores. Unfortunately, adult focus groups hated them.

But Keebler's plant manager, with the inappropriate name of Bill Post, knew that his children loved heating and eating the new pastries. Post was always bringing home cookies and crackers, which his kids "usually turned their noses up at. But they asked me to bring more of those fruit scones." Kellogg took the hint and aimed its marketing squarely at America's youth. To cut waste and lower costs, Kellogg eliminated Pop-Tarts' original rounded corners, which were designed to make them look more like toast. The first Pop-Tarts were also scored along a diagonal to make them easier to break in two, but within a year, the scoring was eliminated.

Kellogg won the *Zeitgeist* sweepstakes when the name Pop-Tarts, chosen for the way they popped out of the toaster, turned out to echo a pair of 1960s cultural movements, pop music and pop art. Post, by contrast, was stuck with Country Squares, a doubly corny name made all the worse since the Beatles had arrived in America less that two weeks before they hit the market. (Post later changed the name to Toast'em Pop Ups.)

As a breakfast specialist, Kellogg had more riding on the success of its product than the conglomerate General Foods, and in 1972 Post abandoned the toaster-pastry business, leaving Kellogg to colonize the breakfast table with 32 flavors of Pop-Tarts at last count, along with Pastry Swirls, Snak-Stix, and even, briefly, Pop-Tarts Crunch Cereal. The huge success of Pop-Tarts caused an explosion of toaster-heated items, which now include such delicacies as cheese steaks, pizza, and scrambled eggs with bacon (all enclosed in crust, of course). In the toaster-pastry category, Pop-Tarts now account for nearly 80 percent of the $431 million Americans spend annually. And the field is still a locus for innovation, as can be seen from what may be the ultimate in mixed nutritional messages, now available in stores: organic toaster pastries.

Source: Reprinted by permission of AMERICAN HERITAGE. Originally appeared in *Invention & Technology* (Fall 2005).

Answers

SPELLING

WORDS OFTEN CONFUSED, SET 1 (PP. 8–12)

EXERCISE 1

1. an, advice
2. a, choose
3. effect
4. already, affect
5. knew
6. its
7. clothes
8. effect
9. accept
10. No

EXERCISE 2

1. are, our
2. course
3. an, a, dessert
4. its
5. due, an
6. knew
7. new
8. fill
9. complement
10. have

EXERCISE 3

1. know, hear
2. It's, except, it's
3. Its, are
4. an
5. a, it's
6. its, knew
7. an
8. a, feel, have, an
9. conscience, due, its
10. break, already

EXERCISE 4

1. already, do
2. clothes, choose
3. have, its
4. course, dessert
5. Due
6. feel, conscious
7. advice
8. have, complimented
9. course, do
10. except

EXERCISE 5

1. an, choose
2. course, it's
3. advice, an
4. effect
5. its, due
6. cloths, no, coarse
7. break
8. all ready, feel, it's
9. compliments
10. clothes

PROOFREADING EXERCISE

~~Its~~ *It's* hard to ~~except~~ *accept* criticism from friends. The other day, my friend Jane told me that my voice is always too loud when I talk on the phone. She said that the way I talk hurts her ears and makes her hold the phone away from her head. I ~~no~~ *know* that she didn't mean to hurt my feelings, but that was the ~~affect~~ *effect* of what she said. I should ~~of~~ *have* told her that she snores whenever we go camping in the ~~dessert~~ *desert*. Next time, I will record her snoring so that she can ~~here~~ *hear* herself. I don't really want Jane's criticism to ~~brake~~ *break* up ~~are~~ *our* friendship, so I'll probably just talk to her and tell her how I ~~fill~~ *feel*.

WORDS OFTEN CONFUSED, SET 2 (PP. 18–22)

EXERCISE 1

1. past
2. principal
3. quiet
4. piece
5. led, right
6. lose, their
7. passed
8. were
9. too
10. passed

EXERCISE 2

1. through
2. You're
3. whose, too, to
4. past, there
5. peace, quiet, their

6. through, they're
7. there, lose, their, right, personal
8. where
9. Then, to, than
10. Whether, you're, quite

EXERCISE 3

1. were
2. weather
3. led
4. past, whether
5. passed

6. past, there
7. quiet
8. lose, two, right
9. through, past
10. piece, weather

EXERCISE 4

1. whether, write
2. who's, You're, your
3. right, through, quite
4. led, too, write, personal
5. past

6. Personnel
7. They're, past, than
8. woman, principal
9. where
10. lose, than, lose

EXERCISE 5

1. principle, your
2. than, to
3. past, quiet
4. there
5. write

6. woman
7. through
8. women, right
9. threw
10. whether, lose

PROOFREADING EXERCISE

In the ~~passed~~ *past,* if you wanted to ~~here~~ *hear* a ~~peace~~ *piece* of music, you turned on ~~you're~~ *your* stereo. Later, you could even listen ~~too~~ *to* tunes on your computer. Now, with the ~~write~~ *right* equipment, you can play music ~~threw~~ *through* a vase of flowers. The sound doesn't come from the vase, but from the flowers themselves. Let's Corp., a company in Japan, has created a gadget called Ka-on, which means "flower sound" in Japanese. With the Ka-on device, sound is ~~past~~ *passed* up the stems of the flowers, into the delicate blossoms, and out into the room. If you touch the petals, you can feel ~~there~~ *their* vibrations. The Ka-on sound is supposed to be softer ~~then~~ *than* music played through ordinary speakers.

THE EIGHT PARTS OF SPEECH (PP. 25–28)

EXERCISE 1

   pro adv   v   n
1. I really love cookies.

    pro   v adj   adj   n
2. They are my favorite snack.

    pro v   pro prep   adj   n conj n
3. I prefer the ones with chocolate chips or nuts.

       n   v   adj conj pro v adj
4. Cookies taste best when they are fresh.

      adv   pro v   n   conj n prep   n
5. Sometimes, I have cookies and milk for breakfast.

     adv adj   adj   n   v   adj   n
6. Now some fast-food restaurants offer fresh-baked cookies.

      adj   n   v   adj   conj pro v adv adj
7. Oatmeal cookies are delicious when they are still warm.

      n   v   adj   n   prep   adj   n
8. Companies release new versions of traditional cookies.

    adj   n prep n   adv v   adj   n
9. One variety of Oreos now has chocolate centers.

     interj v   pro   adj
10. Wow, are they yummy!

EXERCISE 2

     conj   n   v   pro   pro adv   v
1. When babies want something, they often cry.

     adv adj   n   v   adj   n   prep adj   n
2. Now some parents teach sign language to their babies.

     adj   n   prep   n   v   adj   n   prep adj n prep   n
3. One professor of psychology tried sign language with her baby in the 1980s.

     adv pro   v   n   prep   adj   n
4. Then she repeated the experiment with other children.

       n   v   conj prep adj   n   prep n adj   n   v adj
5. The results showed that at twelve months of age, most babies are ready.

    pro   v   v   adj   n   adv   adv
6. They can control their hands fairly well.

conj n   v   n prep adj   n   n   v   v   pro
7. If a parent repeats signs for a few months, a child can learn them.

n   v   n   prep n   pro   v   adj   n
8. Studies report benefits for babies who learn sign language.

adv   adj   adj   adj   n   v   adj
9. Later, their verbal test scores are high.

adv   pro   v   adv adv prep adj n
10. Also, they score very well on IQ tests.

EXERCISE 3

prep   n   prep n   adj   n   v   adj   n
1. In the summer of 2005, London Zoo opened a temporary exhibit.

n   prep   n   v   adj   n
2. The title of the exhibit was "The Human Zoo."

adj   n   v   adj   adj   n
3. Zoo officials selected eight human volunteers.

adv pro v   n   prep n   prep adj   n
4. Then they put the humans on display for several days.

n   prep n   v   v   adv prep   n
5. Dozens of people had applied online for the project.

n   v   adj   n   conj adj   n
6. The exhibit showcased three males and five females.

pro   v   prep adj adj   n   pro   v   adj   n   conj adj   n
7. They dressed in fake fig leaves that covered their shorts and bikini tops.

prep adj adj   n   conj   adj   n   n   v   adv
8. With its rocky ledges and cave-like structures, the enclosure had previously

v   n
housed bears.

adj   n   v   v   n   conj   v   n prep   n
9. The eight humans talked, played games, and received a lot of attention.

prep   n   n   v   n   prep adj   n   n   conj   n
10. Outside the exhibit, the zoo posted signs about human diet, habitat, and behavior.

EXERCISE 4

n   v   n   conj   n
1. Plants need water and sunlight.

adv   n   v   adv
2. Sometimes houseplants wither unexpectedly.

     n   adv   v   pro adv adj   n conj adv adj   n
3. People often give them too much water or not enough water.

  pro v   n   prep   adj   n   adv
4. I saw an experiment on a television show once.

  pro   v   adj   n
5. It involved two plants.

      adj   n   v   adj   n   prep   n   conj   n
6. The same woman raised both plants with water and sunlight.

       n   v prep adj   adj   n
7. The plants grew in two different rooms.

  pro   v prep adj   n   conj   v   adj   n   prep   pro
8. She yelled at one plant but said sweet things to the other.

      adv   adj   n   v   adv   conj   adj pro   v
9. The verbally praised plant grew beautifully, but the other one died.

      n   v   n   adv
10. Plants have feelings, too.

EXERCISE 5

      n   v   n   pro v   adv   adj
1. Rabies is a disease that is usually fatal.

  adv adj   n   prep adj   n   v   adv   v
2. Only five people with rabies symptoms have ever survived.

  adj   n   pro v   v   v   adj   n   conj adj   n   v
3. Most people who are bitten get rabies shots before any symptoms begin.

  adj   n   v   v   adj   n   prep   n
4. These patients can avoid the deadly results of the disease.

      n   prep   n   v   adj
5. Jeanna Giese from Wisconsin is unique.

  pro   adv   v   n   conj   n v pro prep adj   n
6. She recently survived rabies after a bat bit her at her church.
    (Note that *her* plays two different parts of speech in Sentence 6.)

  pro   adv   v   n   prep n   conj pro v prep   n
7. She already showed symptoms of rabies when she went to the hospital.

     n   v adv v   n   adj   n
8. Doctors did not give Giese the rabies vaccine.

  pro   v   n   prep   n   adv
9. They put the teenager into a coma instead.

    adj   n   v   conj pro   v   n prep adj   n prep   n
10. Their treatment worked, and it promised hope for rabies patients in the future.

PARAGRAPH EXERCISE

    adj   n   v   adv   adj n adv   pro   v   adv conj pro   v
    Your eyelids blink regularly all day long. They stop only when you sleep.

    n   v   adj   adj   n prep   n   conj   pro   v   prep
Blinking protects your delicate eyes from injury. When something flies toward

pro adv   adj   n   v   adv   conj   v   adj   n
you, usually your lids shut quickly and protect your eyes.

        n   adv   v   n prep adj   n pro   v   adj   n   adv conj
    Blinking also does a kind of washing job. It keeps your eyelids moist. If

  n prep n   v prep adj   n   adj   adj   n   v pro adv   adj   n
a speck of dirt gets past your lids, your moist eyeball traps it. Then your eyes

 v prep   n   adj   n   v   conj   n   v   adv prep adj   n
fill with water, your lids blink, and the speck washes out of your eye.

ADJECTIVES AND ADVERBS (PP. 32–35)

EXERCISE 1

  1. adjective adding to the noun *trees*

  2. adjective adding to the noun *magnolias*

  3. adjective adding to the noun *flowers*

  4. adjective adding to the noun *petals*

  5. adverb adding to the verb *drop*

  6. adverb adding to the verb *sweep*

  7. adjective adding to the noun *afternoon*

  8. adverb adding to the verb *look*

  9. adjective adding to the noun *ground*

10. adverb adding to the verb *work*

EXERCISE 2

  1. adjective adding to the noun *coupon*

  2. adverb adding to the adjective *one*

  3. adjective adding to the pronoun *I*

  4. adverb adding to the verb *sells*

  5. adjective adding to the noun *software*

6. adjective adding to the noun *hardware*

7. adjective adding to the noun *Spanish*

8. adjective adding to the noun *students*

9. adjective adding to the noun *child*

10. adjective adding to the pronoun *she*

EXERCISE 3

1. close

2. closely

3. close

4. badly

5. bad

6. badly

7. very happily

8. very happy

9. good

10. well

EXERCISE 4

1. the smallest

2. a small

3. smaller

4. the newest

5. newer

6. newer

7. better

8. the best

9. better

10. more important

EXERCISE 5

1. I took a very unusual art class over the summer.
         adv adj adj

2. The intriguing title of the class was "Frame-Loom Tapestry."
     adj   adj

3. We created small colorful tapestries on a wooden frame.
     adj adj   adj

4. We started with four wooden stretcher bars, two long ones and two short ones.
     adj adj   adj   adj adj   adj adj

5. Then we carefully joined them at the corners to make a rectangular frame.
    adv   adv   adj

6. Next, we wound white cotton string around the frame lengthwise.
    adv   adj adj   adv

7. We finally had the basis for our tapestries.
    adv   adj

adv   adj   adj
8. We took brightly colored yarns and fabric strips and wove them between the strings.

adv   adj
9. I was very happy with the results.

adj adj   adj
10. My first tapestry looked like a beautiful sunset.

PROOFREADING EXERCISE

I didn't do very ~~good~~ *well* in my last year of high school. I feel ~~badly~~ *bad* whenever I think of it. I skipped my classes and turned in messy work. My teachers warned me about my negative attitude, but I was ~~real~~ *really* stubborn. Now that I am a college student, I am even ~~stubborner~~ *more stubborn*. I go to every class and do my best. Now, success is ~~only~~ my *only* goal.

CONTRACTIONS (PP. 37–41)

EXERCISE 1

1. There's, that's, doesn't

2. It's, doesn't

3. aren't

4. you'd

5. they're

6. it's

7. can't

8. no contractions

9. don't, it's

10. you're

EXERCISE 2

1. There's

2. it's

3. someone's

4. person's

5. no contractions

6. there's, we'll, we're

7. We'll

8. there's

9. they're

10. That's

EXERCISE 3

1. we'd

2. didn't, I'd

3. couldn't, hadn't

4. wasn't

5. didn't

6. weren't, they're

7. isn't, didn't, I'd

8. no contractions

9. we'd

10. we're, couldn't

EXERCISE 4

1. who's	**6.** wouldn't, we'd
2. I'm	**7.** They're
3. You're	**8.** wasn't
4. that's	**9.** that's
5. It's	**10.** hasn't (*Its* is used twice as a possessive.)

EXERCISE 5

1. there's, I'm	**6.** it's
2. I've	**7.** aren't
3. We've, haven't	**8.** we're, we'll
4. We'll, can't	**9.** That's, I'll, it's
5. she's, we've	**10.** there's

PROOFREADING EXERCISE

~~Ive~~ *I've* just learned about a new Web site created to allow people to share ~~there~~ *their* books with complete strangers. ~~Its~~ *It's* called BookCrossing.com, and when ~~your~~ *you're* finished reading a book, it can be ~~past~~ *passed* on to a ~~knew~~ *new* reader just by leaving it on a park bench, at a cafe, or wherever you like. Before you pass it on, you just register the book on the web site, get its ID number, and tell ~~wear~~ *where* you're going to leave it. Then you place a note or a sticker in the book with ~~a~~ *an* identification number and the web address telling the person ~~whose~~ *who's* going to find it what to do next. This way, people can keep track of the books they decide to "release into the wild," which is how the Web site phrases it. The best part about "bookcrossing" is it's anonymous, and ~~its~~ *it's* free!

POSSESSIVES (PP. 45–47)

EXERCISE 4

1. child's	**6.** stroller's
2. baby's	**7.** bystanders'
3. building's (Note: No apostrophe is needed for the possessive pronoun *its*.)	**8.** parents'
4. nanny's	**9.** no possessive nouns (Note: No apostrophe is needed for the possessive pronoun *Its*.)
5. baby's	**10.** model's

EXERCISE 5

1. Claude Monet's

2. London's

3. fog's

4. weather's

5. no possessive nouns

6. no possessive nouns

7. People's (Note: No apostrophe is needed for the possessive pronoun *its.*)

8. no possessive nouns

9. artist's

10. "Monet's London."

PROOFREADING EXERCISE

My ~~houses'~~ *house's* windows are old and out of style. They have single panes of glass, so they don't provide any insulation from heat or cold. Last ~~months~~ *month's* heating bills were the highest I've ever had. My next-door ~~neighbors~~ *neighbor's* name is Don. ~~Dons'~~ *Don's* house has new windows. At his ~~carpenters~~ *carpenter's* suggestion, Don put in double-paned windows, and it really makes a difference in his energy bills. The new ~~windows~~ *windows'* design includes another fancy feature. They have shades installed between the two panes of glass. Since they're protected by glass, the shades don't get dirty. I plan to replace my old windows with new ones like Don's as soon as I can.

REVIEW OF CONTRACTIONS AND POSSESSIVES (PP. 48–49)

1. There's, Valentine's

2. I'm, You're

3. America's, that's

4. Necco's, they've

5. heart's (or hearts'), it's

6. company's, cookie's

7. candy's

8. country's

9. New Year's, year's, Valentine's

10. they'll

Bowling for Values

Growing up as a child, I didn't have a set of values to live by. Neither my mother nor my father gave me any specific rules, guidelines, or beliefs to lead me through the complicated journey of childhood. My parents' approach was to set me free, to allow me to experience life's difficulties and develop my own set of values.

They were like parents taking their young child bowling for the first time. They hung their values on the pins at the end of the lane. Then they put up the gutter guards and hoped that I'd hit at least a few of the values they'd lived by themselves.

If I had a son today, I'd be more involved in developing a set of standards for him to follow. I'd adopt my mom and dad's philosophy of letting him discover on his own what he's interested in and how he feels about life. But I'd let him bowl in other lanes or even in other bowling alleys. And, from the start, he'd know my thoughts on religion, politics, drugs, sex, and all the ethical questions that go along with such subjects.

Now that I'm older, I wish my parents would've shared their values with me. Being free wasn't as comfortable as it might've been if I'd had some basic values to use as a foundation when I had tough choices to make. My children's lives will be better, I hope. At least they'll have a base to build on or to remodel—whichever they choose.

RULE FOR DOUBLING A FINAL LETTER (PP. 51–52)

EXERCISE 1

1. tossing
2. clipping
3. intending
4. meeting
5. picking
6. buying
7. asking
8. calling
9. mapping
10. targeting

EXERCISE 2

1. sewing
2. reviewing
3. dealing
4. clogging
5. clicking
6. unhooking
7. quizzing
8. pushing
9. aiming
10. delivering

EXERCISE 3

1. snipping
2. buzzing
3. mixing
4. rowing
5. tampering
6. performing
7. conferring
8. gleaming
9. clipping
10. permitting

EXERCISE 4

1. patting
2. sawing
3. feeding
4. playing
5. occurring
6. brushing
7. gathering
8. knotting
9. offering
10. hogging

EXERCISE 5

1. helping
2. flexing
3. assisting
4. needing
5. selecting
6. wishing
7. cooking
8. constructing
9. polishing
10. leading

PROGRESS TEST (P. 53)

1. B. They enjoyed the rest of *their* vacation.

2. B. Their parents felt *bad* about taking them to him.

3. B. He said that my details perfectly *complemented* my ideas.

4. A. I've heard that *you're* looking for a new car.

5. B. The final battle scene could *have* been much shorter.

6. A. Driving a car was easier *than* I thought it would be.

7. A. My computer has a problem with *its* CD drawer.

8. B. I also feel *closer* to my family now.

9. A. Yesterday, our band teacher was absent, so a student *led* the rehearsal.

10. A. College counselors give good *advice*.

SENTENCE STRUCTURE

FINDING SUBJECTS AND VERBS (PP. 64–67)

EXERCISE 1

1. Many people saw the movie *March of the Penguins.*

2. It was one of the most popular films of 2005.

3. The movie followed the lives of a group of emperor penguins.

4. The filmmakers lived in the penguins' world for over a year.

5. Luc Jacquet directed the documentary.

6. Jacquet and his crew recorded the birds' incredible journey to their breeding grounds.

7. The penguins and humans endured extreme storms and hungry predators.

8. There were moments of joy and sadness in the film.

9. In one of the saddest parts, an egg slid away from its parents and froze on the ice.

10. Audiences loved the relationships between the penguin parents and their chicks.

EXERCISE 2

1. Travelers often carry food and other products from one country to another.

2. They ride trains or take planes to their new destinations.

3. Customs officials check passengers for illegal foods or other contraband.

4. Sometimes, customs officers catch smugglers of very unusual items.

5. One woman from Australia made the news recently.

6. There were two odd things about her skirt.

7. It looked very puffy and made a sloshing noise.

8. Customs officers found fifty-one live tropical fish in an apron under her skirt.

9. The apron had special pockets and held fifteen plastic bags.

10. Officials arrested the woman and confiscated her cargo.

EXERCISE 3

1. Chris Lindland had a simple idea.

2. He used an ordinary fabric in an extraordinary way.

3. Lindland invented "Cordarounds."

4. Cordarounds are corduroy pants with a twist.

5. The corduroy ridges go across instead of down the pant legs.

6. These new pants have their own Web site.

7. The Web site is, predictably, cordarounds.com.

8. There are different colors and styles of Cordarounds.

9. They cost a little more than regular corduroy pants.

10. Lindland sees other new styles of clothes in his future.

EXERCISE 4

1. Cats are extremely loyal and determined pets.

2. They form strong attachments to their families.

3. One cat recently showed her love for the Sampson family very clearly.

4. The Sampsons made a temporary move and took Skittles, the cat, with them.

5. The Sampsons and Skittles spent several months 350 miles away from home.

6. Before the end of their stay, Skittles disappeared.

7. The family returned home without their beloved cat and considered her lost.

8. Seven months later, there was a surprise on their doorstep.

9. Skittles somehow navigated her way home but barely survived the 350-mile trip.

10. This incredible story proves the loyalty and determination of cats.

EXERCISE 5

1. There are a number of world-famous trees in California.

2. One of them is the oldest tree on the planet.

3. This tree lives somewhere in Inyo National Forest.

4. The type of tree is a bristlecone pine.

5. Scientists call it the Methuselah Tree.

6. They place its age at five thousand years.

7. The soil and temperatures around it seem too poor for a tree's health.

8. But the Methuselah Tree and its neighbors obviously thrive in such conditions.

9. Due to its importance, the Methuselah Tree's exact location is a secret.

10. Such important natural specimens need protection.

PARAGRAPH EXERCISE

My most valuable possession at the moment is a pair of chopsticks. These chopsticks are not worth a lot of money. In fact, they are the disposable kind and still have the white paper wrapper on them. Their value lies in my memories of an evening with someone very special. It happened almost a year ago. As a favor to my friend Tressa, I agreed to a blind date with her cousin Marcus. Marcus and I met at a restaurant, ate sushi, and talked for hours. That night was the start of a wonderful relationship. On my way out of the restaurant that evening, I looked for a souvenir. There was a tall glass of take-out chopsticks by the door. I grabbed a pair and treasure it to this day.

LOCATING PREPOSITIONAL PHRASES (PP. 70–73)

EXERCISE 1

1. Roald Dahl is the author (of *Charlie and the Chocolate Factory*).

2. (In his youth), Dahl had two memorable experiences (with sweets).

3. One (of them) involved the owner (of a candy store).

4. Dahl and his young friends had a bad relationship (with this particular woman).

5. (On one visit) (to her store), Dahl put a dead mouse (into one) (of the candy jars) (behind her back).

6. The woman later went (to his school) and demanded his punishment.

7. He and his friends received several lashes (from a cane) (in her presence).

8. (During his later childhood years), Dahl became a taste-tester (for the Cadbury chocolate company).

9. Cadbury sent him and other schoolchildren boxes (of sweets) to evaluate. [*To evaluate* is a verbal, not a prepositional phrase.]

10. Dahl tried each candy and made a list (of his reactions and recommendations).

EXERCISE 2

1. A killer whale (at MarineLand) (in Canada) recently invented his own stunt.

2. (After feeding time), gulls often ate the leftover fish (on the surface) (of the water).

3. This orca found a way to benefit (from the gulls' habit). [*To benefit* is a verbal, not a prepositional phrase.]

4. He filled his mouth (with fish chunks) and squirted them (on top) (of the water).

5. Then he sank (beneath the surface) and waited (for a gull).

6. The whale caught the gull and had it (for dessert).

7. This whale then taught his new trick (to some) (of the other whales).

8. One main aspect (of the whales' behavior) fascinates scientists.

9. These whales taught the trick (to themselves) and (to each other) (without human guidance).

10. Luckily, cameras captured all (of the learning) (on film) (for study) (in the future).

EXERCISE 3

1. My family and I live (in a house) (at the top) (of a hilly neighborhood) (in Los Angeles).

2. (On weekday mornings), nearly everyone drives (down the steep winding roads) (to their jobs) or (to school).

3. (In the evenings), they all come back (up the hill) to be (with their families).

4. (For the rest) (of the day), we see only an occasional delivery van or compact school bus.

5. But (on Saturdays and Sundays), there is a different set (of drivers) (on our roads).

6. (On those two days), tourists (in minivans) and prospective home buyers (in convertibles) cram our narrow streets.

7. (For this reason), most (of the neighborhood residents) stay (at home) (on weekends).

8. Frequently, drivers unfamiliar (with the twists and turns) (of the roads) (in this area) cause accidents.

9. The expression "Sunday driver" really means something (to those) (of us) (on the hill).

10. (In fact), even "Saturday drivers" are a nuisance (for us).

EXERCISE 4

1. <u>Most</u> (of us) <u>remember</u> playing (with Frisbees) (in our front yards) (in the early evenings) and (at parks or beaches) (on weekend afternoons).

2. <u>Fred Morrison</u> <u>invented</u> the original flat Frisbee (for the Wham-O toy company) (in the 1950s).

3. <u>Ed Headrick</u>, designer (of the professional Frisbee), <u>passed away</u> (at his home) (in California) (in August) (of 2002).

4. Working (at Wham-O) (in the 1960s), <u>Headrick</u> <u>improved</u> the performance (of the existing Frisbee) (with the addition) (of ridges) (in the surface) (of the disc).

5. Headrick's <u>improvements</u> <u>led</u> (to increased sales) (of his "professional model" Frisbee) and (to the popularity) (of Frisbee tournaments).

6. (After Headrick's re-design), <u>Wham-O</u> <u>sold</u> 100 million (of the flying discs).

7. <u>Headrick</u> also <u>invented</u> the game (of disc golf).

8. (Like regular golf) but (with discs), the <u>game</u> <u>is played</u> (on special disc golf courses) (like the first one) (at Oak Grove Park) (in California).

9. (Before his death), <u>Headrick</u> <u>asked</u> (for his ashes) to be formed (into memorial flying discs) (for select family and friends). [*To be formed* is a verbal.]

10. <u>Donations</u> (from sales) (of the remaining memorial discs) <u>went</u> (toward the establishment) (of a museum) (on the history) (of the Frisbee and disc golf).

EXERCISE 5

1. An engraved <u>likeness</u> (of Pocahontas), the famous Powhatan Indian princess, <u>is</u> the oldest portrait (on display) (at the National Portrait Gallery).

2. (In 1607), <u>Pocahontas</u>—still (in her early teens)—single-handedly <u>helped</u> the British colonists (in Virginia) to survive. [*To survive* is a verbal.]

3. Later, (in 1616), <u>Pocahontas</u> <u>traveled</u> (to England) (after her marriage) (to John Rolfe) and (after the birth) (of their son).

4. She <u>visited</u> the court (of King James I) and <u>impressed</u> the British (with her knowledge) (of English) and (with her conversion) (to Christianity).

5. (For her new first name), <u>Pocahontas</u> <u>chose</u> Rebecca.

6. (During her seven-month stay) (in England), <u>she</u> <u>became</u> extremely ill.

7. (At some point) (before or during her illness), <u>Simon Van de Passe</u> <u>engraved</u> her portrait (on copper).

8. The <u>portrait</u> <u>shows</u> Pocahontas (in a ruffled collar and fancy English clothes) but (with very strong Indian features).

9. Successful <u>sales</u> (of prints) (from the portrait) <u>illustrate</u> her fame abroad.

10. <u>Pocahontas</u> <u>died</u> (on that trip) (to England) (at the age) (of twenty-two).

PARAGRAPH EXERCISE

    Even the Liberty Bell came (to the fair) (during that summer)—after seventy-five thousand St. Louis school children had signed a petition requesting its visit. (On June 8), the cracked bell arrived (on a flat wagon) pulled (by a team) (of horses) and surrounded (by policemen) (from Philadelphia). Crowds lined the edges (of the Plaza) (of St. Louis), hoping to get a glimpse (of this famous artifact). Mayor Rolla Wells pronounced the occasion Liberty Bell Day and called off school (in the city) so that children could come (to the fair).

Notes: *After* begins a dependent clause, not a prepositional phrase, in the first sentence. *To get* begins a verbal phrase, not a prepositional phrase, in the third sentence. *Off* adds to the verb *called* in the final sentence. Together, *called off* means "canceled."

UNDERSTANDING DEPENDENT CLAUSES (PP. 76–81)

EXERCISE 1

1. Two men created a Web site that offers an unusual service.

2. After one of their friends died, they discovered the need for a place online to store a person's important information.

3. Because most people keep this information a secret, family and friends lack necessary details after their deaths.

4. People who subscribe to this service control the release of their private information.

5. The site stores the members' information until they pass away.

6. Members pay about a hundred dollars for the service, which lasts a lifetime.

7. Once people become members, they enter their bank accounts, passwords, life insurance policies, and specifics of their wills.

8. Since current technology is so advanced, pre-written e-mails and pre-recorded video messages are very popular additions to members' last wishes.

9. Members can personally communicate exactly what they want to say to their loved ones in these final messages.

10. Anyone can visit the site, which is called LastWishes.com.

Exercise 2

1. The world is a miserable place when you have an upset stomach.

2. Whether you get carsick, airsick, or seasick, you probably welcome any advice.

3. Motion sickness is most common when people are between the ages of seven and twelve.

4. Motion sickness happens to some people whenever the brain receives mixed messages.

5. If the inner ear feels movement but the eyes report no movement, the brain gets confused.

6. This confusion results in dizziness and the feeling that all is not well.

7. Experts suggest that you sleep well and eat lightly to avoid motion sickness.

8. When you travel by car, you should sit in the middle of the back seat and look straight out the windshield.

9. On an airplane or a boat, the best seat is one that allows a view of the clouds or horizon.

10. Whenever the queasy feeling comes, you should sip small amounts of water.

EXERCISE 3

1. The Breathalyzer is a machine that measures a person's blood alcohol level.

2. Police officers use the device when they suspect a drunk driver.

3. Robert F. Borkenstein was the man who invented the Breathalyzer.

4. Before Borkenstein created the portable measuring device, officers took suspects' breath samples in balloons back to a laboratory for a series of tests.

5. Borkenstein's Breathalyzer was an improvement because all testing occurred at the scene.

6. The Breathalyzer was so reliable and became so feared that one man went to extremes to avoid its results.

7. While this man waited in the back of the police car, he removed his cotton underwear and ate them.

8. He hoped that the cotton cloth would soak up all the alcohol in his system.

9. When the desperate man's case went to court, the judge acquitted him.

10. The judge's decision came after spectators in the court laughed so hard that they could not stop.

EXERCISE 4

1. On June 8, 1924, George Mallory and Andrew Irvine disappeared as they climbed to the top of Mount Everest.

2. Earlier, when a reporter asked Mallory why he climbed Everest, his response became legendary.

3. "Because it is there," Mallory replied.

4. No living person knows whether the two British men reached the summit of Everest before they died.

5. Nine years after Mallory and Irvine disappeared, English climbers found Irvine's ice ax.

6. In 1975, a Chinese climber spotted a body that was frozen in deep snow on the side of the mountain.

7. He kept the news secret for several years but finally told a fellow climber on the day before he died himself in an avalanche on Everest.

8. In May 1999, a team of mountaineers searched the area that the Chinese man described and found George Mallory's frozen body still intact after seventy-five years.

9. After they took DNA samples for identification, the mountaineers buried the famous climber on the mountainside where he fell.

10. The question remains whether Mallory was on his way up or down when he met his fate.

EXERCISE 5

1. I read an article that described the history of all the presidents' dogs.

2. George Washington cared so much about dogs that he interrupted a battle to return a dog that belonged to a British general.

3. Abraham Lincoln, whose dog's name was actually Fido, left his loyal pet in Illinois after the Lincolns moved to the White House.

4. Teddy Roosevelt met and adopted Skip, the dog that he loved best, after the little terrier held a bear at bay in the Grand Canyon.

5. Franklin Delano Roosevelt made a U.S. Navy ship return to the Aleutians to pick up his dog Fala up after the diplomatic party accidentally left the dog behind.

6. Warren G. Harding's Laddie Boy was the most pampered of the presidential dogs since the Hardings gave him birthday parties and ordered a special chair for Laddie Boy to sit in during presidential meetings.

7. Nikita Khrushchev traveled from Russia with Pushinka, a dog that he gave to John F. Kennedy's daughter Caroline.

8. At a gas station in Texas, Lyndon Johnson's daughter Luci found a little white dog, Yuki, whom President Johnson loved to have howling contests with in the Oval Office.

9. Of course, Nixon had his famous Checkers, and George Bush Sr. had a spaniel named Millie, who wrote her own best-selling book with the help of Barbara Bush.

10. And just when it seemed that all presidents prefer dogs, Bill Clinton arrived with Socks, a distinctively marked black-and-white cat.

PARAGRAPH EXERCISE

Why Is the Grass Wet in the Morning?

All day long, the grass is warm and dry. The sun has made it so. Then the sun goes down. And when the sun goes down, the warmth goes away, and the grass grows colder. The air that touches the cold grass leaves little beads of water on it.

All air has water vapor in it. Warm air holds more of this water vapor than cold air does. So when the night air turns colder, it releases its water vapor. The water clings to the blades of grass and forms dew. The dew remains until the sun rises again the next day. Then, as the heat of the sun transforms the beads of water into vapor again, the grass grows warm and dry.

CORRECTING FRAGMENTS (PP. 84–88)

EXERCISE 1
Possible revisions to make the fragments into sentences are *italicized.*

1. Correct

2. *They don't think* about the consequences.

3. Correct

4. Correct

5. About half of the people *change their minds*, to be exact.

6. Correct

7. *It involves* lasers to remove the pigment in the skin.

8. Correct

9. *They are* used on different colors and in different combinations.

10. Correct

Changes used to make the fragments into sentences are *italicized.*

1. Correct

2. Correct

3. *Jerry had to wear the shirt* on TV.

4. *He did it* to help Kramer's friend, a fashion designer.

5. Correct

6. Dorothy's ruby slippers from *The Wizard of Oz are also on display there.*

7. *The museum holds* other famous objects, like the original Kermit the Frog from *Sesame Street.*

8. Correct

9. Correct

10. *It's* because the shirt had the combination of a funny design and a funny name.

Answers may vary, but here are some possible revisions.

1. Finding a parking space on the first day of classes seems impossible. I drive endlessly around campus looking for an empty spot.

2. With the hope that the situation will improve, I always spend forty dollars for a parking permit.

3. My old car's engine doesn't like the long periods of idling. It stalls a lot and won't start up again easily.

4. In order to get a space close to my first class, I always follow anyone walking through the parking lot closest to the science building.

5. I am usually disappointed by this method, however. Most people are just walking through the parking lot to get to farther lots or to the bus stop.

6. I was really lucky on the first day of the semester two semesters ago. I drove right into a spot vacated by a student from an earlier class.

7. Maybe I should get up before dawn myself, for that's a foolproof way to secure a perfect parking place.

8. Every morning, I see these early birds in their cars with their seats back. They sleep there for hours before class but in a great spot.

9. I don't think I can solve the problem this way. I find it hard to get out of bed in the dark.

10. Due to the rise in college populations, campus parking problems will most likely only get worse.

EXERCISE 4

Answers may vary, but here are some possible revisions.

1. We were writing our in-class essays when suddenly the emergency bell rang.

2. Everyone in the class looked at each other first and then at the teacher. He told us to gather up our things and follow him outside.

3. The series of short rings continued as we left the room and noisily walked out into the parking lot beside the main building.

4. The sunlight was very warm and bright compared to the classroom's fluorescent lights, which always make everything look more clinical than natural.

5. As we stood in a large group with students and teachers from other classes, we wondered about the reason for the alarm.

6. I have never heard an emergency alarm that was anything but a planned drill.

7. Without the danger of injury, a party atmosphere quickly developed since we all got a break from our responsibilities.

8. I've noticed that the teachers seem the most at ease because they don't have to be in control during these situations.

9. After we students and the teachers chatted for ten minutes or so, the final bell rang to signal the end of the drill.

10. When we sat down at our desks again, the teacher asked us to continue writing our essays until the end of the hour.

EXERCISE 5

Answers may vary, but here are some possible revisions. (Changes are in *italics*.)

1. *I am surprised* whenever I see a seagull up close.

2. After lunch on Tuesdays, our club *meets* in the gym.

3. After we turned in our research assignments, *the librarians celebrated.*

4. Traveling overseas without a lot of planning *is risky.*

5. The pizza *arrived* within thirty minutes of our call.

6. It *was* the hardest question on the test.

7. *I have discovered* that people often stretch the truth.

8. *Discuss* the topic with the person next to you.

9. Even though "wet paint" signs were still on the walls, *people leaned against them.*

10. *The book explains* how a series of paragraphs becomes an essay.

PROOFREADING PARAGRAPH

Here is one possible revision to eliminate the five fragments.

Fred Astaire was one of the most popular dancers of all time, dancing in over forty movies in his fifty-year career. He was born in Omaha, Nebraska, with the real name of Frederick Austerlitz. Fred Astaire and his sister were stage stars when they were still children. They appeared as a miniature married couple dancing on top of a huge wedding cake and as a lobster and a glass of champagne. Astaire was eventually happily married to his first wife Phyllis for many years. Later in his life, Fred Astaire got married again. This time he married Robyn Smith, a female jockey who was forty-five years younger than Astaire.

CORRECTING RUN-ON SENTENCES (PP. 91–94)

EXERCISE 1

Your answers may differ depending on how you chose to separate the two clauses.

1. Mary Mallon is a famous name in American history, but she is not famous for something good.

2. Most people know Mary Mallon by another name, and that is "Typhoid Mary."

3. The sentence is correct.

4. The sentence is correct.

5. Mary Mallon was the first famous case of a healthy carrier of disease, but she never believed the accusations against her.

6. Mallon, an Irish immigrant, was a cook; she was also an infectious carrier of typhoid.

7. By the time the authorities discovered Mallon's problem, she had made many people ill. A few of her "victims" actually died from the disease.

8. A health specialist approached Mallon and asked her for a blood sample; she was outraged and attacked him with a long cooking fork.

9. Eventually the authorities dragged Mallon into a hospital for testing, but she fought them hysterically the entire time.

10. The lab tests proved Mallon's infectious status, and health officials forced Mary Mallon to live on an island by herself for twenty-six years.

EXERCISE 2

Your answers may differ depending on how you chose to separate the two clauses.

1. Frank Epperson invented something delicious and refreshing, and it comes on a stick.

2. In 1905, Epperson was an eleven-year-old boy. He lived in San Francisco.

3. The sentence is correct.

4. The sentence is correct.

5. There was a record-breaking cold snap that evening, and the drink froze.

6. In the morning, Frank Epperson ate his frozen juice creation; it made a big impression.

7. Epperson grew up and kept making his frozen "Epsicles"; they came in seven varieties.

8. The sentence is correct.

9. Epperson's kids loved their dad's treat, and they always called them "pop's sicles."

10. So Popsicles were born, and people have loved them ever since.

EXERCISE 3

Your answers may differ since various words can be used to begin dependent clauses.

1. *When* I went to the orthodontist last month, she told me that I needed braces.

2. I was happy *because* I always wanted them.

3. The sentence is correct.

4. The sentence is correct.

5. *After* my dentist told me about many types of braces, I wanted the invisible kind.

6. *Once* the dentist said that the invisible ones were perfect for my case, she began the process.

7. The sentence is correct.

8. The company made a series of sets of clear braces, *which* I will wear for several weeks each.

9. *Because* the first set fits my teeth perfectly, they are almost totally invisible.

10. I am glad that orthodontists offer this new type of braces *that* are just right for me.

EXERCISE 4

Your answers may differ since various words can be used to begin dependent clauses.

1. Now that I've been learning about sleep in my psychology class, I know a lot more about it.

2. Sleep has five stages, which we usually go through many times during the night.

3. As the first stage of sleep begins, our muscles relax and mental activity slows down.

4. The sentence is correct.

5. Because stage two takes us deeper than stage one, we are no longer aware of our surroundings.

6. The sentence is correct.

7. Next is stage three, in which we become more and more relaxed and are very hard to awaken.

8. Stage four is so deep that we don't even hear loud noises.

9. The fifth stage of sleep is called REM (rapid eye movement) sleep because our eyes move back and forth quickly behind our eyelids.

10. Although REM sleep is only about as deep as stage two, we do all our dreaming during the REM stage.

EXERCISE 5

Your answers may differ depending on how you chose to connect the clauses.

1. Boston Red Sox fans have a tradition, *which* they celebrate at every home game without question.

2. Very few people know how the tradition began, but most people don't care to know.

3. It happens in the eighth inning, and everyone looks forward to it.

4. *When* the loud speakers at Fenway Park play the song "Sweet Caroline," all of the fans sing along.

5. There is problem with the tradition; the song has no link to Boston or baseball.

6. Neil Diamond sings the thirty-year-old song, but his last name is only a baseball coincidence.

7. In the past, other teams played the song at stadiums, but in 2002, Boston started playing it at every game.

8. The sentence is correct.

9. The Red Sox won the 2004 World Series; no one really expected that.

10. Players and teams in sports are sometimes superstitious. Singing "Sweet Caroline" is a lucky charm that the fans, the players, and the management love.

REVIEW OF FRAGMENTS AND RUN-ON SENTENCES (PP. 95–96)

Your revisions may differ depending on how you chose to correct the errors.

With all of the attention on cleanliness lately in advertising for soaps and household cleaning products, people are surprised to hear that we may be too clean for our own good. This phenomenon is called the "hygiene hypothesis," and recent studies support its validity. For instance, one study shows the benefit of living with two or more pets. Babies may grow up with healthier immune systems and be less allergic if they live with a dog and a cat or two dogs or two cats. The old thinking was that young children would become more allergic living with many pets, but they don't. Somehow the exposure to pets and all their "dirty" habits gives youngsters much-needed defenses. There is sometimes as much as a seventy-five percent lower allergy risk, according to this study.

IDENTIFYING VERB PHRASES (PP. 98–102)

EXERCISE 1

1. For the first time, scientists have successfully cloned a dog.

2. Cloning experts had been attempting this accomplishment for many years.

3. They had had success with horses, cats, and even rats before they could clone a dog.

4. The scientists who eventually succeeded were from Seoul National University in South Korea.

5. They named the cloned dog Snuppy as a tribute to the university where the accomplishment was made.

6. Of course, Snuppy can thank his "parent" dog, a three-year-old Afghan hound, for all of his great features.

7. Both dogs have long glossy black fur that is accentuated by identical brown markings on their paws, tails, chests, and eyebrows.

8. Now that a dog has been cloned, everyone anticipates that some pet owners will want a clone of their dogs.

9. The procedure for dogs involves different steps and may always be more difficult.

10. Cloning pets will definitely cost a lot of money and be a gamble at best.

EXERCISE 2

1. Kris Kliszewicz, a successful businessman in England, has been raising money and interest around the world for a pet project.

2. Kliszewicz wants to build a theme park which will allow people to immerse themselves in the life and times of Shakespeare.

3. Kliszewicz is planning to call the new history-based theme park "Shakespeare's World."

4. He has decided on the perfect location for the first of these parks—on the outskirts of Shakespeare's hometown, Stratford-upon-Avon.

5. At Shakespeare's World, troupes of roaming actors will perform scenes from Shakespeare's plays.

6. According to Kliszewicz, visitors will see the sights and hear the sounds that Shakespeare saw and heard.

7. There will be cobblestoned streets complete with bakeries and butcheries, fields full of animals and farming peasants, and tradespeople who will demonstrate Tudor crafts.

8. Some Shakespeare scholars are not convinced that a Shakespeare theme park is a good idea.

9. But Kliszewicz believes that people might enjoy more exposure to Shakespeare without the purely academic treatment that he is given in classrooms.

10. The idea of Shakespeare's World is also getting some attention in China, Russia, and America, which Kliszewicz plans to make future sites for Shakespeare's World.

EXERCISE 3

1. I have always wondered how an Etch A Sketch works.

2. This flat TV-shaped toy has been popular since it first arrived in the 1960s.

3. Now I have learned the secrets inside this popular toy.

4. An Etch A Sketch is filled with a combination of metal powder and tiny plastic particles.

5. This mixture clings to the inside of the Etch A Sketch screen.

6. When the pointer that is connected to the two knobs moves, the tip of it "draws" lines in the powder on the back of the screen.

7. The powder at the bottom of the Etch A Sketch does not fill in these lines because it is too far away.

8. But if the Etch A Sketch is turned upside down, the powder clings to the whole underside surface of the screen and "erases" the image again.

9. Although the basic Etch A Sketch has not changed since I was a kid, it now comes in several different sizes.

10. Best of all, these great drawing devices have never needed batteries, and I hope that they never will [need batteries].

EXERCISE 4

1. During my last semester of high school, our English teacher assigned a special paper.

2. He said that he was becoming depressed by all the bad news out there, so each of us was asked to find a piece of good news and write a short research paper about it.

3. I must admit that I had no idea how hard that assignment would be.

4. Finally, I found an article while I was reading my favorite magazine.

5. The title of the article was a pun; it was called "Grin Reaper."

6. I knew instantly that it must be just the kind of news my teacher wanted.

7. The article explained that one woman, Pam Johnson, had started a club that she named The Secret Society of Happy People.

8. She had even chosen August 8 as "Admit You're Happy Day" and had already convinced more than fifteen state governors to recognize the holiday.

9. The club and the holiday were created to support people who are happy so that the unhappy, negative people around will not bring the happy people down.

10. As I was writing my essay, I visited the Society of Happy People Web site and, for extra credit, signed my teacher up for their newsletter.

EXERCISE 5

1. Donald Redelmeier was sitting in front of his television a few years ago, and he was not alone.

2. He was enjoying the Academy Awards along with millions of other TV viewers.

3. Redelmeier focused on the nominees as they were waiting for the announcement of the winners' names.

4. Suddenly, he was struck by the good health and lively mannerisms of them all.

5. Redelmeier's experiences as a doctor of ordinary people did not match what he was seeing on TV.

6. He devised a study that would explore the effects of success and recognition on health.

7. He would use the winners and losers of Academy Awards as the pool of subjects for his data.

8. He wondered if Oscar winners would live longer than losers and those who had never been nominated.

9. The results of his study showed that the winners do live an average of four years longer that the losers.

10. Luckily, nominees who lose also live a few months longer than those who are not nominated, so they do get some benefits.

REVIEW EXERCISE

There is something that starts (in the sky) (as one thing) and lands (on earth) (as something else). It is hail. Hail starts (as rain), but before the drops (of water) can fall very far, the wind blows them high up where the air is colder. They freeze and start to fall again. Over and over they fall and are blown back up again. Each time that they fall, a new layer (of water vapor) condenses (on them). And each time that they are blown up (into the freezing layer), this new layer (of water) turns (to ice). Finally, the hailstones become too heavy to be lifted (by the wind), and they fall (to earth). Some hailstones as large as baseballs have been recorded, but usually hailstones do not grow larger than the size (of a pea).

(During the next hailstorm), if you pick up a few pieces (of hail) and cut them in half), you can see the layers that were formed as they fell, collected more moisture, and were swept back up (into the freezing air) again. If you count the layers, you can record the number (of trips) that each hailstone made before it finally landed (on the ground).

USING STANDARD ENGLISH VERBS (PP. 105–109)

EXERCISE 1

1. packs, packed
2. are, were
3. walk, walked
4. has, had
5. need, needed

6. does, did
7. is, was
8. like, liked
9. have, had
10. am, was

EXERCISE 2

1. do, did
2. are, were
3. has, had
4. type, typed
5. counts, counted

6. have, had
7. opens, opened
8. does, did
9. plan, planned
10. am, was

EXERCISE 3

1. do, don't
2. had, decided
3. was, played
4. talked
5. asked, was

6. was
7. were, were
8. enjoyed, liked
9. started, stopped
10. am, plan

EXERCISE 4

1. changed, want
2. had
3. signed, turned
4. was, were
5. did, were, did

6. observed, had
7. watched, helped
8. had
9. imagined, had
10. needs, are, am

EXERCISE 5

1. Last month, my English teacher *assigned* a narration essay.
2. We *had* one week to finish a rough draft.
3. The sentence is correct.
4. They *were* about holiday traditions in different families.
5. In one essay, the writer *explained* the tradition of Thanksgiving at her house.
6. I *liked* the part about making pies for the adults and candy for the kids.
7. The second essay *outlined* the steps another family went through to prepare for Chinese New Year.
8. That one *had* even more details about food and gifts for the children.
9. The sentence is correct.
10. I *finished* my rough draft in one night; it *described* my dad's obsession with Halloween.

Most people believe that they *have* the best pets. I think that we have the cutest pet hamster in the world. Her name is Toots. The name *comes* from the little dog that *dies* in the movie *Lassie Come Home.* Our Toots *doesn't* look like that dog, but she *has* something about her that reminds us of it. The dog in the movie *protects* her owner from some really mean men. When the men try to beat the man who *owns* her, Toots is so brave. She *jumps* in front of her owner and saves him. Our hamster is small but fearless too, so her name is Toots.

USING REGULAR AND IRREGULAR VERBS (PP. 114–118)

EXERCISE 1
1. eat
2. eat
3. eating
4. eaten
5. ate
6. eats
7. eat
8. eaten
9. ate
10. eat

EXERCISE 2
1. buy, bought
2. know, knew
3. is, are
4. agree, agree
5. told, telling
6. sit, sat
7. having, have
8. got, getting
9. need, need
10. am, are

EXERCISE 3
1. took, supposed
2. did, earned
3. called, told, feel
4. thought, was
5. leaving, drove, saw
6. felt, knew, tell
7. tried, went (or got)
8. been, undo
9. wishes, take
10. used, called, does

EXERCISE 4
1. use, puts
2. does, do
3. transfers, spend
4. is, like, choose
5. does, wants
6. trusts, is
7. imagine, made
8. talking, asked, worries
9. looked, said, lived, understand
10. wonder, is

EXERCISE 5

1. lying, fell

2. was, done

3. wearing, shielded

4. lain, woke, realized, happened

5. felt, started

6. passed, turned, began

7. describe, experienced

8. was, felt, saw

9. looked, taped, was, protected, wearing

10. had, felt

PROGRESS TEST (P. 119)

1. B.   (incorrect verb form) As soon as I *finished* the test, the bell rang.

2. A.   (fragment, incomplete verb) School supplies *can be ordered* over the Internet.

3. A.   (run-on) Our assignment required a trip to the museum, and I love museums.

4. B.   (incorrect word form) I should *have* gone to the library sooner.

5. A.   (incorrect word form) We were *supposed* to lock the door after class.

6. B.   (incorrect word form) *They're* going away for spring break, and I'm staying at home.

7. B.   (incorrect word form) We were *surprised* that it was delivered on time.

8. A.   (incorrect verb form) In my math class, we've already *taken* three quizzes.

9. B.   (run-on) Nothing worked, so we all got off the bus and waited for another one.

10. A.   (fragment) I don't like the taste of grapefruits and lemons.

MAINTAINING SUBJECT-VERB AGREEMENT (PP. 122–126)

EXERCISE 1

1. think, picture

2. are, live

3. is

4. encounter

5. goes, looks

6. have, defend

7. tease, taunt, gives, leaves

8. run, make

9. is, flicks, kicks

10. work, swoop, pounce

EXERCISE 2

1. is, call
2. is, are, has
3. is, are, is
4. have, is
5. are, are
6. experiences, has
7. are, functions
8. determine
9. seems
10. affect, tend

EXERCISE 3

1. wrinkles
2. is
3. absorbs
4. absorb
5. soak, have
6. swells, expands
7. result
8. doesn't
9. block
10. take, get

EXERCISE 4

1. are, involve
2. suffer
3. are
4. come, lead
5. start, works, plays
6. starts
7. are
8. cause
9. is
10. warn

EXERCISE 5

1. is
2. has
3. starts
4. puts, wants
5. likes
6. have, looks
7. let, wants
8. have
9. helps, turn
10. am, is

PROOFREADING EXERCISE

I exercise in the gardens near my house several times a week. The fresh air and pretty scenery ~~refreshes~~ *refresh* me and make me happy. There ~~is~~ *are* several paths I can follow each day. One of my favorite walks ~~go~~ *goes* up a steep hill and down through a grove of ferns. The droplets of water on the ferns ~~splashes~~ *splash* on me as I brush past them. Then the path ~~open~~ *opens* into a grassy area that ~~take~~ *takes* my breath away sometimes. The late afternoon sunlight ~~shine~~ *shines* through the branches of a few large trees, and it ~~create~~ *creates* beautiful shadows on top of the grass. Another of the paths goes straight between a row of tall, narrow trees. The trunks of the trees ~~is~~ *are* smooth, but their leafy tops ~~sways~~ *sway* in the wind because they are so high. I love my afternoon walks in the gardens.

AVOIDING SHIFTS IN TIME (PP. 128–129)

1. Plastic surgery helps many people look better and feel better about themselves. Of course, there *are* stories of unnecessary surgeries and even heartbreaking mistakes. People *can* make their own decisions about whether plastic surgery *is* right for them. Dogs, however, can't communicate what they want. Nevertheless, some people *take* their dogs in for cosmetic surgeries, such as tummy tucks and face-lifts. Just like humans, dogs sometimes *need* surgery to correct painful or unhealthy conditions. A dog with a low-hanging tummy *can* get an infection from scratches that *are* caused by rocks on the ground. And another dog may require a face-lift to help it stay clean when it eats. Animal lovers *are* worried that some canine plastic surgeries *are* done without good reasons.

2. The paragraph is correct.

3. I really enjoyed my winter break this year. It was too short, of course, but I *made* the most of the time I had. My extended family had a reunion at my aunt's house in St. Louis. I didn't pack enough coats and sweaters, but the loving atmosphere *kept* me warm. Once I *was* back in the same room with my cousins, we goofed off just the way we used to when we were kids. One night my four closest cousins and I *stayed* up after everyone else *was* in bed. We played board games and ate buttery popcorn and got the game pieces all greasy just like the old days. Overall, my trip to St. Louis with its late-night game marathon *was* the highlight of my winter vacation.

RECOGNIZING VERBAL PHRASES (PP. 131–135)

EXERCISE 1

1. Some travelers want [to know how [to behave in other countries]].

2. *Behave Yourself!* is a book [written to help such people].

3. It outlines what [to do] and what not [to do] in countries around the world.

4. In Austria, for example, [cutting your food with a fork] is more polite than [cutting it with a knife].

5. In Egypt, [nodding the head upward]—not [shaking the head from side to side]—means "no."

6. In the Netherlands, [complimenting people about their clothes] is not a good idea.

7. An Italian diner will fold lettuce into a bite-size piece with the fork and knife instead of [cutting it].

8. A common mistake that people make in many countries is [to stand with their hands on their hips].

9. This posture and [pointing at anything with the fingers] are thought [to be very rude] and even [threatening].

10. Travelers should study any country before [visiting it] in order [to avoid [confusing] or [offending] anyone].

EXERCISE 2

1. [Finding the exact origin of the game of poker] is probably impossible.

2. Some think that it started as a game [played in China around a thousand years ago].

3. Others have a theory [placing its origins in an ancient Persian game] that involves [using twenty-five cards with five suits].

4. Poker also has similarities to the game "poque," [played by the French when they colonized New Orleans in the 1700s].

5. [Betting] and [bluffing] were both aspects of poque.

6. So was a deck of cards [containing the four suits] [used in modern poker]: diamonds, hearts, spades, and clubs.

7. In the 1800s, Jonathan H. Green wrote about a pastime [called the "[cheating] game."]

8. He observed that people [traveling down the Mississippi river] enjoyed this card game.

9. Green used the name "poker" for the first time [to identify it].

10. Since human [beings] have always loved games, [tracing the history of one game] can be difficult.

EXERCISE 3

1. The idea of [home-schooling children] has become more popular recently.

2. Many parents have decided [to teach kids themselves] instead of [sending them to public or private school].

3. There are many different reasons [to choose [home-schooling]].

4. In Hollywood, for instance, child actors often must use [home-schooling] due to their schedules.

5. The [home-schooling] option allows for one of their parents, or a special teacher, [to continue] [to instruct them on the set].

6. Other parents simply want [to be directly involved in their child's [learning]].

7. Many school districts <u>have</u> special independent study "schools," [offering parents the structure and materials] that they <u>need</u> [to provide an appropriate curriculum on their own].

8. Children <u>do</u> all of their [reading] and [writing] at home, with their parents [guiding them along the way].

9. The family <u>meets</u> with the independent study school's teacher regularly [to go over the child's work] and [to clarify any points of confusion].

10. Many parents <u>would like</u> [to have the time] to home-school their children].

1. [Mixing light of different colors] sometimes <u>produces</u> [surprising] results.

2. It <u>is</u> an entirely different process from [mixing colored paints].

3. For example, [mixing red and green paints] <u>produces</u> a dark brown color.

4. But [mixing red and green light] <u>produces</u> yellow light.

5. [Mixing paints] <u>is</u> an example of a process [called color subtraction].

6. [Mixing colored light] <u>is</u> an example of color addition.

7. White light <u>is made</u> up of [colored] light.

8. When [looking at a rainbow], you <u>are seeing</u> sunlight.

9. The band of color in a rainbow <u>is called</u> a spectrum, [containing seven basic colors]—red, orange, yellow, green, blue, indigo, and violet.

10. Light of these colors <u>can be recombined</u> [to form white light].

1. John Steinbeck, author of *The Grapes of Wrath,* <u>was</u> the first native of California [to receive the Nobel Prize for literature].

2. [Calling his hometown of Salinas "Lettuceberg,"] Steinbeck's [writing] <u>made</u> the area famous.

3. At the time, not everyone <u>liked</u> the attention [brought by his portrayals of life in *Cannery Row* and other works].

4. Steinbeck's father <u>was</u> the treasurer of Monterey County for ten years, [working also for the Spreckels company].

5. John Steinbeck <u>tried</u> [to find satisfaction in his birthplace], [enrolling in and quitting his studies at Stanford University many times].

6. Finally, Steinbeck moved to New York, [distancing himself from his California roots].

7. Steinbeck won the Nobel Prize in 1962, [revealing the literary world's esteem for his work].

8. Not [writing anything of the caliber of the Salinas stories] while [living in New York], Steinbeck did return to California before he died in 1968.

9. In 1972, the Salinas library changed its name, [to be known thereafter as the John Steinbeck Library].

10. And the house Steinbeck was born in became a restaurant and then a full-[fledged] museum [chronicling the life of Salinas' most [celebrated] citizen].

PARAGRAPH EXERCISE

Mars glows like a [burning] ember [embedded in the night], and as a result it has long been linked with the color red. . . .

Nonetheless, Mars is not red. It is russet and brown, an autumnal, rust-[colored] world, as *Viking 1* dramatically showed. The rocky soil is the color of clay, thanks to the presence of iron oxides, and the sky, [suffused with large particles of dust], is neither blue, as we might imagine, nor black, as some scientists had expected, but apricot, salmon, and peach.

The air on this coral-[colored] world is 95 percent carbon dioxide, so it is impossible [to breathe]. . . .

Mars is beautiful in its way, even though, [compared to the blue and verdant Earth], it is a harsh and unlivable steppe. On the other hand, [compared to the [blistering] hell of Venus], it is not half bad.

SENTENCE WRITING

Your sentences may vary, but make sure that your verbals are not actually the main verbs of your clauses. You should be able to double underline your real verbs, as we have done here.

[Shopping for holiday food] is fun.

[Earning enough money for a vacation] can take a long time.

I like [giving my dog a bath].

My dog <u>hates</u> [wearing a leash].

We <u>tried</u> [to drive all the way up the coast in one day].

Neither of them <u>knows</u> how [to sew].

They <u>need</u> [to talk about their problems].

[Given a chance], I could <u>climb</u> that rope.

The [baked] apples <u>tasted</u> delicious.

Projects [built by Habitat for Humanity] are <u>supported</u> by the community.

CORRECTING MISPLACED OR DANGLING MODIFIERS (PP. 136–139)

Answers may vary. Corrections are in *italics*.

EXERCISE 1

1. They finally found their lost credit card; *it had been lying under the table for a week.*

2. *Walking down the hall, she located the door to the auditorium.*

3. The sentence is correct.

4. *My doctor told me to drink extra water after taking an aspirin.*

5. The sentence is correct.

6. Our mail carrier *tripped on a crack in the sidewalk and fell.*

7. *Since we argued nonstop,* the road trip was not as much fun as we hoped it would be.

8. The sentence is correct.

9. The sentence is correct.

10. The students immediately liked their substitute teacher, *who smiled nicely at everyone.*

EXERCISE 2

1. *As I was walking up the stairs,* I found a cell phone.

2. *Because that play was full of surprises, we loved it* and want to see it again.

3. *The tires on his car* need to be replaced.

4. *Because I scribbled it quickly,* I could not read the phone number.

5. The sentence is correct.

6. With outdated functions and styling, *my cell phone needs to be upgraded.*

7. *After I took several photographs,* the shadows on the trees disappeared.

8. The sentence is correct.

9. The sentence is correct.

10. *After he talked to the doctor,* his ear started to feel better.

EXERCISE 3

1. The sentence is correct.

2. The sentence is correct.

3. *In the store,* she kicked her mother by accident.

4. *Searching outside the house,* the inspector found a few termites.

5. The sentence is correct.

6. *Waiting in line at the new restaurant, I couldn't wait to taste the food.*

7. The sentence is correct.

8. *The State of California offers a test for students who are sixteen to get out of high school early.*

9. The sentence is correct.

10. The sentence is correct.

EXERCISE 4

1. *After I got a headache from the fumes,* the ferry finally made it across the river.

2. *That carnival sold cotton candy full of empty calories, but it was the best I'd ever tasted.*

3. *Two months after we moved out,* our old apartment is still empty.

4. *In her e-mail message,* she promised to return the library books.

5. *Sitting in small groups,* the students took the notes.

6. *Before we said goodnight,* the porch light burned out.

7. Our hostess showed us her favorite room; *it was decorated beautifully.*

8. *I saw a tiny gray mouse* scampering along the baseboards of the cabin.

9. The sentence is correct.

10. All along the highway, volunteers *wearing special T-shirts* planted trees.

EXERCISE 5

1. Feeling the excitement of the first day of school, *I left my backpack behind.*

2. We saw the new movie that everyone is talking about; *it was full of explosions.*

3. My cousins and I, *wearing our pajamas,* always wrapped our gifts on the night before the holiday.

4. *Now that he practices for an hour a day,* his tennis has improved.

5. *Rising and falling several times a year,* the price of gasoline fluctuates.

6. The sentence is correct.

7. *Hiking in the nearby mountains,* they discovered a new trail.

8. She felt pressure *from her parents* to get good grades.

9. The sentence is correct.

10. The sentence is correct.

PROOFREADING EXERCISE

Corrections are *italicized.* Yours may differ slightly.

Hoping to become famous and wealthy, a man in Edinburgh, Scotland, has invented a device. *Located just above the trunk and visible from behind,* the device is a variation on the center-mounted brake light used in the design of many new cars. Instead of just a solid red brake light, however, this invention displays to other drivers *words* written in bold, red-lighted letters.

With simplicity in mind, *the inventor limited the machine's vocabulary* to three words: "Sorry," "Thanks," and "Help." After making an aggressive lane change, *we could use the machine* to apologize. Or after being allowed to go ahead of someone, we could thank the considerate person responsible. Of course, *with the use* of the "Help" display, we could summon fellow citizens for assistance.

And there is no need to worry about operating the device while driving. With three easy-to-reach buttons, *we could activate the messages* without taking our eyes off the road.

FOLLOWING SENTENCE PATTERNS (PP. 142–146)

EXERCISE 1

1.   S   LV   Desc
Horatio Greenough was a sculptor (in the 1800s).

2.   S   AV   Obj
Greenough created a controversial statue (of George Washington).

3.   S   AV   Obj   S   LV   Desc
The statue weighed twelve tons, but its weight was not the reason (for the controversy).

               S   AV   Obj

4. The controversial aspect (of the statue) involved Washington's clothes.

        S   AV   Obj

5. The statue portrayed Washington (in a toga-like garment).

            S   S   S   LV   Desc   Desc

6. His stomach, chest, and arms were bare and very muscular.

        S   AV

7. One part (of the toga) draped (over the statue's raised right arm).

             S   AV

8. The bare-chested statue (of Washington) stood (in the rotunda) (of the Capitol) (for only three years).

      S   AV   Obj

9. Officials moved the statue many times.

            S   AV

10. (In 1962), it arrived (in its final home) (at the American History Museum).

EXERCISE 2

         S   AV   Obj

1. Many people get migraine headaches.

           S   LV   Desc

2. These headaches can be extremely painful.

     S   AV

3. People (with migraines) may also suffer (from nausea and dizziness).

           S   AV   Obj   Obj

4. Migraine sufferers avoid bright lights and loud sounds.

          S   AV   Obj

5. These sensations cause a different kind (of discomfort).

           S   AV   Obj

6. Some medicines reduce the pain (of migraine headaches).

          S   AV

7. Other drugs help (with the additional symptoms).

             S   LV Desc

8. No migraine treatment is perfect (for everyone).

     S   AV   Obj

9. Scientists have been studying migraine headaches (for years).

     S   LV   Desc

10. A cure (for migraines) is long overdue.

EXERCISE 3

         S   LV   Desc
1. <u>Sleep</u> <u>is</u> an important part (of life).
          S   S   AV   Obj
2. <u>Animals</u> and <u>humans</u> <u>use</u> sleep (as a vacation) (for their brains and bodies).
           S   AV   Obj
3. Some <u>facts</u> (about sleep) <u>might surprise</u> people.
          S   AV   Obj   S   AV
4. Large <u>animals</u> <u>require</u> less sleep than small <u>animals</u> <u>do</u>.
           S   AV
5. A typical <u>cat</u> <u>will sleep</u> (for twelve hours) (in a day).
               S   AV
6. An ordinary <u>elephant</u> <u>will sleep</u> (for only three hours).
            S   AV   Obj   Obj
7. Smaller <u>animals</u> <u>use</u> their brains and bodies (at higher rates).
              S   AV   Obj
8. Therefore, <u>they</u> <u>need</u> many hours (of sleep).
            S   LV Desc
9. The <u>reverse</u> <u>is</u> true (for large animals).
         S   AV
10. <u>Humans</u> <u>fall</u> (between cats and elephants) (for their sleep requirements).

EXERCISE 4

       S   LV   Desc   Desc
1. <u>Cakes</u> <u>can be</u> plain or fancy.
                  S   S   AV Obj
2. Most grocery <u>stores</u> and almost all <u>bakeries</u> <u>sell</u> cakes.
        S   AV
3. <u>They</u> <u>range</u> (in price) depending (on size, occasion, and amount of decoration).

   [*Depending* begins a verbal phrase.]

        S   AV
4. A <u>cake</u> (with a "Happy Birthday" inscription) <u>will</u> usually <u>cost</u> thirty (to fifty)

   Obj
   dollars.

          S   LV   Desc
5. Wedding <u>cakes</u>, however, <u>are</u> often very expensive.
                 S   AV   Obj
6. An elaborate wedding <u>cake</u> <u>may cost</u> several hundred or even a thousand dollars.

                                                S   LV
7. The multilayered traditional white wedding <u>cake</u> still <u>seems</u> the most popular

Desc
kind.

                              S   AV   Obj
8. These delicate <u>structures</u> <u>need</u> special care (during transportation).

                    S   AV   Obj
9. Some <u>couples</u> <u>order</u> two or more smaller cakes (for the occasion).

              S   AV   Obj   Obj
10. <u>People</u> sometimes <u>save</u> a slice or section (of their wedding cake) (as a memento).

EXERCISE 5

                              S   AV   Obj
1. (In 1998), Sotheby's auction <u>house</u> <u>sold</u> a piece (of 60-year-old **wedding cake**)
(for an amazing price).

        S   AV
2. <u>It</u> <u>had belonged</u> (to the Duke and Duchess) (of Windsor).

                                S   AV
3. (On June 3, 1937), the famous <u>couple</u> <u>married</u> (in France).

                                        S   AV   Obj
4. (On the day) (of their wedding), <u>they</u> <u>put</u> a piece (of cake) (in a pink box) and

      AV   Obj
<u>tied</u> a pink bow (around it).

        S   AV   Obj   S   AV
5. <u>They</u> <u>identified</u> its contents as "a piece of our wedding cake"; <u>they</u> <u>initialed</u> and

      AV   Obj   S   AV Obj
<u>dated</u> the box, and <u>they</u> <u>kept</u> it (as a memento) (for the rest) (of their lives).

                          S   S   AV   LV Desc
6. This couple's <u>relationship</u>, which <u>began</u> (in the 1930s), <u>was</u> one (of the most
famous love affairs) (in history).

              S   AV   Obj
7. The <u>Duke</u> (of Windsor) <u>gave up</u> the throne (of England) to be (with Wallis

                                      S   AV
Simpson), the woman that <u>he</u> <u>loved</u>. [*To be* begins a verbal phrase.]

                          S   LV   Desc
8. Unfortunately, <u>she</u> <u>was</u> a divorced American woman and <u>could not</u>, therefore,

      AV   Obj   S   AV
<u>marry</u> the king (of England), so <u>he</u> <u>abdicated</u>.

S

9. The pre-auction <u>estimate</u> (for the box) containing the piece (of their wedding

      LV   Desc

cake) <u>was</u> five hundred (to a thousand) <u>dollars</u>. [*Containing* begins a

verbal phrase.]

                S   AV   S   LV

10. When the <u>gavel</u> <u>came down</u>, the high <u>bid</u> (by a couple) (from San Francisco) <u>was</u>

   Desc

$29,900.

PARAGRAPH EXERCISE

     S   LV   Desc   S   AV

<u>Color</u> <u>is</u> perhaps the most powerful tool (at an artist's disposal). <u>It</u> <u>affects</u> our

  Obj   AV   Obj

emotions (beyond thought) and <u>can convey</u> any <u>mood</u>, (from delight) (to despair).

S   LV   Desc   Desc   AV   Obj   AV   Obj

<u>It</u> <u>can be</u> subtle or dramatic, <u>capture</u> attention or <u>stimulate</u> desire. [Used more

                                          S   AV   Obj

boldly and freely today than ever before], <u>color</u> <u>bathes</u> our vision (with an infinite

variety) (of sensations),(from clear, brilliant hues) (to subtle, elusive mixtures).

   S   LV   Desc

<u>Color</u> <u>is</u> the province (of all artists), (from painters and potters) (to product

designers and computer artists).

AVOIDING CLICHÉS, AWKWARD PHRASING, AND WORDINESS (PP. 150–151)

Your revisions may differ.

1. If I had to choose my favorite class from high school, it would be the cook-ing class that I took in tenth grade. The class was an independent study, so I got to choose my own meals to cook and eat. The assignments were all the same: re-search a meal from a particular country or culture, buy the ingredients for the meal, and learn to cook it. To get a grade, I brought my teacher a sample of the food along with my report about making it. Then I received my grade.

2. *While You Were Sleeping* is one of my favorite holiday movies. I love the scenes in the snow and at holiday parties. In the story, Sandra Bullock's character saves a man's life after he is injured at the train station where she works. He goes into a coma, and she pretends to be his fiancée. While he is unconscious, she gets close to his whole family, especially his brother. Suddenly, the man in the coma wakes up. Eventually, everyone realizes that Bullock's character and the man's brother belong together, and the story ends happily.

3. Ancient civilizations mummified the remains of adults, children, and animals. Mummification was a way to help these beings enter into the next world and to show them respect. One mummy of an Eskimo baby found in Greenland dated back to the 1400s. It was wrapped in beautiful fur to protect it from the cold. In Egypt, archeologists discovered the mummies of cats, crocodiles, cows, baboons, and birds. In Alaska, experts found a huge, perfectly preserved bison mummy that was over 35,000 years old. A big lion's tooth in its neck revealed how it probably died.

CORRECTING FOR PARALLEL STRUCTURE (PP. 153–157)

Your answers may differ from these possible revisions.

EXERCISE 1

1. I have read about many foods that can help people stay healthy and live longer.

2. Eating whole wheat bread benefits the brain and increases energy.

3. Apples contain ingredients to aid memory, keep lungs healthy, and prevent cancer.

4. Kidney beans can reduce cholesterol, increase energy, and stabilize moods.

5. Oranges fight inflammation and loss of eyesight.

6. Substances found in fish can prevent heart problems, depression, and high cholesterol.

7. Milk boosts the nervous system and postpones aging.

8. Antioxidants in red grapes benefit the heart, protect the brain, and prevent cancer.

9. The sentence is correct.

10. By eating these foods, people can live longer, stay stronger, and be happier.

EXERCISE 2

1. The sentence is correct.

2. The process involves two steps: planning and gathering certain supplies.

3. The sentence is correct.

4. The sentence is correct.

5. Where would you go, and how would you get there?

6. The sentence is correct.

7. The adults, teenagers, and children in a family should carry those phone numbers with them.

8. The most important supplies for emergencies include water, food, a flashlight, a radio, and batteries.

9. First-aid kits can be made or purchased.

10. Reading, understanding, and updating insurance policies is the final step in the process.

EXERCISE 3

1. I like coffee and tea.

2. I've heard that coffee is bad for you, but tea is good for you.

3. It must not be the caffeine that's bad because both coffee and tea have caffeine.

4. The sentence is correct.

5. All teas are supposed to be healthy, but green tea is supposed to be the healthiest.

6. The sentence is correct.

7. I love orange pekoe tea with tons of milk and sugar.

8. The sentence is correct.

9. I know that all coffee comes from coffee beans, but I didn't know that all tea comes from *Camellia sinensis* leaves.

10. The sentence is correct.

EXERCISE 4

1. I was washing my car two weeks ago and noticed a few bees buzzing around the roof of my garage.

2. I didn't worry about it at the time, but I should have.

3. The sentence is correct.

4. The sentence is correct.

5. They flew in a pattern as if they were riding on a roller coaster or over waves.

6. The sentence is correct.

7. There was nothing I could do but wait in my car until they went away.

8. Finally, the bees flew straight up into the air and disappeared.

9. Once inside my house, I opened the phone book and called a bee expert.

10. The sentence is correct.

EXERCISE 5

Your revisions may differ.

1. Experts give the following tips to those who want to get the most out of a doctor visit.

2. First, avoid getting frustrated if you have to wait a long time in the reception area or the exam room.

3. Always answer the doctor's questions first; then ask a few of your own.

4. Inquire about a referral to a specialist if you think you need one.

5. Find out about other treatments besides the one the doctor first recommends.

6. Ask about any tests that the doctor orders and determine how to get in touch with the doctor about the results.

7. Take the time to ask about prescription drugs' side effects and optional medicines.

8. Try to be calm in your discussions with the doctor.

9. Finally, be prepared to wait in a long line at the pharmacy.

10. If you follow these suggestions when visiting a doctor, you will be more informed and feel more involved in your own treatment.

PROOFREADING EXERCISE
Your revisions may differ.

Shirley Temple was born in 1928 and discovered in 1931 when she was just three years old. Someone recognized her natural talent at a dance lesson and asked her to be in movies. She starred in many films that are still popular today. Among them are *Heidi, Rebecca of Sunnybrook Farm,* and *Curly Top.* Directors loved Shirley's acting style and her ability to do a scene in only one take, but not everyone trusted Shirley Temple. Graham Greene was sued when he claimed that Shirley was really about thirty years old and a dwarf. Little Shirley's parents helped with her career and earned money for their efforts. In the early days, the studios paid her mother several hundred dollars a week to put fifty-six curlers in Shirley's hair each night. That way, her famous ringlets would always be perfect and consistent. Shirley's father managed her money, so much money that at one point Shirley Temple was among the ten highest paid people in America. It was 1938, and she was only ten years old.

USING PRONOUNS (PP. 162–165)

EXERCISE 1

1. I
2. I
3. she and I
4. she
5. she and I

6. I
7. she
8. her and me
9. her
10. me

Your revisions may differ.

1. its

2. its

3. its

4. their

5. One day last week, the passengers had to gather their belongings . . . .

6. their

7. their

8. The passengers did their best to hide their annoyance . . . .

9. As the passengers stepped off the bus at the end of the line, the driver thanked them for their patience and understanding.

10. it

EXERCISE 3
Your revisions may differ.

1. its

2. he

3. Students will buy their own materials for the sculpture class.

4. their (for players) *or* its (for tournament)

5. she

6. Everyone in the class was allowed to turn the essay in late thanks to the extended deadline.

7. me

8. You and I

9. them

10. I

EXERCISE 4
Your revisions may differ.

1. My burrito exploded as I was cooking it in the microwave.

2. The student didn't understand what the librarian was saying and told her so.

3. The decorations blew away while we were putting them on the tables.

4. Our cat sleeps all the time, so she is a boring pet.

5. Samantha asked her friend, "Why wasn't I invited to join the debate team?"

6. The sentence is correct.

7. He finished printing his book report, turned off the printer, and put his report in his folder.

8. Max told his brother, "My bike has a flat tire."

9. Buying my parking pass early gave me one less thing to worry about.

10. Irene's mom lets Irene break school rules by using her cell phone on campus.

EXERCISE 5

1. As the raccoon was walking across the tree limb, the limb fell.

2. Groups of children can be hard to manage.

3. I signed the application with a pen and put the application in an envelope.

4. When I placed the bowls on top of the plates, the plates broke.

5. Sheila told her friend Helen, "I have made a mistake." *or* Sheila told her friend Helen, "You have made a mistake."

6. Studying hard for the test didn't guarantee we would get a good grade.

7. The sentence is correct.

8. Luke's tutor noticed that Luke's pencil was dull, so he asked Luke to sharpen it. *or* The tutor asked, "Luke, will you sharpen my pencil?"

9. Taking a lot of tests in that class is exhausting.

10. The sentence is correct.

PROOFREADING EXERCISE
Corrections are *italicized*.

My daughter and *I* drove up the coast to visit a little zoo I had heard about. *The zoo was a hundred miles away, and the drive took* about two hours. Once *she* and I arrived, we saw the petting zoo area and wanted to pet the baby animals, but *the zoo employees* wouldn't let us. They said that it was the baby animals' resting time, so we couldn't pet them. Then we got to the farm animals. There was a prize-winning hog. *When the huge pig was lying down, it was as big as a couch.* My daughter liked the hog best of all, and as she and I drove home in the car, *that big pig* was all she could talk about.

AVOIDING SHIFTS IN PERSON (PP. 166–167)

1. Americans have always had more than they actually need. Americans have gotten used to having as much food, water, and clothes as they want. Restaurants throw away plates and plates of food every day. If people don't want something, they throw it in the trash. But a lot of people have started to think differently. Recycling doesn't just involve aluminum cans and plastic bottles. Americans can re-cycle food, water, and clothes if they think more creatively and responsibly than they've been doing in the past. People can change the society's view of recycling by just doing it.

2. The paragraph is correct.

3. If I had a choice to live in the city or the country, I would choose the city. I would choose the city because I am surrounded by other people there, and it feels friendly. The country is too quiet. There is dirt everywhere, flies flying around in the sky, bugs—which I hate—crawling on the floor inside and out. The city is a place where the lights are always on. Yes, I deal with pollution, smog, and crowds, but it just feels like home to me. A city house can be any size, shape, and color. All the houses in the country look the same to me. No matter who the country people are, they have a white house and a big red barn. I have to admit that I have only been to the country a couple of times to visit my relatives, but the city would have to be the place for me.

REVIEW OF SENTENCE STRUCTURE ERRORS (PP. 168–170)

Your corrections may differ.

1. B. not parallel (We saw a play on Broadway, walked down Fifth Avenue, *and visited the Statue of Liberty.*)

2. A. wordy (*The problem is that* the ATM machine sometimes runs out of cash.)

3. A. run-on sentence (I planned to go on the field trip to the museum, but my car broke down.)

4. B. incorrect pronoun (She stayed with my lab partner and *me* during our whole experiment.)

5. A. pronoun agreement error (Everyone in the graduation ceremony received *a* fake diploma.)

6. B. cliché (I knew that it was *better to turn it in late than not at all.*)

7. A. subject-verb agreement error (Each of the reference books I needed *was* checked out.)

8. B. run-on sentence (I do well in math classes; I also love to read the biographies. . . .)

9. B.   incorrect pronoun (*He and I* agreed that I needed to improve my footwork.)

10. A.   fragment (*The construction company who will build the new auditorium came to campus for the groundbreaking ceremony.*)

11. B.   shift in person (The tissues in *the* lungs slowly repair themselves.)

12. A.   cliché (My car *is very unpredictable.*)

13. B.   fragment (*We had* cold mashed potatoes, overcooked broccoli, and tough pork chops.)

14. B.   shift in time and awkward (Everyone's eyes *were* watering, and *everyone was* coughing.)

15. A.   dangling modifier (A brick fell on his right foot *when he was four.*)

PROOFREADING EXERCISE

Mother Tells All

I have learned the most memorable lessons about myself from my children. A mother is always on display; she has nowhere to hide. And children are like parrots; they repeat whatever they hear. If I change my mind about something, they will remind me of every word I said.

For example, last summer I told my kids that I planned to take an exercise class and lose about forty pounds. I did lose some weight, and I attended an exercise class. But I started to feel like a balloon losing air. I decided that I did not want to lose any more weight or exercise anymore. I expected my children to accept my decision.

When I stopped, one of my sons said, "Mom, you need to go back to exercise class." Then they all started telling me what to eat, and I felt horrible. I had given up these things because I wanted to, but my words were still being repeated like a nonstop alarm clock. Finally, my kids got bored with the idea of my losing weight. Sometimes, when one of them makes a joke about my "attempt" to lose weight, it hurts me that they don't understand.

From this experience, I have learned not to tell my children about a plan unless I am going to finish it. Otherwise, they will never let me forget.

PUNCTUATION AND CAPITAL LETTERS

PERIOD, QUESTION MARK, EXCLAMATION POINT, SEMICOLON, COLON, DASH (PP. 172–176)

Your answers may vary slightly, especially in the use of optional pieces of punctuation (the exclamation point and the dash).

EXERCISE 1

1. Have you heard of the phenomenon known as a "milky sea"?

2. Sailors throughout history have described this eerie condition.

3. A milky sea occurs when ocean water turns almost completely white.

4. What accounts for this milky color?

5. It is due to huge amounts of bacteria that glow with white light.

6. Until recently, no one had photographs or other visual proof of this condition.

7. In 1995, however, people took the first pictures of a milky sea off the coast of Somalia.

8. Scientists later reviewed satellite images from the same period and discovered their own startling documentation that milky seas exist.

9. The satellite photos clearly showed a long glowing white stretch of ocean water.

10. It was the size of the state of Connecticut. (or !)

EXERCISE 2

1. Wasn't the company's holiday party nice this year?

2. At first, I wasn't sure that I wanted to go; now I'm glad I did.

3. The music—especially the harp music—made everyone so calm and contented.

4. The twinkling lights in the trees on the patio gave off a beautiful light.

5. Even the cubicles around our desks looked festive.

6. The boss announced our new Employee of the Year: Ted Haynes.

7. With so many of us doing the same job, there is a lot a competition; however, all that was put aside for the party.

8. The boss's husband is nicer than I thought he would be; I enjoyed meeting him.

9. I talked with coworkers that I haven't had any fun with in a long time—even Charlie!

10. I hope that everyone will still be in a holiday spirit once we get back to work on Monday.

EXERCISE 3

1. People can learn foreign languages in several new ways these days: by practicing with a partner, by studying on long plane flights, and by listening to foreign news on the radio or watching movies in other languages.

2. The Internet allows people—especially those who want to learn a language—to correspond easily with people from other countries.

3. The exchange goes something like this: one person wants to know French; he contacts a person in France who wants to learn English.

4. The two exchange e-mails; then, as they correct each other's phrasing, they learn more about the other's language.

5. Certain audio programs and books have been designed for one purpose: to offer airline passengers a quick course in a foreign language.

6. Portable music devices usually hold book-length works; therefore, these in-flight language programs are easy to use.

7. The sentence is correct.

8. It's easy to find foreign news sites on the Internet; these radio programs feature reporters who speak clearly and use many common phrases.

9. There is a variation that anyone with a DVD player can use: most DVD menus include the option of listening to the movie dubbed in another language.

10. In this way, movies can be even more entertaining; they can also be more educational.

EXERCISE 4

1. Nancy Cartwright is a well-known actress on television; however, we never see her when she is acting.

2. Cartwright is famous for playing one part: the voice of Bart Simpson.

3. Besides her career as the most mischievous Simpson, Cartwright is married and has children of her own—a boy and a girl.

4. The sentence is correct.

5. The sentence is correct.

6. The sentence is correct.

7. Bart is perpetually ten years old; Cartwright is in her forties.

8. Bart is a boy; Cartwright is obviously a woman.

9. The sentence is correct.

10. When they yell for her to "Do Bart! Do Bart!" she declines with Bart's favorite saying: "No way, man!"

EXERCISE 5

1. What do math and origami—Japanese paper folding—have to do with each other?

2. Erik Demaine and other origami mathematicians would answer, "Everything." (or "Everything!")

3. If you have never heard of the field of origami mathematics, you're not alone.

4. Origami math is a relatively new field; back in 2003, Demaine won a "genius" award partly due to his work with origami and its applications in many fields.

5. The MacArthur Foundation awarded Demaine more than just the title "genius"; it awarded him half a million dollars. (or !)

6. At twenty, Demaine was hired as a professor by the Massachusetts Institute of Technology; he became the youngest professor MIT has ever had.

7. Erik Demaine has his father to thank for much of his education: (or ;) Martin Demaine home-schooled Erik as the two of them traveled around North America.

8. Erik was always intensely interested in academic subjects; during his travels, he and his father would consult university professors whenever Erik had questions that no one else could answer.

9. Erik Demaine continues to investigate one area in particular: the single-cut problem.

10. This problem involves folding a piece of paper—then making one cut; the result can be anything from a swan to a star, a unicorn, or any letter of the alphabet.

PROOFREADING EXERCISE

The ingredients you will need for a lemon meringue pie are lemon juice, eggs, sugar, cornstarch, flour, butter, water, and salt. First, you combine flour, salt, butter, and water for the crust and bake until lightly brown; then you mix and cook the lemon juice, egg yolks, sugar, cornstarch, butter, and water for the filling. Once the filling is poured into the cooked crust, you whip the meringue. Meringue is made of egg whites and sugar. Pile the meringue on top of the lemon filling; place the pie in the hot oven for a few minutes, and you'll have the best lemon meringue pie you've ever tasted!

COMMA RULES 1, 2, AND 3 (PP. 178–183)

EXERCISE 1

1. My cousins and I used to go fishing with our grandfather, but we rarely enjoyed it.

2. He told long stories about his old friends, and we rolled our eyes.

3. The sentence is correct.

4. Sometimes he asked us about our friends, or he told us stories about our parents when they were children.

5. Then we became interested, for the stories about our moms and dads were very funny. (Note: *For* means "because" in this sentence and is a *fanboys.*)

6. One time my cousin Joey threw a whole can of bait in the water, and my grandfather chased him all around the edge of the lake.

7. Now I know how special those times were, and I wish I could go fishing with him again.

8. The sentence is correct.

9. My cousins remember those fishing trips too, and we feel bad about how we acted sometimes.

10. Our grandfather isn't with us anymore, but we think about him all the time.

EXERCISE 2

1. I graduated from high school on June 25, 2002, in San Antonio, Texas.

2. I was lucky to have an English teacher in high school who was young, enthusiastic, and highly motivated.

3. We read essays, stories, poems, and research articles in her class.

4. One time we read a short play, chose parts to memorize, and gave a performance of it in front of the whole school.

5. The sentence is correct.

6. She was trying to teach us how to follow directions, how to explain something clearly, and how to think about what she called our "tone of voice" when we wrote.

7. We had to write a real letter of complaint about a product, a service, or an experience that was unsatisfactory to us.

8. Then we sent a copy of our letter to the company's business address, to our home address, and to Ms. Kern's school address.

9. Ms. Kern assured us that we would receive a response from the company if we explained our complaint well, asked for a reasonable solution, and used an appropriate tone.

10. In the big envelope from my company was a letter of apology, a bumper sticker, and an impressive discount coupon to use at any of the company's stores.

EXERCISE 3

1. Most people don't know how coffee is decaffeinated, do you?

2. Although there are three methods used to decaffeinate coffee, one of them is the most popular.

3. The most popular method is called water processing, drawing the caffeine from the coffee beans into a water solution and removing most of it.

4. After going through the natural water processing method, the coffee may be a little less flavorful.

5. To decaffeinate coffee another way, manufacturers add a chemical solution to the beans and then steam them to remove the leftover chemicals.

6. Compared to the water processing method, the chemical method is more "scientific" and removes more of the caffeine.

7. Finally, there is the method that infuses coffee beans with carbon dioxide gas to get rid of the caffeine.

8. Since carbon dioxide is plentiful and nontoxic, this process is also popular.

9. Even though the carbon dioxide method is the most expensive of the three ways to decaffeinate coffee, it also removes the most caffeine.

10. Whenever I drink a cup of decaf in the future, I'll wonder which method was used to remove the caffeine.

EXERCISE 4

1. When the government issued the Susan B. Anthony dollar coin on July 2, 1979, it met with some disapproval.

2. People didn't dislike the person on the coin, but they did dislike the size and color of the coin.

3. It was nearly the same size as a quarter, had a rough edge like a quarter's, and was the same color as a quarter.

4. It differed from a quarter in that it was faceted around the face, was lighter in weight, and was worth four times as much.

5. Due to these problems, the Susan B. Anthony dollar was discontinued, and in January 2000, the government issued a new golden dollar.

6. Like the Anthony dollar, the new coin portrayed the image of a famous American woman.

7. She was the young Native American guide and interpreter for the Lewis and Clark expedition, and her name was Sacagawea.

8. Although the Sacagawea dollar was roughly the same size as the Anthony dollar, it had a smooth wide edge, and its gold color made it easy to distinguish from a quarter.

9. Sacagawea's journey included hardship, suffering, and illness, but it also revealed her incredible knowledge, courage, and strength.

10. While the men on the expedition had only themselves to worry about, Sacagawea made the treacherous journey to the Pacific with her baby strapped to her back.

EXERCISE 5

1. In the past, people believed that emeralds held magical powers.

2. They were supposed to cure disease, lengthen life, and protect innocence.

3. Part of their appeal was their rarity, for emeralds are even rarer than diamonds.

4. Geologists have been mystified by emeralds because they are produced through a unique process, the blending of chromium vanadium and beryllium.

5. These substances almost never occur together, except in emeralds.

6. In South Africa, Pakistan, and Brazil, emeralds were created by intrusions of granite millions of years ago.

7. These areas are known for their beautiful gems, but emeralds from Colombia are the largest, greenest, and most sparkling of all.

8. In Colombia, the makeup of the sedimentary rock accounts for the difference.

9. Instead of the granite found in other emerald-rich countries, the predominant substance in Colombia is black shale.

10. Even though emeralds can be synthesized, a real one always contains a trapped bit of fluid, and jewelers call this tiny imperfection a "garden."

PROOFREADING EXERCISE

I couldn't believe it, but there I was in the pilot's seat of an airplane. I had casually signed up for a course in flying at the aviation school and hadn't expected to start flying right away. The instructor told me what to do, and I did it. When I turned the stick to the right, the plane turned right. When I turned it to the left, the plane went left. Actually, it was very similar to driving a car. Most of my practice involved landing, bringing the plane in softly and safely. After many hours of supervised flying, my time to solo came, and I was

really excited. I covered the checklist on the ground, took off without any problems, and landed like a professional. On May 8, 2005, I became a licensed pilot,
so now I can pursue my dream of being a private pilot for a rock star.

SENTENCE WRITING

Here are some possible combinations. Yours may differ.

> I take ski trips in the winter, but I go hiking in the summer, so I like hiking
> better.

> Tutors will not correct a student's paper, but they will explain how to clarify
> ideas, add stronger details, and improve organization.

> When Charles bought his first car, he bought a big one and got a good
> price, but Charles should have thought more about gas mileage because
> now he spends over a hundred dollars a month on gas.

COMMA RULES 4, 5, AND 6 (PP. 186–190)

EXERCISE 1

1. This year's Feast of Lanterns in Pacific Grove, I think, was better than last year's.

2. The sentence is correct.

3. The sentence is correct.

4. Certainly, the weather was perfect this year.

5. The sentence is correct.

6. Laurie and Jane, who decorated their houses, were among the unsung heroes
   of the weeklong festival.

7. The sentence is correct.

8. Adrienne and Andrea, two volunteers at the Pet Parade, were also dancers in
   the ballet.

9. The salads at the Feast of Salads, I have to say, were better last year.

10. The sentence is correct.

EXERCISE 2

1. We trust, of course, that people who get their driver's licenses know how to
   drive.

2. The sentence is correct.

3. The sentence is correct.

4. Mr. Kraft, who tests drivers for their licenses, makes the streets safer for all of us.

5. The sentence is correct.

6. Therefore, we may understand when we fail the driving test ourselves.

7. The driver's seat, we know, is a place of tremendous responsibility.

8. The sentence is correct.

9. The sentence is correct.

10. No one, we believe, should take that responsibility lightly.

EXERCISE 3

1. The sentence is correct, or commas could be used around "Ms. Gonzalez."

2. The sentence is correct.

3. My daughter's friend Harry doesn't get along with her best friend, Jenny.

4. My daughter's best friend, Jenny, doesn't get along with one of her other friends, Harry.

5. The tiger, which is a beautiful and powerful animal, symbolizes freedom.

6. The sentence is correct.

7. The sentence is correct.

8. Kim and Teresa, who helped set up the chairs, were allowed to sit in the front row.

9. My car, which had a tracking device, was easy to find when it was stolen.

10. The sentence is correct.

EXERCISE 4

1. Arthur S. Heineman, a California architect, designed and built the world's first motel in the mid-1920s.

2. He chose the perfect location, the city of San Luis Obispo, which was midway between Los Angeles and San Francisco.

3. Heineman, an insightful man of business, understood the need for inexpensive drive-in accommodations on long motor vehicle trips.

4. Hotels, which required reservations and offered only high-priced rooms within one large structure, just didn't fulfill the needs of motorists.

5. Heineman envisioned his "Motor Hotel," or Mo-Tel, as a place where the parking spaces for the cars were right next to separate bungalow-style apartments for the passengers.

6. Heineman's idea was so new that, when he put up his "Motel" sign, several residents of the area told him to fire the sign's painter, who couldn't even spell the word *hotel*.

7. The sentence is correct.

8. Heineman's Milestone Mo-Tel, the world's first motel, opened in San Luis Obispo in 1925.

9. Before Heineman's company, the Milestone Interstate Corporation, could successfully trademark the name "Mo-Tel," other builders adopted the style and made *motel* a generic term.

10. Much of the original Milestone Mo-Tel building, now called the Motel Inn, still stands on the road between L.A. and San Francisco.

EXERCISE 5

1. I bought a book, *The Story of the "Titanic,"* because I am interested in famous events in history.

2. This book, written by Frank O. Braynard, is a collection of postcards about the ill-fated ocean liner.

3. The book's postcards, four on each page, can be pulled apart and mailed like regular ones.

4. The sentence is correct.

5. The blank sides, where messages and addresses go, include brief captions of the images on the front of the cards. (Note: This sentence could be left without commas.)

6. The book's actual content, the part written by Braynard, offers a brief history of each image relating to the *Titanic*.

7. One of my favorite cards shows the ship's captain, Edward Smith, and its builder, Lord Pirrie, standing on the deck of the *Titanic* before it set sail.

8. Another card is a photograph of *Titanic* passengers on board the *Carpathia,* the ship that rescued many survivors.

9. There is also picture of two small children, survivors themselves, who lost their father in the disaster but were later reunited with their mother.

10. The most interesting card, a photo of the ship's gymnasium, shows that one of the pieces of exercise equipment for the passengers was a rowing machine.

PROOFREADING EXERCISE

Do you know, Ryan, that there is a one-unit library class that begins next week? It's called Library 1, Introduction to the Library, and we have to sign up for it before Friday. The librarians who teach it will give us an orientation and a series of assignment sheets. Then, as we finish the assignments at our own pace, we will turn them in to the librarians for credit. Ms. Kim, the librarian that I spoke with, said that we will learn really valuable library skills. These skills, such as finding books or articles in our library and using the Internet to access other databases, are the ones universities will expect us to know. I, therefore, plan to take this class, and you, I hope, will take it with me.

SENTENCE WRITING

Here are some possible combinations. Yours may differ.

Soup, especially chicken noodle soup, tastes best when it's hot.

Chicken noodle is one soup that tastes especially good when it's hot.

We should, I believe, start a savings account to help us prepare for financial emergencies.

I believe we should start a savings account to help us prepare for financial emergencies.

Leslie, my roommate, got a job in the bookstore to get good discounts on books.

My roommate Leslie got a job in the bookstore to get good discounts on books.

COMMA REVIEW EXERCISE (P. 191)

I'm writing you this reminder, Lisa, so that you won't forget our date to go to the museum this Saturday. [4] I know we're still friends, but lately some of our plans have slipped your mind. [1] After we decided to meet in the library last weekend, you forgot all about it. [3] I'm taking this opportunity, therefore, to refresh your memory. [5] I know that you're busy with work, with school, and with family. [2] I've made a reservation to have lunch in The Greenhouse, an expensive little restaurant at the museum, as a special treat. [6] I know that you'll love it. See you Saturday!

QUOTATION MARKS AND UNDERLINING/*ITALICS* (PP. 193–197)

EXERCISE 1

1. "Do you need any help with your homework?" my father asked.

2. In William Zinsser's book On Writing Well, he explains that "Readers want the person who is talking to them to sound genuine."

3. Sigmund Freud had this to say about the intensity of a particular dream: "The dream is far shorter than the thoughts which it replaces."

4. Cat People and The Curse of the Cat People are two movies about people who turn into panther-like cats.

5. "All for love, and nothing for reward" is a famous quotation by Edmund Spenser.

6. Forrest Gump made many sayings famous, but "Life is like a box of chocolates" is the most memorable.

7. My teacher wrote "Well done!" at the top of my essay.

8. Poker expert Phil Gordon admits that "Everyone makes mistakes." "A bad poker player," he adds, "will make the same mistake over and over again."

9. Donna asked, "What time is the meeting?"

10. My family subscribes to The New Yorker, and we all enjoy reading it.

EXERCISE 2

1. Emilie Buchwald once noted, "Children are made readers on the laps of their parents."

2. Have you read Mark Twain's book The Adventures of Tom Sawyer?

3. I took a deep breath when my counselor asked, "How many math classes have you had?"

4. "Let's start that again!" shouted the dance teacher.

5. Last night we watched the Beatles' movie Help! on DVD.

6. "Books," wrote Jonathan Swift, "are the children of the brain."

7. Voltaire stated in A Philosophical Dictionary that "Tears are the silent language of grief."

8. Why do dentists ask questions like "How are you?" as soon as they start working on your teeth?

9. "Time is the only incorruptible judge" is just one translation of Creon's line from the Greek play Oedipus Rex.

10. My favorite essay that we have read this semester has to be "The Pie" by Gary Soto.

EXERCISE 3

1. "Marks" is the title of a poem by Linda Pastan.

2. I'll never understand what "No news is good news" means.

3. The student asked the librarian, "Can you help me find an article on sponta-neous human combustion?"

4. Whatever happened to The Book of Lists?

5. My Antonia is the title of one of Willa Cather's most famous novels.

6. "Let's begin," the relaxation expert said, "by closing our eyes and imagining ourselves in an empty theater."

7. Television series like Frontier House and Colonial House have made PBS a real competitor for reality-TV-hungry audiences.

8. "I can't keep this a secret anymore," my neighbor told me. "Your son has a tattoo that he hasn't shown you yet."

9. Phil Gordon's Little Green Book is the whole title of his book, and the subtitle is Lessons and Teachings in No Limit Texas Hold'em.

10. I was shocked when my high school English teacher told us, "Most of Shakespeare's stories came from other sources; he just dramatized them bet-ter than anyone else did."

EXERCISE 4

1. Alfred Tonnelle defined art this way: "The artist does not see things as they are, but as he is."

2. I found a vintage children's book called Baby Island at the thrift store; it was a fascinating story.

3. A Russian proverb says, "When money speaks, the truth is silent."

4. When someone suggested that Walt Disney run for mayor of Los Angeles fol-lowing the success of Disneyland, Disney declined, saying, "I'm already king."

5. About trying new foods, Swift said, "It was a bold man who first ate an oyster."

6. Mark Twain noted about California, "It's a great place to live, but I wouldn't want to visit there."

7. There is a French expression *L'amour est aveugle; l'amitié ferme les yeux,* which translates as follows: "Love is blind; friendship closes its eyes."

8. "Let's keep our voices down," the librarian said as we left the study room.

9. One of Emily Dickinson's shortest poems begins, "A word is dead/When it is said/Some say."

10. Dickinson's poem ends like this: "I say it just/Begins to live/That day."

1. In Booker T. Washington's autobiography <u>Up from Slavery</u>, he describes his early dream of going to school.

2. "I had no schooling whatever while I was a slave," he explains.

3. He continues, "I remember on several occasions I went as far as the school-house door with one of my young mistresses to carry her books."

4. Washington was incredibly attracted by what he saw from the doorway: "several dozen boys and girls engaged in study."

5. "The picture," he adds, "made a deep impression upon me."

6. Washington cherished this glimpse of "boys and girls engaged in study."

7. It contrasted directly with his own situation: "My life had its beginning in the midst of the most miserable, desolate, and discouraging surroundings."

8. "I was born," he says, "in a typical log cabin, about fourteen by sixteen feet square."

9. He explains, "In this cabin I lived with my mother and a brother and sister till after the Civil War, when we were all declared free."

10. As a slave at the door of his young mistress's schoolhouse, Booker T. Washington remembers, "I had the feeling that to get into a schoolhouse and study in this way would be about the same as getting into paradise."

PARAGRAPH EXERCISE

I've been reading the book <u>How Children Fail</u> by John Holt. I checked it out to use in a research paper I'm doing on education in America. Holt's book was published in the early 1960s, but his experiences and advice are still relevant today. In one of his chapters, "Fear and Failure," Holt describes intelligent children this way: "Intelligent children act as if they thought the universe made some sense. They check their answers and their thoughts against common sense, while other children, not expecting answers to make sense, not knowing what is sense, see no point in checking, no way of checking." Holt and others stress the child's self-confidence as one key to success.

CAPITAL LETTERS (PP. 199–202)

EXERCISE 1

1. J.K. Rowling is a very famous British writer.

2. Her Harry Potter novels are among the most popular books ever written.

3. The series begins with the book *Harry Potter and the Sorcerer's Stone.*

4. In England, the first book is called *Harry Potter and the Philosopher's Stone.*

5. Next comes *Harry Potter and the Chamber of Secrets,* which introduces the character of Tom Riddle.

6. In *Harry Potter and the Prisoner of Azkaban,* everyone is trying to catch the supposed criminal named Sirius Black.

7. The fourth book in the series is *Harry Potter and the Goblet of Fire.*

8. Harry's friends Ron and Hermione aggravate him in *Harry Potter and the Order of the Phoenix.*

9. Readers learn more about Harry's nemesis, Voldemort, in *Harry Potter and the Half-Blood Prince.*

10. Rowling's seventh and final book will no doubt pair Harry with another fabulous subtitle.

Exercise 2

1. Now that DVDs are more popular than VHS tapes, I am updating my movie library.

2. My friends say that I shouldn't waste my money on repeat titles.

3. But my friend Jake is on my side because he and I are usually the ones who watch movies together.

4. Even though I have good VHS copies of famous films such as *Chinatown, Jaws,* and *Blade Runner,* the DVD versions offer behind-the-scenes footage and original trailers that VHS tapes don't include.

5. Of course, I'm aware that another technology will replace DVDs before too long.

6. Then I guess I'll just have to commit to that new format.

7. There are always collectors who want the old stuff.

8. In fact, I know someone who has a collection of video discs and 8-track cassette tapes.

9. I may be leaning that way myself.

10. I haven't disposed of my VHS duplicates yet, and I've been buying old record albums at thrift stores.

EXERCISE 3

1. When my art teacher asked the class to do research on Frida Kahlo, I knew that the name sounded familiar.

2. Then I remembered that the actress Salma Hayek starred in the movie *Frida*, which was about this Mexican-born artist's life.

3. Frida Kahlo's paintings are all very colorful and seem extremely personal.

4. She painted mostly self-portraits, and each one makes a unique statement.

5. One of these portraits is called *My Grandparents, My Parents, and I*.

6. Kahlo gave another one the title *The Two Fridas*.

7. But my favorite of Kahlo's works is *Self-Portrait on the Borderline between Mexico and the United States*.

8. In an article I read in *Smithsonian* magazine, Kahlo's mother explains that after Frida was severely injured in a bus accident, she started painting.

9. Kahlo's mother set up a mirror near her daughter's bed so that Frida could use herself as a model.

10. In the *Smithsonian* article from the November 2002 issue, Kahlo is quoted as saying, "I never painted dreams. I painted my own reality."

EXERCISE 4

1. Hidden beneath the church of St. Martin-in-the-Fields in London is a great little place to have lunch.

2. It's called The Café in the Crypt, and you enter it down a small staircase just off Trafalgar Square.

3. The café is literally in a crypt, the church's resting place for the departed.

4. The food is served cafeteria-style: soups, stews, sandwiches, and salads.

5. You grab a tray at the end of the counter and load it up with food as you slide it toward the cash register.

6. Although the café is dark, the vaulted ceilings make it comfortable, and you can just make out the messages carved into the flat tombstones that cover the floor beneath your table.

7. One of London's newspapers ranked The Café in the Crypt high on its list of the "50 Best Places to Meet in London."

8. The Café in the Crypt can even be reserved for private parties.

9. The café has its own gallery, called—what else?—The Gallery in the Crypt.

10. So if you're ever in London visiting historic Trafalgar Square, don't forget to look for that little stairway and grab a bite at The Café in the Crypt.

EXERCISE 5

1. My mom and dad love old movie musicals.

2. That makes it easy to shop for them at Christmas and other gift-giving occasions.

3. For Mom's birthday last year, I gave her the video of Gilbert and Sullivan's comic opera *The Pirates of Penzance*.

4. It isn't even that old; it has Kevin Kline in it as the character called the Pirate King.

5. I watched the movie with her, and I enjoyed the story of a band of pirates who are too nice for their own good.

6. Actually, it is funnier than I thought it would be, and Kevin Kline sings and dances really well!

7. Dad likes musicals, too, and I bought him tickets to see the revival of *Chicago* on stage a few years ago.

8. He loves all those big production numbers and the Bob Fosse choreography.

9. Thanks to Baz Luhrmann and others, movie musicals are making a comeback.

10. *Moulin Rouge* and the film version of *Chicago* are just two recent examples.

REVIEW OF PUNCTUATION AND CAPITAL LETTERS (P. 203)

1. The Alamo is a famous historical site in Texas.

2. Have you ever seen the first episode of The Simpsons?

3. They've remodeled their garage, and now their daughter uses it as an apartment.

4. "How much will the midterm affect our grades?" the nervous student asked.

5. We have refunded your money, Ms. Jones, and will be sending you a confirmation letter.

6. One of the teachers who visited the library left a textbook on the checkout counter.

7. The United Parcel Service, better known as UPS, was hiring on campus yesterday.

8. Even though I am enjoying my Latin class, I should have taken Spanish instead.

9. You always remember the date of my birthday, March 20, but you forget your own.

10. Pink is a calming color—but not if it's hot pink. (or !)

11. Pam, Martha, Justin, and Luke left class early to practice their presentation in the hallway.

12. Finding a good deal for a new car online takes time, patience, and luck.

13. My friend is reading a Shakespeare play in her women's studies class.

14. I wonder how much my <u>History of Textiles</u> book will cost.

15. Steve Jobs is CEO of Apple Computer Inc.; he deserves a lot of credit for the success of the iPod products. (Note the special capitalization of iPod.)

COMPREHENSIVE TEST (PP. 204–205)

1. (c) When you step inside a greenhouse, the air feels so refreshing.

2. (shift in person and wordy) People should check their online accounts regularly *for a breach in security.*

3. (adv) We all feel *bad* about the way we treated the substitute.

4. (s-v agr) Either the title or the main points *need* to be changed.

5. (adj) She was getting the *highest* grades in the class.

6. (ww) The twins spent *their* summer vacation in Canada.

7. (wordy and awk) *I have questions* about the return policy.

8. (cap) I love *fall* and *spring;* they are my favorite seasons.

9. (pro) The cadet gave my friend and *me* a ticket for parking without our permits.

10. (ro) Campers can have fun, or they can be miserable.

11. (apos) My counselor's advice has served me well.

12. (cs) I consider myself creative; however, I have no interest in becoming an artist.

13. (mm) *My friend found a sticker under the lid of the bottle* that said "Winner."

14. (cap) We read the essay called "Once More *to the* Lake," by E.B. White.

15. (pro agr) *Members of the jury were able to express their own opinions.*

16. (ww) I took their comments about my essay as *compliments.*

17. (ww and cliché) His research paper is more developed *than* mine, but mine has a better title.

18. (ww/apos) *It's* not easy to take two final exams in one day.

19. (wordy) Thanks to my petition, the school allowed me to repeat the class.

20. (shift in time) The students broke into groups and *started* discussing the poem.

WRITING

ORGANIZING IDEAS (PP. 224–225)

EXERCISE 1 THESIS OR FACT?

1. FACT	**6.** FACT
2. FACT	**7.** FACT
3. THESIS	**8.** THESIS
4. FACT	**9.** THESIS
5. THESIS	**10.** THESIS

TRANSITIONAL EXPRESSIONS (PP. 227–228)

EXERCISE 2 ADDING TRANSITIONAL EXPRESSIONS

Whenever I plan a trip that involves driving long distances, I go through the following routine. *First*, I make sure that I have a recent map of the highways so that if I get lost along the way, I won't panic. *Next*, even if I do have a map to the city of my destination, I go online to get specific driving directions to the hotel from the highway. *Another* way that I prepare is to check my car's tires and get its engine serviced, if necessary. I know how important cell phones are on long drives; *therefore*, I never forget to bring mine. *Finally*, before I leave my house on the day of the trip, I call the Highway Patrol hotline to see if there are any highway closures. This routine has always worked for me. *However*, I would give it up for a car with its own computerized navigation system.

WRITING ABOUT WHAT YOU READ (PP. 241–242)

ASSIGNMENT 17

100-WORD SUMMARY OF "ELVIS ON CELLULOID"

Elvis Presley's film career disappointed many people but none more than Elvis himself. Elvis had dreams of becoming a real actor. He wanted people to let him show his serious side. But because he was such a popular celebrity, Elvis was forced to make a lot of silly musicals just so that everyone could watch him sing. His films were really popular then, and they still are today. But that never mattered to Elvis and his family and friends. It doesn't seem to impress critics either since most of them think of Elvis's movies as just fluff without any substance.

Index